On the Intelligibility
of Political Philosophy

On the Intelligibility
of Political Philosophy

Essays of Charles N. R. McCoy

edited by James V. Schall
and John J. Schrems

The Catholic University of America Press
Washington, D.C.

Copyright © 1989
The Catholic University of America Press

LIBRARY OF CONGRESS CATALOGING-IN-PUBLICATION DATA
McCoy, Charles N. R. (Charles Nicholas Reiten), 1911–1984.
   On the intelligibility of political philosophy : essays of Charles
N. R. McCoy / edited by James V. Schall and John J. Schrems.
      p.   cm.
Includes index.
1. Political science—History.   2. Church and social problems—
Catholic Church.   i. Schall, James V.   ii. Schrems, John J., 1936–
iii. Title.
JA81.M388   1989   88–31601
320'.01'1—dc19
ISBN 0–8132–0679–0

Contents

III. American Political Thought

IV. Catholic Social Questions

V. Conclusion

Acknowledgments

The editors gratefully acknowledge permission to include in this volume the following works by Charles N. R. McCoy:

1. "American Political Thought after 1865," *Thought* 21 (1946), 249–71.
2. "The Doctrine of Judicial Review and Natural Law," 6 *Cath. U. L. Rev.* 7 (1956).
3. "Democracy and the Rule of Law," *Modern Schoolman* 25 (November 1947), 1–10.
4. Review of Ernst Cassirer, *Myth of the State*, in *Modern Schoolman* 25 (May 1948), 271–8.
5. "Historical Position of Man Himself," in *Mélanges à la Memoir de Charles de Koninck* (Presses de l'Université Laval, 1968), 219–31.
6. "Humanae Vitae: Perspectives and Precisions," *The New Scholasticism* 44 (Spring 1970), 265–72.
7. "Note on the Problem of the Origins of Political Authority," *The Thomist* 16 (1953), 71–81.
8. "Political Philosophy," in *New Catholic Encyclopedia* (McGraw-Hill Book Co., 1968), Vol. 11, 510–16.
9. "Social Justice in *Quadragesimo Anno*," *Social Order* 7 (June 1957), 258–63.
10. "Value-Free Aristotle and the Behavioral Sciences," *Western Political Quarterly* 23 (March 1970), 57–73.
11. "American Federalism: Theory and Practice," *The Review of Politics*, II (January 1970), 105–17.
12. "On the Revival of Classical Political Philosophy," *The Review of Politics*, 27 (July 1943), 161–79.

The editors are grateful also to the estate of Charles N. R. McCoy for permission to use his notes on liberation theology and on the counter culture.

Chronology of the Life of Charles N. R. McCoy

1911	Born, August 7, Brooklyn, New York
1930–1932	Rufus Choate Scholar, Dartmouth College
1932	B.A., Dartmouth College, Phi Beta Kappa
1938	Ph.D., Political Science, University of Chicago
1941	Ordained, May 31, St. Paul, Minnesota
1941–1947	Professor, College of St. Thomas, St. Paul, Minnesota
1951	Ph.D., Philosophy, Laval University, Quebec
1947–1953	Associate Professor, St. Louis University, St. Louis, Missouri
1953–1963	Professor, The Catholic University of America, Washington, D.C.
1954–1963	Chairman, Department of Politics, The Catholic University of America, Washington, D.C.
1959–1960	Visiting Professor of Political Science, Stanford University, Stanford, California
1963–1964	Lecturer, General Studies Program, Stanford University, Stanford, California
1963–1976	Professor, Santa Clara University, Santa Clara, California
1984	Died, October 11, Santa Clara, California

On the Intelligibility
of Political Philosophy

Introduction

This volume contains the published scholarly essays and previously unpublished writings of Charles N. R. McCoy. It is intended for individuals unfamiliar with McCoy as well as for those who know of his remarkable work but who are not aware of its extent. In fulfilling this intention, it is important to recall and emphasize the centrality of McCoy's one book, *The Structure of Political Thought*.[1] This book is an incisive, unique, basic contribution to political philosophy and its theoretic understanding. Political philosophy, to be understood correctly, must like all other things be grasped as a whole and in the relationship of its parts to its whole. McCoy grasped both. *The Structure of Political Thought* is McCoy's expression of his understanding of the whole. This particular collection is intended to illustrate McCoy's grasp of the parts, a grasp which is evident from his very earliest writings to his last.

The essays and previously unpublished articles contained in this volume can each be read and appreciated independently of one another and independently of *The Structure of Political Thought*, though naturally a knowledge of that book will be of enormous help in guiding the reader to McCoy's central concerns in each particular essay. Thus, these writings variously initiate, develop, or complete arguments found in *The Structure of Political Thought*. They demonstrate McCoy's ability to penetrate to the core of an issue in political philosophy. They offer as much insight today (more perhaps) as when they were first written. There is a certain striking abidingness in McCoy's arguments.

1. Charles N. R. McCoy, *The Structure of Political Thought* (New York: McGraw–Hill, 1963). See James V. Schall, S.J., " 'Man for Himself': On the Ironic Unities of Political Philosophy," *Political Science Reviewer*, XV (Fall 1985), 67–108, for an analysis of McCoy's contribution.

Each of McCoy's essays is related in some direct way to the central treatment of political philosophy and its importance for human reality. It is to this reality that Charles N. R. McCoy devoted his intellectual life. Subsequent events in political philosophy, American culture, and Christian theology demonstrate the acuteness of McCoy's analyses of the nature and direction of the main issues of political theory. A careful reading of McCoy will take one directly and quickly to the heart of political philosophy. Likewise, it will present a profound and original analysis of what political philosophy actually is, an analysis, that is, in many ways, unique in the discipline. The failure to grasp the significance of McCoy's work when it originally appeared (a failure this collection seeks to redress) was, in part, responsible for many ideological trends that subsequently appeared both in political practice and in theology.

This collection is directed to four specific audiences:

(1) The political philosophers themselves, who are concerned with the content and intelligibility of their discipline, are the first thinkers to whom McCoy's work is directed. Granted Leo Strauss's remark that we are lucky if one or two great thinkers are alive during the time in which we are alive, nonetheless, there are many writers and politicians who consider themselves to philosophize about politics. Included in this asscmblage of McCoy's essays, then, are Marxist, liberal, and conservative theories, which he analyzed so well. Included also are critiques of the existentialist and behavioral theorists, whose work essentially concerned philosophy and political science during McCoy's lifetime. The students of those writers engaged in the revival of classical theory—writers such as Leo Strauss, Eric Voegelin, Hannah Arendt—are likewise part of this audience. These philosophers, like McCoy, were concerned with the same problems within modern theory and with the origin of these concerns. McCoy's work should be attended to as unique in dealing in a positive way with the problems of revelation analyzed in the brilliant works of Strauss, Voegelin, Arendt, and their schools. McCoy's work in its parts, as detailed in these essays, will more and more provide a structure of principles for all of political philosophy.

(2) Christian philosophers and theologians are a second audience for this volume. McCoy saw strains in Christian philosophy and theology, which had lost contact with the central flow of political philosophy itself and its inner relation to revelation, and

consequently ended up embracing the sort of modern positions most inimical to revelation. McCoy's writing will interest those involved in this experience as well as those who observe it. A large portion of religious and philosophical thought today is taken up either with going beyond thought to political action or in disputing those who hold more classical positions. Aristotle and Aquinas, political philosophy and the questions addressed to it by revelation, theologies of liberation and radical Christian economic theories, can be better understood in their interrelatedness through numerous works contained in this volume.

(3) The third audience consists of scholars interested in the intellectual nature of modernity and modern political philosophy as such, its order and manifestations in liberalism, conservatism, behavioralism, socialism, or existentialism. In all of his writings, McCoy was aware of the modern implications of whatever he focused upon. This attention revealed the political philosopher, as opposed to the philosopher or theologian *per se*, in him. He could do this because he was aware that political philosophy had its own history and yet it did not stand by itself in isolation from metaphysics, knowledge theory, or theological premises. These theoretical premises were presupposed by political philosophy. Questions arose in political thought that had to be directed to these higher disciplines. From the beginning of his writings, McCoy was neither a metaphysician who came to write about political philosophy, nor a political scientist who sought viable theological or philosophical generalizations with which to explain contemporary concerns. He was from the start a political philosopher who had no difficulty seeing the proper place of his discipline in the division of the sciences. His grasp of the place of political philosophy made it possible for him to show the context through which modern developments could be understood and appreciated.

(4) The above remarks suggest a fourth audience about which we are especially concerned. This final group may indeed be a subset of the first three. It is the younger generation of students of political philosophy and of other theoretical disciplines who are open to wonder about the orientation and the overall implications of this area of knowledge. In this audience are graduate students and young scholars, those who have studied political philosophy formally, those in any area of political science or the social sciences, students and scholars of philosophy, theology, literature, or the physical sciences, all who begin to wonder about the whole. These

students are individuals who have not yet settled the larger questions and are willing to entertain fundamentals not found in their passing academic milieu. Literary students of Marion Montgomery's *Reflective Journey Toward Order* or philosophical students of E. F. Schumacher's *Guide for the Perplexed* would be among the first to see the import of McCoy's work.[2] An enormous change has taken place in political philosophy in recent years, thanks largely to the students or heritage of thinkers like Strauss or Voegelin or Arendt, to scholars like Sheldon Wolin, John Hallowell, Michael Oakeshott, Russell Kirk, Joseph Cropsey, Gerhart Niemeyer, Ernest Fortin, Dante Germino, Ellis Sandoz, Francis Canavan, and others. Political philosophy is seen again to lie at the center of any defense of our culture. Without it, there is no objection to the relativism, "globalism," socialism, and Marxism which in some way influence our intellectual culture. The fundamentals, the context, the breadth of treatment, the grasp of classical, modern, and contemporary thought by McCoy provide to this audience an unparalleled opportunity for expansion and development of understanding of political things and how they relate to "higher" and "lower" concerns.

Philosophically, it is not enough to know that there are different periods or authors or movements in political philosophy itself. We must also know how the periods, authors, and movements relate to one another. For this knowledge, the works of Charles N. R. McCoy are of unique value, for what most concerned him was not just the individual periods or strands of thought, but the whole, how everything fit together.

This volume is much more than a mere convenience to save time from collecting the separate pieces from their original sources. The essays come from scattered sources which McCoy himself had lost track of. McCoy's estate had no record of the material nor of the bibliography presented here. Seeing them together in one place, the overall impact of his thought can be reflected upon and studied in detail. The total amount of writing of Charles N. R. McCoy is not especially large. Volume or quantity alone is deceptive, however. The richness he gave to each essay requires scrutiny of each word, phrase, sentence, paragraph, and page. Only after much

2. Marion Montgomery, *Reflective Journey Toward Order* (Athens, GA., 1978); *The Prophetic Poet and the Spirit of the Age* (La Salle, IL., 1982–84); and E. F. Schumacher, *A Guide for the Perplexed* (New York, 1977).

time will the full impact of what has been read be appreciated. It is a rewarding experience.

It must be added that McCoy was primarily concerned with the truth of the discipline. This truth, he argued, required meticulous and accurate attention to error. McCoy was fully in the tradition of the great thinkers who are able to state the objections to their positions better than the objectors themselves. From Plato to Marx and Heidegger, McCoy saw clearly their positions in exact philosophic context. He was insistent that each philosopher stood for some intelligible position that followed, however obscurely, from what went before in philosophy. At the same time, McCoy was able to relate the deviation to its source in truth so that the whole was what made sense. The weaving of truth from error can be seen in his writings on Plato—perhaps his most controverted position—Feuerbach, Rousseau, or Machiavelli. A similar perspective can be seen in his writings on contemporary topics of social science, papal encyclicals, the counter culture, modern liberalism, and liberation theology.

The writings collected in this volume are topical in organization. They begin with modern political philosophy and its classical roots. The beginning treats of St. Thomas and political science, democracy, the origin of political authority, and Rousseau. The second part treats of contemporary political philosophy—including liberalism, existentialism, behavioralism, Leo Strauss, and the Counter Culture. The third part contains McCoy's often unknown (even by his closest students) essays on American political philosophy. Here are important writings on federalism, judicial review, and the Gilded Age. The fourth part concerns aspects of Catholic political philosophy and deals with papal encyclicals on social justice and birth control, and the more recent phenomenon of liberation theology. The final part of this collection contains McCoy's basic essay on the core of political philosophy.

We have omitted from this volume what are perhaps the most delightful things McCoy ever wrote, namely, his many book reviews in the *Modern Schoolman*, the *Catholic Historical Review*, and other journals. These reviews are included in the bibliography and are worth considerable attention, for McCoy reviewed many of the major books in political theory published in his time. If he did not like something, he made it evident why. On the other hand, we have included one lengthy review, that of Ernst Cassirer's *The*

Myth of the State, since Cassirer was of such fundamental influence on McCoy's thought.

Footnotes from the original essays, appearing under differing forms in various journals, have been redone in a consistent form, though these footnotes remain substantially as they appeared in their initial form. Left out of some footnotes were simple direct quotations. This was done to save space and was justified on the assumption that a footnote is intended to give a reference which any reader can verify for himself. When the original footnote contained something McCoy himself added or commented on, as was often the case, the footnote was left as it appeared. Where incomplete, bibliographical information for many footnotes has been completed when possible. The citations McCoy used from Aristotle were almost always from the McKeon-Ross, Random House Edition of *The Basic Works of Aristotle.* The translations of Aquinas were usually McCoy's own. McCoy often cited passages from Marx from the German original, especially the *Economic and Philosophical Manuscripts, 1844.* Since he wrote, English versions of this work have appeared. These have been noted where appropriate.

Throughout *The Structure of Political Thought* and these essays, McCoy came back again and again to the same texts, from Aristotle, Aquinas, Hume, Grotius, Feuerbach, Marx, or Heidegger, as well as those from Cassirer, de Koninck, Erich Fromm, or David Riesman. These are more than repetitions. In context, they represent McCoy's method of teaching and reflecting. They stress ideas that get into the heart of political philosophy, ideas McCoy made his own, such as the notions of "humanitas" as a denial of transcendence, or nature as a "substitute intelligence," or Marx's "generic being," or man's loss of an "intellectual center" from Cassirer, or the "return of myth and magic" in political philosophy, again from Cassirer. Grotius's dictum "that the natural law would be the natural law even supposing that God did not exist," was often cited by McCoy as the beginning of a wrong turn in political thought. The attentive scholar from any of the four audiences mentioned above will pay particular attention to such recurrences, even in small book reviews or short asides. McCoy's writings have that quality of precision that a comma, a quotation mark, a word, a phrase, a question mark, an exclamation (though rare), must be understood completely before meaning can be assigned by the reader.

Despite the arduous attention required to follow McCoy's ar-

guments, there remains throughout these essays a kind of sub-
merged excitement that is not totally in evidence until the reader
has begun to catch something of the vast enterprise in which
Charles N. R. McCoy was engaged. That enterprise was a complete rethinking of political philosophy in the proper line of Aristotle and Aquinas. Thus, there is an exhilaration of intellectual
discovery in McCoy that is almost impossible to describe to anyone
not making these same discoveries for himself. Students attending
his lectures felt this enthusiasm, his sense of the deepest concern,
though McCoy himself seemed little aware of it.

The origins of McCoy's attachment to the classical philosophical
tradition, so evident in all of his essays, are not easy to trace. He
had graduated, Phi Beta Kappa, from Dartmouth in 1932, after
having been a Rufus Choate scholar there. Shortly thereafter his
first two essays in *The Commonweal* were published. McCoy's more
strictly academic publications started in 1939 shortly after he received his Ph.D. from Chicago in 1938. What is noteworthy about
his early years and publications is how easily and extensively he
used the works of those two principle classical authors, Aristotle
and Aquinas, who were to dominate his entire life of publication.

In 1951, McCoy received a Ph.D. in political philosophy at Laval,
studying under Charles de Koninck, but by this time his thinking
was already significantly in line with de Koninck. McCoy's Ph.D.
at Chicago had been in the area of constitutional law—as a way
of avoiding Charles E. Merriam, who taught an altogether different form of political theory at Chicago at the time. As a Catholic
priest, ordained in 1941, it might be assumed that his seminary
training was the source of his understanding of Aristotle and Aquinas. Two considerations seem to rule against such an origin: first,
his attachment to Aristotle and Aquinas was already in evidence
by the time of his first academic writings; and second, he had been
known to remark that one reason for the negative attitude toward
Aquinas among many priests and priest-educators was the poor
teaching in seminaries.

Jerome Kerwin, of the University of Chicago, a friend for many
years, may have been an influence, but once again the attachment
appears to predate the association with Kerwin, and McCoy's use
of the classical authors seems greater than Kerwin's. The primary
discoverable source of McCoy's classical penchant, then, seems to
have been his Dartmouth experience; or, perhaps he acquired it
entirely on his own. That is an intriguing origin for a man who

was to profoundly criticize the autarchy of "man for himself" and who was to spend his entire academic career, except for visiting lectureships at Stanford, at Catholic universities.

McCoy's 1940 article on "Federalism" (Chapter 13) was a theoretical expression of his constitutional law dissertation. The dissertation was tightly reasoned, as were all of his writings, but it was legalistic, and very competently so. It carefully follows the constitutional law side of political science, but it had classical theory within its lines just waiting to burst forth. The federalism article shows how easily he turned competence in one area into profundity in another. In the larger context of political philosophy, the article, by examining the mistaken expressions of the compact theory, addressed a central issue of the very possibility of government in the United States.

Father McCoy's subsequent articles and book reviews continued his fundamental classical examination. One finds, however, sprinkled within his 1943 "Machiavelli" and his 1946 "American Political Philosophy" (Chapter 14) articles, as well as his 1943 to 1945 book reviews, concern with the contemporary world issues of Hitler and world war. Each article throughout his career deals in a significant way with an important area of historical or theoretical interest, but each also deals with some relationship to matters of contemporary concern. He relates Plato and Aristotle to Marx, for example. The post-Aristotelian turning point in political philosophy is related to the seventeenth- and eighteenth-century turning point and to modern thought (Bibliography, 1950), and Rousseau to the breakdown of classical thought and to Marx (Chapter 5).

Each thinker or idea McCoy deals with he relates, in the words of the title of his book, to the "structure of political thought." He never dealt with the "variable truth of contingent operables," as he described sociological or behavioral type examinations at one point. Instead, he chose to focus on the working out of eternal verities. It is as if each writing had a teleology to it and was not a strictly exegetical treatment of an author or work. It may have been because of this teleological style that Strauss and Cropsey replaced McCoy's "Augustine" and "Aquinas" chapters in the first edition of their *History of Political Philosophy* with a different, albeit excellent, author in the second and third editions.[3] The Strauss style,

3. Leo Strauss and Joseph Cropsey, *History of Political Philosophy* (Chicago, 1963, "St. Augustine," 151–59, "St. Thomas," 201–26). Because of their similarity to the

legitimate in its own right, is more an exegesis with a less direct teleology. Contrasting the two editions of the Strauss work makes the differing styles striking. Though an approximate contemporary of Strauss dealing with roughly the same topics, McCoy, employing different hermeneutics, produced perhaps a more long-lasting, though a less immediate, result.

The structure of political thought, as with classical teleology, was given and was best, but it was not guaranteed and could be destroyed. It was precisely this destruction, through the exercise of the liberty of contrariety, that McCoy understood Marx. McCoy saw much of modern thought to derive from this source. McCoy wished to preserve the structure, the teleology of natural law, understood as a reason put into things by the divine art. It is small wonder then that the last three works McCoy wrote, three of the previously unpublished pieces found in this volume, combine a most profound treatment of political philosophy with an analysis of contemporary issues. Two of the articles deal with the Counter Culture (Chapters 11 and 12) and the third is concerned with liberation theology (Chapter 18).

The manuscript used for this posthumous publication of the smaller Counter-Culture chapter is apparently that submitted to a journal (*Western Political Science Quarterly*) and either used for subsequent classroom reference or edited for possible resubmission. Some of the editing comments of the referees had been noted, and changes were reflected in the draft manuscript. It should be made clear that the articles published in this volume are as close as possible to what Charles N. R. McCoy intended. There is no question that these unedited chapters are published without benefit of his final review, although the executor of his estate, James E. McCoy, III, has graciously given permission for their publication here. These essays are the work of a deep analytical mind. They have a larger potential appeal than any of his other writings, and for that reason they are offered here.

The fourth of McCoy's unpublished essays included here, "Liberation Theology and Political Philosophy" was evidently his last effort before he died, since one of the writings cited in this handwritten manuscript was published in April, 1984, just six months before McCoy's death. McCoy began this essay by saying that he

---

discussion of St. Augustine and St. Thomas in *The Structure of Political Thought,* Chapters IV and V, these two essays were not included in this volume. They remain, however, well worth reading in themselves.

did not intend to judge "except indirectly liberation theology, with which indeed, I have some sympathy." However, this sympathy did not go so far as to ignore the context, in this instance, the company which liberation theology keeps. According to McCoy, liberation theology attracts Christian supporters who are unaware of the richness of their own tradition; it is, furthermore, heir of those seventeenth- and eighteenth-century philosophies that saw political philosophy as another means of advancing the "essentiality of man."

Liberation theology's conjuring a spurious spirituality had all the hallmarks of that religious or seminary training which failed to convey the richness of its own classical-Christian tradition. This gave substance to McCoy's view that the neglect of political philosophy can be disastrous for theology itself. In his earlier essays on Augustine, Aquinas, and in his discussion of Christianity in his *Structure of Political Thought*, McCoy had made it clear, recalling words of George Sabine, that he saw a revolutionary significance to religion. The obligation "to effect the good of earthly peace itself" according to the universally revealed model of Goodness is Christianity's mandate in the political world. Insofar as liberation theology would seek to fulfill this mandate, one would have sympathy with it. But insofar as it, not unlike Feuerbach or Marx, saw spirituality itself as "man-made," a type of Christian Counter Culture, McCoy could not abide it.

Two principles that are found in both Aristotle and Augustine appear to epitomize and summarize the corpus of McCoy's thought: one, politics and the state would be the highest if man were the best thing in the universe; two, men should be god-like in their actions. The two propositions are not in conflict. Man is *not* the best thing in the universe, and men should imitate "the most just Disposer" (God) in their behavior, but they should not play God.[4] Both propositions fit well into an appreciation of what McCoy was saying in the Counter-Culture and liberation theology pieces. Indeed they are propositions that fit the whole of McCoy's publications and, indeed, of his life.

A classmate of Father McCoy's from Dartmouth days wrote in the May, 1985, Dartmouth *Newsletter*:

1932: "We are all getting too close to the front of the class. I had a premonition about Reverend Charles N. R. McCoy, having heard little

4. *The Structure of Political Thought*, 114.

about him in recent years. He and I were friendly competitors in Political Science for four years, but he never failed to burn a candle for each of us before major exams. I, in turn, introduced him to that underground store across the river in Vermont, so familiar in '32. He was, in my opinion, not so much a leader at Dartmouth, but certainly a major contributor to the goodness that does exist in our society. We spent four years arguing the good and bad of our society. It comes out a tie."[5]

It is not exactly clear in what arena the tie exists. But McCoy's many former and new students, and not least the editors of this volume, will always think of him as unmatched. His essays which we re-present here will, we think, remind us that when we neglect a major political philosopher, we miss a key insight into reality— that such incisive minds as that of Charles N. R. McCoy were given to us in order that we might further probe the reality that constitutes our being.

5. *Dartmouth Alumni Newsletter* (Hanover, N.H., May 1985).

1. Classical and Medieval Political Philosophy

1. Aristotle and the Medieval Tradition

[This chapter (written before 1958) is an essay distributed by Father McCoy in his class. It contains a description of the nature of the speculative and practical sciences. This analysis is treated as an aspect of the differences and similarities between the divine and human intellects with respect to knowing and producing. A theme that constantly came up in McCoy's work, the idea that nature is a "substitute intelligence," is treated and explicated. The position of the human intellect deserves special treatment because the human intellect is able to know and be measured by what is already made. The complicated treatment of the nature of law is begun from this consideration. Of particular interest is McCoy's insistence that law in the case of human beings not only can treat the universal but also is capable of reaching particular actions. In this sense, divine law serves as a guide to the end of law itself in the case of each particular person subject to it. In this essay, McCoy began the recurring theme of the common good and how this can both be a higher good and reach to the good of each individual subject to it. McCoy suggested what the idea of providence meant, that is, the divine knowledge of particular acts, but acts which are free. The systematic relation of all law to eternal law has its foundation in the proper understanding of nature, its origins, and how the human intellect begins not from itself, but from a given reality it did not make.]

The Division of Sciences: Speculative and Practical

Plato was prompted to hold the Doctrine of Ideas because he had observed that all knowledge takes place through some kind of similitude; and that since it is a fact that things as understood in the intellect are understood under conditions of immateriality and immobility, it seemed to Plato that things must similarly exist in themselves. The consequence of this view was that all knowledge was reduced to a kind of metaphysics or mathematics, for according to Plato there was no reality except the archetypal Ideas, which he seemed to identify, too, with mathematical numbers. Now the great contribution of Aristotle was to show that while it is true that all knowledge takes place through some kind of similitude, the conditions of immateriality and immobility under which the intellect receives the species of material and movable bodies does not imply that the species of material and movable bodies are themselves without matter: for what is received is in the receiver according to the mode of the receiver. This is very clear to us in the case of sense knowledge: for the color green is not in the eye in the same way as it is in the colored surface which is seen. So too the intellect, whose act of understanding is universal, and characterized by a certain necessity, receives according to its own mode the species of material and movable things.

According to Aristotle, the human intellect, although not the act of an organ, is a power of a soul which is substantially united to a body, and for that reason it is proper to it to know an essence existing individually in corporeal matter but *not as* existing in this individual matter; i.e., to know "man," which is an essence existing in individual matter (e.g., in Paul) but to know it *as common* to all men. Aristotle called this operation "abstraction," for to know what is in individual matter, yet not as existing in such matter is to abstract the essence from individual matter. It was this analysis of the process of abstraction that enabled Aristotle to distinguish the various sciences, for now it was possible to show that the intellect, although knowing what it knows in an immaterial mode, can, by different degrees of abstraction, distinguish different subject-matters in accordance with their relation to matter.

The division of sciences by Aristotle is most clearly explained and presented by St. Thomas Aquinas in the following way:

[A]ccording to the order of abstraction from matter and motion, the speculative sciences are distinguished. *First degree of abstraction.* There are certain objects of speculation which are dependent upon matter as to their existence, since they cannot exist except in matter, and these are distinguished because they depend on matter both really and logically, such as things whose definition posits sensible matter. Hence, they cannot be understood without sensible matter, as for example, in the definition of man it is necessary to include flesh and bones; and with things of this kind physics, or natural science, is concerned.

Second degree of abstraction. But certain other things, although they depend upon matter as to their existence, do not so depend as far as the intellect is concerned; because in a definition of them sensible matter is not included, as in the case of lines and numbers with which mathematics deals.

Third degree of abstraction. But there are still other objects of speculation that do not depend upon matter for their existence, because they can exist without matter: either they are never found in matter, as God and the angels, or they are sometimes in matter and in other cases not, as substance, quality, potency, act, one and many, and things of this sort.[1]

These sciences—physics, mathematics, metaphysics—are called *speculative* sciences because the objects with which they are concerned are not anything that can be made or done by our efforts. The end of the speculative intellect is truth only, and not any action to be accomplished. The speculative sciences are distinguished from those sciences that are practical and have to do with action for an end.

St. Thomas makes clear this division of the sciences into speculative and practical as follows:

[I]t must be said that the theoretical or speculative intellect is to be distinguished from the operative or practical intellect by this peculiar fact: that the speculative intellect has for its end the truth which it considers; the practical, on the contrary, ordains the truth considered in respect to some operation as to its end. . . . Since, therefore, the matter ought to be proportionate to the end, the matter of the practical sciences should be those things that can be made or done by our work, so that knowledge of them can be ordered to operation as to an end.

But the matter of the speculative sciences ought to be things that cannot be made by our effort; therefore the consideration of them is not ordained to an end.[2]

But now we must here observe that man himself with his specific nature falls under the consideration of natural science or physics.[3] If physics then is a speculative science, how do we say that there are certain sciences concerned with human actions that are practical and deal with "operable matter"?

At the beginning of *Physics* II, Aristotle defines *nature* as "the principle and cause of movement and rest in that to which it belongs primarily, in virtue of itself and not in virtue of a concomitant attribute."[4] In the course of this same work, Aristotle demonstrates in many ways that nature acts for an end. In the light of this demonstration, St. Thomas defines nature as "a reason (*ratio, logos*)

1. Thomas Aquinas, *Commentary on the De Trinitate of Boethius*, V, 1.
2. *Ibid.*
3. The terminus of the considerations of natural science is reached, Aristotle shows in the Second Book of the *Physics*, with those forms which are in some manner separable from matter. See Thomas Aquinas, *Commentary in II Physics*, Lect. 4.
4. Aristotle, *Physics*, II, 1, 192b21.

put in things by the Divine Art, so that they are able to act for an end." But now although natural things act for an end they do so without knowledge of the end, a sign of which is that nature acts always or for the most part in the same way: that ants and spiders act for an end, but not by virtue of any intellectual principle, is evident, Aristotle points out, from the fact that they operate always in the same way. All spiders make their webs in the same way; all swallows build their nests in the same way. And this would not be the case if they operated by intellect and art, for architects do not all build the same kind of house, because an architect can make judgment about the form of artefacts and can vary them. Hence it is evident that although natural things act to an end, the principle of their being moved for an end is not in them but in something else by which the principle of action toward an end is imprinted on them.

Now man has, in common with all other natural things, an intrinsic principle of movement; but unlike any other nature, he is said to move himself precisely because he has knowledge of the end.[5] Hence all those things to which a man has a natural inclination are naturally apprehended by reason as being good, and consequently as objects of pursuit, and their contraries as evil, and objects of avoidance. All such things are operable matters for man and the subject of "practical" as distinguished from "speculative" science. Now the first principles of all such operable matters are taken from the order of natural inclinations.

For there is in man, first of all, an inclination to good in accordance with the nature which he has in common with all substances, inasmuch, namely, as every substance seeks the preservation of its own being, according to its nature; and by reason of this inclination, whatever is a means of preserving human life, and of warding off its obstacles [is natural to man]. Secondly, there is in man an inclination to things that pertain to him more specially, according to that nature which he has in common with other animals; and in virtue of this inclination those things are said to [be natural] *which nature has taught to all animals*, such as sexual intercourse, the education of offspring and so forth. Thirdly, there is in man an inclination to good according to the nature of his reason, which nature is proper to him. Thus man has a natural inclination to know the truth

---

5. Irrational animals are said also to move themselves, but imperfectly, since their apprehension of the end is had without knowing it under the aspect of end of the relationship of an act to the end. Therefore, they are not said properly speaking to move themselves, but to be moved to their end by some principle outside—namely, the Divine Art. See Thomas Aquinas, *Summa Theologiae*. I–II, 6, 2.

about God, and to live in society; and in this respect, whatever pertains to this inclination [is natural for man], e.g., to shun ignorance, to avoid offending those among whom one has to live, and other such things regarding the above inclination.[6]

Practical Sciences Operative According to the Imitation of Nature

Having set forth the distinction of speculative and practical science, we have now to push our inquiry back further before we can profitably proceed to the specific matter of political science. In the *Prologue* to his *Commentary on the Politics of Aristotle*, St. Thomas shows that Aristotle's procedure in the *Politics* is based on the principle that the arts of man are imitative of the works of nature. He writes:

As the philosopher teaches in the second book of the *Physics*, art imitates nature. The reason for this is that as principles are related to each other so the operations and effects of principles are proportionately related. But the principle of those things that are done according to art is the human intellect which by a certain similitude is derived from the divine intellect which is the principle of natural things. Whence it is necessary that the operations of art imitate the operations of nature; and that those things which are done according to art imitate those things which are done according to nature. For if anyone were to prepare a work of art he would do well to become the disciple of a master from whom he could receive the art and finally be capable of working after the manner of the master. And therefore the human intellect which receives its intelligible light from the divine intellect has necessarily to inform itself in those things that are made naturally.

And therefore it is for this reason that the Philosopher says that if art made those things which nature makes it would not make them differently from the way nature makes them; and conversely, if nature made those things which are made by art it would make them in the way in which they are made by art. But nature does not perfect the things that are of art. It merely prepares certain principles and offers an exemplar. And art inspects the things of nature and is able to use them for the perfecting of its own work; but the things of nature are not themselves perfected by art. Whence it is clear that human knowledge of those things that are according to nature is "cognositive" only, but of those things that are according to art it is both cognositive and productive; whence it is that human sciences concerned with natural things are speculative, but those which are concerned with things done by man are practical, or operative according to the imitation of nature.

6. *Ibid.*, I–II, 94, 2.

If this is Aristotle's procedure in the *Politics*, it is important that we have some understanding of it.

The first thing to notice is that the subject-matter of what, from the point of view of our own intellect, we designate as *speculative* (the whole created universe) is "operable" by the divine intellect, and hence is the work of God's practical knowledge. The following diagram illustrates the relationship:

Divine Nature—Divine Art—Nature—
Speculative Science—Human Art

The knowledge of God is to all created things what the knowledge of an artist is to the things made by his art. And thus natural things stand midway between the knowledge of God and our knowledge in the way, for example, that a house that has been built stands midway between the knowledge of the builder who made it and the knowledge of one who gathers his knowledge of the house from the house already built.

Now we observe that nature proceeds from the simple to the composite, as is clear in the example of any whole in relation to its parts; mixed bodies are made up of simple elements, sentences of words, words of syllables, and syllables of letters. And in the prosecution of knowledge science proceeds by dividing the composite into its irreducible elements. We observe further a double order in natural things: the order of the parts to each other, and the order of the parts to the whole which is ordained to some end. An example drawn from the arts again makes this clear; the parts of a house are ordered to one another and they are all ordered in relation to the whole house which is ordained to a certain end. Now the ordering of the whole universe bespeaks this principle.

Aristotle puts it in the following way:

We must consider also in which of two ways the nature of the universe contains the good and the highest good, whether as something separate and by itself, or as the order of the parts. Probably in both ways, as an army does; for its good is found both in its order and in its leader, and more in the latter; for he does not depend on the order, but it depends on him. And all things are ordered together somehow, but not all alike— both fishes and fowls and plants; and the world is not such that one thing has nothing to do with another, but they are connected. For all are ordered together to one end. . . . I mean, for instance, that all must at least come to be dissolved into their elements, and there are other functions similarly in which all share for the good of the whole.[7]

7. Aristotle, *Metaphysics*, XII, 10, 1075a12.

A fuller understanding of these principles is to be had from a study of the following text of St. Thomas:

Now if we wish to assign an end to any whole, and to the parts of that whole, we shall find, firstly, that each and every part exists for the sake of its proper act, as the eye for the act of seeing; secondly, that the less honorable parts exist for the more honorable, as the senses for the intellect; . . . and thirdly, that all parts are for the perfection of the whole, as the matter for the form, for the parts are, as it were, the matter of the whole. Furthermore, the whole man is on account of an extrinsic end, that end being the fruition of God. So therefore, in the parts of the universe also every creature exists for its own proper act and perfection, and the less noble for the nobler, as those creatures that are less noble than man exist for the sake of man, whilst each and every creature exists for the perfection of the entire universe. Furthermore, the entire universe, with all its parts, is ordained towards God as its end, inasmuch as it imitates, as it were, and shows forth the Divine goodness, to the glory of God.[8]

We have already seen that St. Thomas, following Aristotle's demonstration that nature acts for an end, defines nature as "a reason put in things by the Divine Art, so that they are able to act for an end" (*Ratio cuiusdam artis, scilicet divinae, indita rebus, qua ipsae res moventur ad finem determinatum*). All the good that is in things—both as regards their very substance and their order to an end—is from God; "Aristotle agrees with this," St. Thomas explicitly says.[9] The ordering of things to an end precisely constitutes government, as St. Thomas makes clear in the following passage:

This good of order existing in created things is itself created by God. Now God is the cause of things by His intellect, and therefore it is necessary that the exemplar of every effect should pre-exist in Him. . . . Hence, the exemplar of the order of things towards their end must necessarily pre-exist in the divine mind; and the exemplar of things ordered towards an end is, properly speaking, providence. For providence is the chief part of prudence. . . . Now it belongs to prudence, according to the Philosopher, *to direct other things towards an end*, whether in regard to oneself . . . or in regard to others. . . . In this second way prudence or providence may suitably be attributed to God. . . . Hence, the very exemplar of the order of things towards an end is in God called providence. Whence Boethius says that *Providence is the divine reason itself which, seated in the Supreme Ruler, disposes all things*, which disposition may refer either to the exemplar of the order of things towards an end, or to the exemplar of the order of parts in the whole.[10]

8. Thomas Aquinas, *Summa Theologiae*, I, 65, 2.
9. *Ibid.*, I, 6, 4.
10. *Ibid.*, I, 22, 1. Aristotle's position is cited also in the following passage: "Now

This very notion of the government of things in God the ruler of the universe has the nature of law. For law is a rule and measure of acts, and we have seen that the knowledge of God stands in relation to all created things as the knowledge of an artist does to the things made by his art, and that moreover he governs all the acts and movements that are to be found in things. "Therefore, just as the exemplar of the divine wisdom, inasmuch as all things are created by it, has the character of an art, a model or an idea, so the exemplar of the divine wisdom, as moving all things to their due end, bears the character of law."[11] For just as human law, as a rule and measure of acts whereby man is induced to act or is restrained from acting, takes its principle from human reason which is the rule and measure of human acts, so the rule and measure of all the acts and movements that are to be found in each single created thing has its principle in the Divine reason by which all created things are ruled and measured. Hence this law which is the exemplar of divine wisdom as directing all actions and movements is called the "eternal law"; and this same law, as found in the things that are ruled and measured by it, is called the "natural law"; "Since all things subject to divine providence are ruled and measured by the eternal law . . . it is evident that all things partake in some way in the eternal law, insofar as, namely, from its being imprinted on them, they derive their respective inclinations to their proper acts and ends."[12]

The law, therefore, by which the entire universe is governed directs all the parts of the universe to the common good of the whole in such a way that the parts attain their own proper operation and perfection by referring, as it were, to themselves, as parts of the good of the whole.[13] Indeed, in any practical science, as St.

---

things partake of the divine goodness by way of likeness, in being themselves good. But the greatest good in the things made by God is the good consisting in the order of the universe, which is most perfect, as the Philosopher says, with whom divine Scripture also agrees (*Genesis*, 1, 31): *God saw all the things that He had made, and they were very good*; whereas of each single work it was said simply *that they were good*. Consequently, that which is chiefly willed and caused by God is the good consisting in the order of the things of which He is the cause. But to govern things is nothing else but to impose order on them. Therefore, God by His intellect and will governs all things." Thomas Aquinas, *Summa Contra Gentiles*, III, 64. (The reference to Aristotle is to *Metaphysics*, XII, 10, 1075a12).

11. Thomas Aquinas, *Summa Theologiae*, I–II, 93, 1.

12. *Ibid.*, I–II, 91, 2.

13. To the objection that one loves a thing only insofar as it is one's own good and that therefore the parts cannot be said to love (by either an intellectual, or a

Thomas points out, it is especially its work that it make manifest how each single part can be perfected; and from the point of view of the Divine Art, the whole universe is the work of the divine practical science.[14]

The art, then, by which man governs himself and others, proceeds by imitating the government of things found in the universe. But before we proceed to the study of the art of politics, there is a final matter of importance that must be considered. Of all the creatures of the corporeal universe, man alone can have the art of government because as part of that universe he holds a special place; for he has a share not only in the execution of Divine Providence but, through governing himself and others, he has a share in the very disposition of Divine Providence. For providence, as we have seen, simply means the ordering of things to an end, whether in regard to oneself or in regard to others; and we have seen too, that man not only has an intrinsic principle of motion but moves himself because of having knowledge of the end, and hence is capable of ordering things with regard both to himself and to others. Thus man's self-government and his liberty consist precisely in this—that he shares in the disposition of Divine Providence by being capable of an art by which he disposes himself well with regard to the end fixed for him in his nature by the Divine Art.

---

rational, or an animal, or a natural love) the common good more than their individual good, St. Thomas replied that while it is indeed true that one loves a thing only insofar as it is one's own good, that does not mean that the common good is loved by referring it to the good of the part, but it is loved by the part referring itself to the good of the whole. *Ibid.*, II–II, 26, 3.

14. Thomas Aquinas, *Commentary on the Politics of Aristotle*, Prologue.

2. St.Thomas and Political Science

[This clear, forceful essay on St. Thomas first appeared in 1947 as a chapter in Theodore Brauer's collection *Thomistic Principles in a Catholic School*. It is different in many ways from McCoy's chapters on St. Thomas in *The Structure of Political Thought* and the chapter, "St. Thomas Aquinas," in the Strauss-Cropsey *History of Political Philosophy*. Father McCoy went through the principal doctrines from Aristotle about man as a social and political being. He next discussed how these are treated in St. Thomas's "Treatise on Law" in the *Summa Theologiae*. This effort was an examination of the nature and limits of politics. McCoy was especially attentive to the naturalness or validity of politics, yet also to the limits of politics. He noted several times that St. Thomas made original contributions to political philosophy, but that his main purpose was theological. This approach necessarily involved him in a discussion of why politics could not achieve certain higher ends of man and why, even in its own order, politics was, historically, so often unsuccessful in bringing about peace or that sufficiency of goods that Aristotle maintained was necessary for persons to practice virtue. McCoy was especially concerned to relate Aristotle to Aquinas through a careful analysis of the common good. Likewise, there is a brilliant discussion of the relation of the Church to the state. This essay is primarily a theoretical discussion which concentrated on the reasons why political philosophy could become an ideology or substitute theology. This analysis required an elaboration of the highest and secondary ends of man.]

Introduction

Politics is the name given by Aristotle to that science under which falls the consideration of the whole of human affairs; for this reason St. Thomas, following Aristotle, calls politics the first of the practical sciences. Just as in the division of speculative sciences metaphysics subordinates to itself all other speculative sciences having for their objects particular determinations of being (physics, the study of being as qualitative and mobile; mathemat-

24

ics, the study of being as quantitative), so in the division of practical sciences politics subordinates to itself all other practical sciences having for their objects ends inferior to and included within the end of politics, the common good. There is no activity of man, nor any association natural or conventional, which does not bear upon the common good of all; economic organizations, fraternal organizations, religious bodies, recreational groups, all have their specific and limited ends, and their specific and limited ends all converge upon the common good of all. The common good is, then, as it were, the convex of the whole good, whose concave is the proper good of individuals and groups composing the state.

The community that realizes the common good is clearly a perfect community. A perfect community is one whose end includes the ends of all other groups and whose end is not included in the end of any other group.[1] This definition has behind it the tremendous effort of the human intellect working toward a clarification of the relation between ethics and politics. Initiated by Plato, it was achieved by Aristotle, and the work of St. Thomas was to remove from Aristotle's achievement certain ambiguities and latent errors. Enlightened by the revealed truths of faith, the genius of St. Thomas brought Aristotle's achievement to sure perfection, and that perfection belongs essentially (as a truth intelligible to the natural light of reason) to the natural order of things.

1. See Josephus Gredt, *Elementa Philosophiae Aristotelico-Thomisticae* (Freiburg, 1932), II, n. 1027. We must understand here, first of all, that (for St. Thomas) it is theology and not politics which is, simply speaking, the principal science. In his *Commentary on the Ethics of Aristotle*, St. Thomas observed that it is only in the genus of practical sciences concerned with human matters that politics is said to be the principal science, and that divine science considers the ultimate end of the whole universe and is therefore the principle science, simply speaking. Secondly, we must understand that politics, as the most arthitectonic science, subordinates to itself both practical and speculative sciences, but differently. Politics prescribes for the practical sciences not only with respect to their employment, but also with respect to the very determination of their work; the state, for example, actually prescribes the roads to be built, the armaments to be made, and the manner of making them. But politics prescribes for the speculative sciences only with respect to the qualifications and requisites of those teaching and learning. "Sed scientiae speculativae praecipit civilis solum quantum ad usum, non autem quantum ad determinationem sui operis." (St. Thomas, *In Aristotelis Stagiritae, Nonnullos Libros Commentaria*, 1867, IV, 5). St. Thomas pointed out in the text cited that truth depends upon the very nature of things and not upon the will of man. Truth, the proper object of the speculative science, is thus not subject to the voluntary action of men and hence must be safeguarded from distortion at the hands of the state.

Man by Nature a Political and Social Animal

Since the good proper to man as an individual is not realized apart from the good of the whole community, evidently by his very nature man is a social and political animal. The least meaning which can be given to the proposition that man is by nature a political animal is that man cannot live well (which is his natural end) apart from the state. A nature is understood when the perfection toward which it tends as toward its proper end is grasped; since man's end, to live well, is accomplished through ordered association, the state is said to be natural to man. Thus it is primarily by virtue of his perfection that man seeks the companionship of his fellows.

St. Thomas makes it clear that man's rational nature does not itself adequately account for his social and political nature. He says:

Were man intended to live alone, as many animals do, he would require no other guide to this end [than the light of reason]. . . . However, it is natural for man to be a social and political animal, to live in a group, even more so than all other animals, as the very needs of his nature indicate. . . . Man was created without any natural provision for these things [his physical needs]. But, instead of them all he was endowed with reason. . . . But one man alone is not able to procure them for himself; for one man could not sufficiently provide for life, unassisted. It is, therefore, natural that man should live in company with his fellows.[2]

From St. Thomas's reasoning it clearly follows that the state cannot be conceived as an artificial or conventional association established originally and simply by contract; for clearly, man's reason is employed to procure his needs, so that from the point of view of man's indigences and from that of his perfections, man's rational nature is seen to be at the same time social. Since the reason of any one man, together with his other endowments, is insufficient for procuring all his needs, it is natural for man to live in the company of his fellows.

Individual Good and the Common Good

Man as a political and social animal can realize his own individual good only through organized community life. In short, the first

2. Thomas Aquinas, *On the Governance of Rulers*, trans. Gerald B. Phelan (Toronto, 1938), 34.

principle of natural justice, which is to seek the good and to avoid evil, must primarily be determined by a rule which has reference to the whole state. Aristotle's distinction between natural justice and legal justice is adopted by St. Thomas. Natural justice, Aristotle says, is "that which everywhere has the same force and does not exist by people's thinking this or that." It is distinguished from legal justice, which Aristotle describes as being "that which is originally indifferent, but when it has been laid down it is not indifferent, e.g., that a prisoner's ransom shall be a mina . . . and again all the laws that are passed for particular cases."[3] Thus it is according to natural justice that stolen goods are to be restored, that evil-doers are to be punished; but it is legal justice that determines the kind of penalty that will be exacted. Legal justice is, as Aristotle says, originally a matter of indifference, in the sense that legal enactments are determinations or specifications of the precepts of natural justice, and as such differ from one country to another and from one time to another. Now if man is by nature a social and political animal, evidently the primary determination of the precepts of natural justice must be directed to the common good. The law is this determination of the principles of natural justice directed to the common good.

The Essence of Law

St. Thomas says: "Law is a rule and measure of acts, whereby man is induced to act or is restrained from acting. . . . Now the rule and measure of human acts is the reason, which is the first principle of human acts." This point is established by showing that the principle of any genus, such as unity in the genus of numbers, is the rule and measure of that genus. By a comparison of the speculative and practical reason, St. Thomas further establishes his proportion about the essence of law. He says that the relationship between propositions and conclusions in the speculative reason holds between operations as the end term of the practical reason and the propositions in the practical reason from which actions proceed; "and such-like universal propositions in the practical intellect that are directed to actions have the nature of law." Now although human actions are concerned with particular matters, law is not ordained to some particular good, but to

---

3. Aristotle, *Nicomachean Ethics*, V, 7, 1134b18–23.

the common good. Against the proposed objection that if law is based on reason then any precept which is founded on reason and directed to some private good will be a law, St. Thomas replies by observing that such precepts may be directed to the common good and that in this way only do they share in the nature of law. How does St. Thomas show that law is directed to the common good?

He has just shown that law as a measure and rule of human acts must pertain to the reason, for reason, being the principle in the genus of human acts, is the rule and measure of such acts. Now he continues:

As reason is a principle of human acts, so in reason itself there is something which is the principle in respect of all the rest: wherefore to this principle chiefly and mainly law must needs be referred. Now the first principle in practical matters . . . is the last end. And the last end of human life is bliss or happiness. Consequently the law must needs regard principally the relationship to happiness. Moreover, since every part is ordained to the whole, as imperfect to perfect, and since one man is a part of the perfect community, the law must needs regard properly the relationship to universal happiness.[4]

Two further elements are necessary before St. Thomas is able to give a complete definition of law: (1) It is necessary to establish competence to make laws, and (2) it is necessary that a law be promulgated. Who is competent to make law? Since law, "properly speaking, regards first and foremost the order to the common good," it cannot be left to anyone at all in the community to make laws; to order anything to the common good belongs either to the whole people or to someone who is vicegerent of the whole people.[5] In all matters the directing of anything to an end concerns

4. Thomas Aquinas, *Summa Theologiae*, I–II, 90, 2. It is important to understand that the unity of the civil multitude of which man is a part is unity of order and not of continuity or composition. In this kind of unity the part can have an operation which is not the operation of the whole. And in the case of the whole which has this unity of order, it is not the same science which considers the whole and the parts. To ethics, not to politics, belongs the consideration of the operations of the individual man ordained to the realization of man's good as a person; politics considers the activity of a civil multitude ordained to the realization of the common good. Thus the political science of St. Thomas guarantees the true liberty of the person, for it insists that politics may not arrogate to itself a simple unity and destroy the rightful autonomy and function of man; on the contrary, the unity of the civil multitude is merely a unity of order, according to which the good proper to the individual is directed to the common good. Therefore, irrespective of forms of government, the state by its very nature exists to safeguard and foster the rightful autonomy of individuals and groups, and to direct their proper activities to the common good. See Thomas Aquinas, *Commentary on the Ethics of Aristotle*, Bk. I.
5. Thomas Aquinas, *Summa Theologiae*, I–II, 90, 3.

the person to whom the end belongs. It is evident, then, that the law, which is established for the good of all, can be established only by the people themselves or by the person who has charge of the commonwealth. Nor is the law effective unless it is promulgated by the lawmaker; since the law is a rule and measure of human acts, those whose acts are to be regulated must be made aware of the application of the law; and this is done by promulgation. These considerations bring St. Thomas to his final definition of law: "Law is an ordinance of reason for the common good, made by him who has care of the community, and promulgated."[6]

St. Thomas's analysis of law allows him to make a very illuminating commentary on the famous description of the quality of law given by St. Isidore of Seville. St. Isidore had expressed the qualifications of a good law as follows: "Law shall be virtuous, just, possible to nature, according to the custom of the country, suitable to place and time, necessary, useful: clearly expressed, . . . framed for no private benefit, but for the common good of the people."[7] St. Thomas inquires whether this long description is not less exact than a previous and shorter description given by St. Isidore. According to the earlier description, law was said to be good if "founded on reason, provided that it foster religion, be helpful to discipline, and further the common weal." St. Thomas shows us by his exact analysis that the later description is an amplification of the earlier one. In a searching examination of its contents, St. Thomas exhibits the second description as a commentary upon the first. He writes: "All the other conditions mentioned [by St. Isidore] are reduced to these three [that the law foster religion, be helpful to discipline, and further the common weal]. For it is called virtuous because it fosters religion. And when he goes on to say that it should be 'just, possible to nature, according to the customs of the country, adapted to time and place,' he implies that it should be helpful to discipline." How does St. Thomas show that these qualities conduce to discipline?

Human discipline depends first on the order of reason, to which he refers by saying 'just'; secondly, it depends on the ability of the agent; . . . and should be according to human customs since man cannot live alone in human society; . . . thirdly, it depends on certain circumstances, in respect of which he says, 'adapted to place and time.' The remaining words, 'necessary,' 'useful,' etc., mean that law should further the common weal;

6. *Ibid.*, I–II, 90, 4.   7. *Ibid.*, I–II, 95, 3.

so that necessity refers to the removal of evils; usefulness to the attainment of good; clearness of expression, to the need of preventing any harm ensuing from the law itself.[8]

The Constitution of a State

It has been already remarked that man's nature as a political and social animal makes it necessary that the first principles of natural justice be determined primarily by a rule which has reference to the whole state. Evidently the very first determination of the principles of natural justice should establish the kind of government by which all the parts of the state (individuals, families, social and economic groups) are ordered to the common good.

This first determination of the principles of natural justice is the constitution of a country. By a constitution neither St. Thomas nor Aristotle understood a written document which describes the organization of government and guarantees certain rights and privileges. A constitution, in the sense in which St. Thomas and Aristotle use the term, is best described as the mode of life of a state; and the mode of life is primarily determined by the nature of the ruling class. Aristotle expresses his notion of a constitution in the following way: "A constitution is the arrangement of magistracies in a state, especially the highest of all. The government is everywhere sovereign in the state, and the constitution is, in fact, the government. For example, in democracies the people are supreme, but in oligarchies the few; and therefore we say that these two forms of government are different: and so in other cases."[9]

There are only three possibilities in the arrangement of the supreme magistracy of a state: that the power be located in one man, or in several men, or in all of the people. In all these cases the government is good if the ruling class governs for the sake of the common good. If one man rules for the common good, the government is called monarchy; if several rule for the common good, the government is called aristocracy; and if the multitude of the people rule for the common good, the government is called polity. Conversely, when the ruling class governs for its private interest rather than in behalf of the common good, the government is a

8. *Ibid.*
9. Aristotle, *Politics*, III, 6, 1278b10–14.

tyranny if in the hands of one man, an oligarchy if in the hands of several, and a democracy if in the hands of the multitude of the people.

Relative Merit of the Good Forms of Government

The question concerning the relative merit of the good forms of government must be answered as a corollary to the basic question: What is the purpose of government? "The welfare and safety of a multitude formed into a society," says St. Thomas, "is the preservation of its unity, which is called peace, and which, if taken away, the benefit of social life is lost."[10] It follows that the ruling class is chiefly concerned with the establishment and protection of the unity of peace. That government, then, is best which is most efficacious in keeping the unity of peace.

If this were all that St. Thomas had to say, it would simply follow that that government which could in fact most efficaciously procure the unity of peace would be the best government. But St. Thomas adds: "It is manifest that what is itself one can more efficaciously bring about unity than several. . . . Therefore the rule of one man is more useful than the rule of many."[11] This, St. Thomas says, is clear from the fact that when several rule, agreement is necessary among them, and this means that the several must approach being one; therefore, again, as a principle, the rule of one is more useful than the rule of many.

It is altogether imperative that we do not hamper St. Thomas's doctrine by the limitations of the historical perspective from which he wrote. Freed from these limitations, the principle is clear that all governments become more efficacious in the task of procuring the unity of peace to the extent that the government is itself unified.

Modern democracies employ innumerable devices to achieve unified action and centralized responsibility: we need only mention the British cabinet system, majority rule, the combination of party leadership and executive responsibility in the United States. It does not by any means follow from St. Thomas's principle that modern democracies are manifestly less good than monarchy; as though their imitations and approximations of the unity of mon-

10. Thomas Aquinas, *On the Governance of Rulers*, 40.
11. *Ibid.*, 41.

archy constitute proof of their demerit. And for this reason: it can quite well be that that equality of condition which de Tocqueville said characterizes modern democracy has resulted, not in a reversal of the principle which St. Thomas lays down, but in a reversal of its concrete realization. Equality of condition makes it necessary, if any one man is to act as one, that he approach the unity of the equal many, that he defer to the will of the multitude.[12] So that in the modern world monarchy is in fact not in itself one but must depend for its unity of action upon the many; and the many is more nearly in itself one because of the equality of condition of which de Tocqueville spoke.

In this light we can see that St. Thomas's choice of monarchy was suggested by a twofold consideration: (1) by the basic principle that that government is best which most efficaciously achieves the unity of peace; and (2) by the historical consideration that the unity which monarchy symbolizes was in fact best achieved in the social structure of medieval Europe by monarchical rule. In the Middle Ages the monarchical regime was part of the historical milieu, and, by reason of the historical fact that Western culture had not as yet been marked by those revolutionary movements which brought about the destruction of an artificial class system based on blood and real property, the monarchical regime was appropriate enough. The equality of men came with the abolition of slavery, the breakdown of feudalism with its attendant divorce of political power from land tenure, the commercial revolution and the consequent mobility of exchange and of men. By the logic of its inner development, especially by the extension of the suffrage, democracy has encouraged a more equitable distribution of wealth and has made possible a "unity of social race based on the common condition of all men bound to labor."[13]

The End of the State

The benefit of social life, which is guaranteed by the preservation of its unity, is virtuous living. As a social and political animal, man differs from other animals not only in his use of reason for pro-

12. Even the Nazi and communist dictatorial regimes were primarily characterized by the need of the dictator's deferring to the popular will. See Charles E. Merriam, *What Is Democracy?* (Chicago, 1941).
13. Jacques Maritain, *True Humanism* (New York, 1938), 193.

curing the material necessities of life, but primarily by virtue of the specifically rational end of his social life, namely, virtuous living. St. Thomas offers as evidence of the truth of this observation the fact "that only those who render mutual assistance to one another in living well truly form a part of an assembled multitude. For if men assembled merely to *live,* then animals . . . would form a part of the civil body. And if men assembled only to acquire wealth, then all those who traded together would belong to one city."[14] The same truth is likewise obvious from a consideration of the nature of the ruler or rulers of a state. If the end for man were corporeal, such as life and health of the body, the governor would before all else be a physician. Again, "if that ultimate end were an abundance of wealth, then some financier would be king of the multitude."[15] But rulers are called "fathers of people" because they have regard for all the necessities of all of the people: they must be men of wisdom and goodness.[16]

The state, then, through its constitution and laws seeks to establish not only the particular justice attained by an equitable distribution of material goods,[17] but ultimately to bring about that complete virtue known as "universal justice." Universal justice Aristotle defines as the exercise of all the virtues in relation to one's neighbors.[18] Indeed, it is because the law seeks universal justice that universal justice is said to be "the lawful," in the sense that "practically the majority of the acts commanded by the law are those which are prescribed from the point of view of virtue taken as a whole."[19] Citing Aristotle to the effect that "the law prescribes the performances of the acts of a brave man . . . and the acts of a temperate man . . . and the acts of the meek man: and in like manner as regards the other virtues and vices, prescribing the former, forbidding the latter," St. Thomas makes a distinction— the significance of which will presently be made clear—between the acts of all the virtues and all the acts of every virtue. Since law is ordained to the common good, and since the objects of all the virtues can be referred to the common good of the multitude, it follows that there is no virtue whose acts cannot be prescribed by

---

14. Thomas Aquinas, *On the Governance of Rulers,* 97.
15. *Ibid.*   16. *Ibid.,* 39. See *ibid.,* I, 8.
17. This "particular justice" embraces distributive justice and commutative justice. Distributive justice consists in the division of material goods among two or more persons on the basis of some order of merit; commutative justice is concerned with rectifying wrongs done to those who already hold goods.
18. Aristotle, *Ethics,* V, 1, 1129b25.   19. *Ibid.,* 1130a9–10.

the law. Human law, then, does prescribe some acts of all the virtues, namely, all acts which are ordainable to the common good.

Peace, good habits, and a sufficiency of earthly goods are indispensable for durable virtue. Peace, which is the tranquillity of order, must first of all be established in the individual man by the rulership of his reason. Gilson appositely says that "not until the social order becomes the spontaneous expression of an interior peace in men's hearts shall we have tranquillity."[20] The peace of a society is procured by the efforts of the ruler in uniting the multitude of the people: it thus follows and is an imitation of the interior peace which should exist in men's hearts. Secondly, virtuous living requires not simply the performance of isolated acts of virtue, but the development of good habits; it requires that "the multitude thus united in the bond of peace, be guided to good deeds."[21] Finally, man's need for a sufficiency of earthly goods is evident upon consideration of the fact that his nature as a social and political animal requires that he first live before he can live well. Having achieved the unity of peace, the ruler will look to its permanence by the careful selection of administrative officials, by rewarding exemplary citizens and punishing criminals, and by defending his people against external enemies.

The Church and the State

It has been pointed out that St. Thomas, in asking the question whether the law prescribes acts of all the virtues, distinguishes between acts of all the virtues and all the acts of every virtue. In dealing with this specific question he says that, since the objects of all the virtues can be referred to the common good of the multitude, there is no virtue whose acts cannot be prescribed by the law. The precise weight of this statement is perhaps more easily appreciated when we understand it to mean that human law does prescribe some acts of all virtues. The reason why the law does not prescribe all the acts of all the virtues becomes clear from the following considerations: In the natural order the law can and does prescribe those acts of each virtue which pertain either immediately or mediately to the common good—"either immediately, as when certain things are done directly for the common good; or

20. Etienne Gilson, *The Spirit of Medieval Philosophy* (New York, 1940), 399.
21. Thomas Aquinas, *On the Governance of Rulers*, 103.

mediately, as when a lawgiver prescribes certain things pertaining to good order, whereby the citizens are directed in the upholding of the common good of justice and peace."[22] The law does not, therefore, prescribe acts of virtue ordained to the private good as such, of individuals. Further, human law can deal with those matters only in which men are competent to judge; "but man is not competent to judge of interior movements, that are hidden, but only of exterior acts which appear."[23]

The law then cannot prescribe the interior acts of virtue. Nor, again, can human law prohibit all vices. Law, being a measure of human acts, should be homogeneous with that which it measures; "wherefore laws imposed on men should also be in keeping with their condition, for . . . law should be possible both according to nature, and according to the customs of the country. Now possibility or faculty of action is due to an interior habit or disposition, since the same thing is not possible to one who has not a virtuous habit as is possible to one who has. Now human law is framed for a number of human beings, the majority of whom are not perfect in virtue. Wherefore human laws do not forbid all vices, from which the virtuous abstain, but only the more grievous vices, from which it is possible for the majority to abstain; and chiefly those that are to the hurt of others, without the prohibition of which human society could not be maintained."[24] The state has certainly for its object the common good of all; and this common good is the virtuous living of each member of the community; but a man cannot be truly virtuous unless he practice not only exterior acts of virtue but the interior acts as well. Nor can he be truly virtuous unless he repress all vices in his life.[25] How, then, is the state to attain its proper end if it cannot prescribe all the acts of all the virtues, and if it cannot repress all vices? This difficulty was in some measure understood by Aristotle, for in the Fifth Book of his *Ethics*, after saying that "the law bids us practice every virtue and forbids us to practice any vice," he adds: "But with regard to the education of the individual as such, which makes him without qualification a good *man*, we must determine later whether this is the function of the political art or of another."[26]

The hearts of men are known only to God; if men are to be

22. Thomas Aquinas, *Summa Theologiae*, I–II, 96, 3.
23. *Ibid.*, I–II, 91, 4.   24. *Ibid.*, I–II, 96, 2.
25. *Ibid.*, I–II, 91, 4.
26. Aristotle, *Nicomachean Ethics*, V, 2, 1130b27–8.

educated in truly virtuous living they will have to be guided by divine authority. Man, considered "in the absolutely peculiar and incommunicable quality of his liberty and as ordered directly to God as to his eternal end, . . escapes inclusion in the political ordination. *Homo non ordinatur ad communitatem politicam secundum se totum et secundum omnia sua.*"[27] Cognizant of the problem, Aristotle did not understand the distinction between ethics and politics, by which politics, as "ordered to the whole of the terrestrial state" is subordinated to ethics, which is "ordered to the transcendant common good of the whole universe," God Himself.[28] This distinction between ethics and politics holds good within the natural order itself; its realization, however, was made possible by Christianity, which not only has shown that it is impossible for the state to realize its own proper goodness without the help of divine guidance, but has given to men a goal beyond any temporal good, namely, eternal happiness.

This brings us to the last and most important reason why the state is of itself inadequate to the task of bringing men to virtuous living. While it is true, as has been pointed out, that there is no virtue whose acts cannot be prescribed by the law, the state remains inadequate on two grounds: it cannot prescribe all the acts of all the virtues nor repress all vices; and it is of itself incapable of bringing men to their final beatitude. And since with respect to the first case the state cannot attain its proper end unless all virtue is fostered and all vice repressed, and with respect to the second case, the state's proper end, the terrestrial common good of the multitude, is subordinated to the eternal good of men, it becomes necessary for the state to be assisted by the divine authority of the Church, and, in matters of faith and morals, to be educated by the Church.

Inasmuch as the moral virtues necessarily bear upon the last end of man, the justice of the common good is specified integrally by being properly ordinated to the last end. "Since man, by living virtuously, is ordained to a higher end, which consists of the enjoyment of God," it follows that the ultimate end of an assembled multitude is not "to live virtuously, but through virtuous living to attain to the possession of God."[29] St. Thomas continues: "Fur-

27. Jacques Maritain, *The Things That Are Not Caesar's* (New York, 1939), 4. The italicized words are from St. Thomas, *Summa Theologiae*, I–II, 21, 3. This does not involve a denial of man's social nature.
28. Maritain, *The Things That Are Not Caesar's*, 2.
29. Thomas Aquinas, *On the Governance of Rulers*, 97 ff.

thermore if it could attain this end by the power of human nature, then the duty of a king would have to include the direction of men to this end. . . . But because a man does not attain his end, which is the possession of God, by human power, but by divine power, . . . therefore the task of leading him to that end does not pertain to human government but to divine. Consequently, government of this kind pertains to that king who is not only a man, but also God, namely, to our Lord Jesus Christ, who by making men sons of God, brought them to the glory of heaven. . . . Hence a royal priesthood is derived from Him, and what is more, all those who believe in Christ, in so far as they are His members, are called kings and priests. Consequently, in order that spiritual things might be distinguished from earthly things, the ministry of this kingdom has been entrusted not to earthly kings, but to priests, and in the highest degree to the chief priest, the successor of St. Peter, the Vicar of Christ, the Roman Pontiff, to whom all the kings of Christian peoples are to be subject as to our Lord Jesus Christ Himself."[30]

In summary, then, the end of the state is a true but intermediate end. With respect to the realization of this end the state is not entirely adequate because the law cannot extend to the interior acts of man and therefore cannot effectively prescribe virtuous living; but further, the proper end of the state, being an intermediate end, is ordained to a further end, namely, the possession of God; and since the task of leading men to that end does not pertain to human government but to divine government, the Church, which has this spiritual power, has an indirect power over temporal things insofar as they affect the spiritual order of salvation.

Conclusion

The interest of St. Thomas Aquinas in politics is primarily a theologian's interest. *On the Governance of Rulers* is properly considered a theological treatise rather than a treatise in political philosophy; not only does St. Thomas's demonstration rest primarily on the authority of sacred scripture, but his interest in the state as a perfect natural community is essentially directed not to an analysis of forms and techniques, but to the nature of the state as defined by its own end, virtuous living, and as ordered to man's

30. *Ibid.*, 99.

final end, eternal happiness. Similarly, St. Thomas's masterly treatise on law is properly a theological treatise, as is evident from the very opening passage, in which law and grace are said to be means by which the extrinsic principle moving men to the good (and the extrinsic principle is God) instructs and assists us. The theological character of these treatises does not, of course, imply that they are devoid of doctrines demonstrable by natural reason; on the contrary, St. Thomas develops many philosophical doctrines which he puts at the disposal of his theological teaching.[31]

Political science is properly concerned with an analysis of the forms and techniques by which the temporal common good is attained, yet the history of political philosophy since the time of St. Thomas has been a history of successive failures to relate ethics to politics and of successive attempts to find a substitute for theology—either in politics itself, as fascism does, or in economics as marxism does. Men are today oppressed by false theologies erected into political systems, and those who are not so oppressed are in risk of becoming so oppressed by an intellectual and moral inability to defend themselves. St. Thomas's political science will not give us the answers to problems of hydro-electric development or technological unemployment; but it will give us the answer to the most vital of contemporary problems: how to secure the rational foundations of humane living.

31. See Gerald Phelan's Preface to Thomas Aquinas, *On the Governance of Rulers.*

3. Democracy and the Rule of Law*

[This treatment is an excellent example of Charles N. R. McCoy's ability to analyze critically a position in political thought in the light of its principles and history. The notion of democracy is central to political science. The word itself bears many meanings which must be distinguished and judged. The basic question is whether "democracy" means an acknowledgment of a rule of law, presupposing theoretical rectitude which does not derive merely from the will of a single ruler or from the wills of the multitude. McCoy understood how important it was to rethink Aristotle over against his interpreters. In this, the rule of law was not something autonomous to itself, but something given, to which every sort of citizen was obliged and which obligation freed him from both his own passions and those of others. McCoy argued that for Aristotle the proximate rule of action or morality could not be someone else, but likewise it could not merely be a reason presupposed to no order. The dignity of the citizen was itself a function of the citizen's obligation to the truth. Truth was not something subject to the decision of the multitude or to the power of the few. Constitutionalism was an aid to human action and to truth. When it lacked this relationship, it easily became a way to build a polity presupposed only to itself.]

Within the last half century democracy and government according to law have come increasingly to be identified in the thought of political scientists. Since the substance of political philosophy admittedly derives from the great pioneer work of Aristotle, political scientists have made some efforts to read in Aristotle either a prophecy of this identification of democracy and the rule of law or an announcement of it. But no great effort was required. Two reasons at least may account for the case and surety with which this interpretation of Aristotle has been made. First of all, Aristotle in his *Politics* contrasts rule according to law with rule by one best

*This essay originally appeared in *Modern Schoolman*, 25 (November 1947), 1–10.

man; this opposition might lead one to conclude that the rule of law is possible only under the rule of the many. Secondly, the new historical spirit is apt to be misled in rendering judgment upon ages in which our modern historical relativism was unknown; and the rendering of judgments on matters of political doctrine is complicated by the widely held opinion that democracy is somehow the unique political expression of cultural relativity. Thus, if the historical sense suggests to us that no one could really believe in eternal truths or universal values, or that at least such belief is intelligible only when considered as one of the phenomena of culture belonging to a particular environment, it suggests to us further that every great thinker must fundamentally have spoken in behalf of democracy. This approach to the history of ideas has had the absurd result that scholars have hailed even Machiavelli as a great lover of the people, of liberty, and of democracy.[1] It has also been suggested that the inevitability of democracy is such that Hitler's Nazi state could not escape the implications of democracy.[2] In this approach to the history of ideas we have the clue to the modern interpretation of Aristotle's doctrine of constitutionalism, which seeks the foundation of that doctrine in the notion of a growing popular wisdom that determines from one historical epoch to another the ideals and aims of society. Professor Sabine well illustrates this manner of understanding Aristotle. Doubtless having in mind Aristotle's introduction into Western philosophy of the distinction between speculative and practical science, Professor Sabine understands this advance over Plato's idealism to involve the supposition that the customs of a people must be the ultimate measure of practical action; Aristotle had found the Platonic concern with the claims of the wise man to be a wholly academic preoccupation and had moved on to seek political ideals in the analysis and description of actual constitutions. Consequently, "Aristotle accepted the point of view that in any good state . . . the law must be the ultimate sovereign and not any person whatsoever."[3] Professor Michael Foster also seems to understand Aristotle's fundamental political doctrine to be that

1. Ernst Cassirer properly convicts those scholars who have attempted to rehabilitate Machiavelli in *The Myth of the State* (New Haven, 1946). See also my "The Place of Machiavelli in the History of Political Thought," *American Political Science Review* 27 (August 1943), 626–41. (See Chapter IV of McCoy's *The Structure of Political Thought*, and below, Chapter 9.

2. Charles E. Merriam, *What Is Democracy?* (Chicago, 1941), 7.

3. George H. Sabine, *A History of Political Theory* (New York, 1937), 93.

mankind experiences a genuine growth in the knowledge of the end and purpose of society.[4] This view Professor Foster contrasts with Plato's doctrine "that scientific knowledge makes a man superior to rules; so that if a man fully understood the principles underlying legislation, he would be superior to the written laws in which those principles were embodied."[5] That Professor Foster conceives the difference between Plato and Aristotle in the manner I have just suggested is clear from the fact that Professor Foster admits that "there is one place (in *Politics* III, chap. 13) in which Aristotle seems to propound a similar doctrine" (similar to Plato's doctrine that scientific knowledge makes a man superior to rules); but, Professor Foster explains, "I have ignored it as an isolated passage which is unsupported by his general doctrine."[6] Professor Foster evidently, then, assumes that the general doctrine of Aristotle supports the view that the speculative understanding of the end of man and society takes its measure from practical regulation. We may remark that if, as Professor Foster says, Aristotle propounds a doctrine that is similar to Plato's and obviously therefore not the same, how does Professor Foster know, if he has ignored it, that it is unsupported by Aristotle's general doctrine?

Nor, paradoxically, has the most significant historical evidence on the meaning of Aristotle been sufficient to overcome the prejudice of the historical sense. I do not refer to the philological problems which have caused scholars many uncertainties about the order of the books of the *Politics*, because the outcome of that question—tentative and uncertain as it is—could not in any case seriously affect the dialectical character of the discussion in the *Politics* of individuals in association.[7] I refer to the fact that the most exhaustive and searching commentary that has ever been made on the *Politics*—and made in the light of equally exhausting and searching commentaries on all of the major works of Aristotle—shows us that the rule of law in democracy, so far from having been conceived by Aristotle as a kind of measuring rod of a growing social intelligence, was conceived in precisely the opposite fashion as an approximation of a fixed limit, which limit moreover was set forth ideally by Aristotle in his conception of the heroically virtuous man. For Aristotle, the whole point about the rule of law

4. Michael Foster, *Masters of Political Thought* (Boston, 1941).
5. *Ibid.*, I, 161.   6. *Ibid.*, I, 161–62.
7. See Richard P. McKeon, "Aristotle's Conception of Moral and Political Philosophy," *Ethics*, 51 (April 1941), 253–90.

in a democracy was indeed that it kept the multitude or any group or any one among them from running away pell-mell with political power under high-sounding claims and titles like "growing social intelligence."[8] It is incredible in a sense that the reverse of this should now be so widely put forth as the doctrine of Aristotle. And it is ironical that scholars whose intention it has evidently been to provide out of Aristotle a defense of democracy have succeeded in producing a theory that by identifying democracy and rule of law involves the destruction of both.

Apparently the point of departure (if there is any) for this curious misconstruction is Aristotle's distinction between speculative and practical science. Those scholars who adopt the "approach" to Aristotle's *Politics* that I have been discussing must imagine that because Aristotle did not agree with Plato's opinion that scientific knowledge makes a man superior to rules he must have held that practical regulation is practical because it is in no way the object of scientific knowledge. I say that these men must imagine this because they fail to give a supporting argument from Aristotle for their bizarre conclusion. But the argument which is implicit in their conclusion is that since practical matters are distinguished from speculative matters in that the former are subject to the will of man, "truth" in practical matters can only be whatever man finds to be within his competence to do; and since, obviously, different civilizations have had very different ideas on these matters—ideas largely affected by the state of applied science—the only conclusion is that there is a "growing stock of social intelligence" which indicates the "truth" about ends and purposes in human society. Obviously, therefore, Plato misconceived the nature of politics when he supposed that scientific knowledge could render a man superior to rules; and in repudiating this idealistic doctrine Aristotle introduced the notion of the practical, and with it the notion that the customs, habits, and opinions of a people are the ultimate norm of "truth" in practical matters. Attractive and plausible as all this may possibly sound, it is simply not the teaching of Aristotle; nor is there even an adumbration of it in Aristotle, unless the misunderstanding of a doctrine may be taken as an adumbration of it.

"Rule of law" has in Aristotle a very profound meaning. Possibly

8. Advance may indeed be made in social intelligence, but it is made in respect to the means available for the achievement of an end already fixed by the nature of man.

it can best be grasped by understanding it in contrast to the rules of an operative art. The laws of a polity, Aristotle observes, have to do with human actions directed toward the end of the polity, and therefore deal with things which affect the perfection of the soul.[9] The rules of an operative art, such as medicine, are directed to the perfection of some material object. In productive work—the sphere of art—the artist is free to choose the end which he desires to realize. The truth of an artistic judgment depends then simply upon the conformity of the intelligence with the end chosen. But the laws of a polity are directed to an end that is fixed by the rectitude of the appetite in relation to the good (the appetible), so that the truth of a prudential judgment in choosing the means to the end does not depend primarily on the intelligence but on the conformity of the appetite with an end known to be truly good. This is not to say that the prudential judgment does not at all depend upon speculative rectification; indeed it presupposes it, as the phrase "right appetite" signifies, for a "right appetite" is one which is in conformity with reason, and this presupposes that we know in some fashion the nature of man and the end of man's activity. Aristotle's point is simply that in human actions speculative truth is not sufficient (for example, that the good is to be done); what is necessary is practical truth about practical knowledge, and this demands rectitude of the appetite. Therefore in repudiating Plato's teaching that scientific knowledge renders a man superior to rules, Aristotle is simply saying that scientific knowledge of practical matters is not enough—and not that it is not necessary.

The means to the attainment of the good are precisely what men are free to choose, and the means are infinite in number, varying according to all sorts of conditions and circumstances. It is the customs and habits of a people by which they concretely manifest their choice of means to the end of virtuously living in community. Since the positive law of the community is ordained to the common good, it must necessarily conform to the fundamental customs and habits by which a people have concretely made their choice of means to virtuous living. This, Aristotle explicitly tells us, is how and why laws differ from the rules of an operative art, which can be quite readily changed to conform with any end that the artist chooses. At the same time, it is the virtuous man who is the mea-

9. Aristotle, *Politics*, III, 16, 1287a16–87b8.

sure and rule of human actions; but he is said to be the measure and rule in a remote and exemplary way, not proximately. No man can be the proximate measure or rule of action for another man—nor for a whole society—because of Aristotle the proximate measure is one's own prudence. The only sense in which the virtuous man can be said to be the measure and rule of another man's actions is in a remote and exemplary way; otherwise one's individual liberty and the liberty of a civil multitude would be destroyed. It is for this reason that law must be not only just in itself but also suitable to the customs of the country and the habits of the people. This is the profound meaning of rule of law that distinguishes it from rule of art; the ruler is not an artist in the proper sense and cannot impose his own will upon the "matter" under his direction. It is this fundamental meaning of rule of law that makes Aristotle's royal rule a "constitutional" and not an absolute rule.[10]

Now it is in a derived sense that the notion of rule of law is applied by Aristotle to democracy. There are many factors, Aristotle tells us, that are to be considered in the organization of a state. Although the virtuous man will apprehend properly the comparative relevance of these factors, claims are nonetheless made absolutely by the partisans of wealth, of freedom and equality, and of nobility of birth on the basis of the principle, "Qualis unusquisque est, talis ei finis videtur."[11] Political history attests the extreme difficulty of organizing the state on the basis of the highest precepts; and therefore the perfect state is for the most part a limiting case whose constitutionalism must be imitated in much the same way as the temperate man is imitated by the continent man.[12] In the virtuous man, Aristotle points out, the reason governs the appetites "with a constitutional and royal rule."[13] The analogy with civil rule is quite direct; for just as the appetitive power has its proper object and can be set in motion by the sense as well as by the intellect, so individuals and groups within the

10. This is the philosophical foundation of that distinction between *gubernaculum* and *jurisdictio* which was central to the legal theory and practice of the medieval period. See Charles H. McIlwain, *Constitutionalism: Ancient and Modern* (Ithaca, 1940). [For McCoy's review of McIlwain, see bibliography.]

11. Aristotle, *Nicomachean Ethics*, III, 7, 1151b20–21.

12. The continent man performs the acts of the temperate man, but he performs them without pleasure; the incontinent man performs the acts of the self-indulgent man, but he performs them with reluctance.

13. Aristotle, *Politics*, I, 5, 1254b4.

state have their proper functions, and their activities are not principally of the whole community.[14] Now the rectitude of the appetite in the virtuous man establishes a perfect constitutional rule; so much so, indeed, that the virtuous man is said to be above the law. In a similar way Aristotle's royal rule is said also to be "legibus solutus" precisely because of the perfection of the rule of law.[15] But in the merely continent man the end which he seeks—virtuous action—cannot be had without setting up very special devices by which he attempts to insure himself against the perversity of his appetite. In a similar way, therefore, the most generally practicable kind of state seeks to prevent the perversity of man's appetites from gaining mastery of the community. It is for this reason that Aristotle's analysis of the best practicable state is not carried out in terms of the nature and final cause of the state, but in terms rather of proportions and functions of the component elements of the state. His chief objective here is to avoid the extremes of oligarchy and democracy, and this is accomplished by balancing birth, wealth, education, and position with sheer number. In practice the polity places supremacy in the hands of the class that lies between the extremes of the very rich and the very poor, and its success is made to depend largely on the numbers and political strength of this intermediate class. But now it should be observed that the contrivance by which the middle class insures the stability of the state no more provides a measure and rule for the actions of the citizenry than does the condition of continence provide a measure and rule for the action of the individual. Aristotle's analysis of the most generally practicable state prescinds from the formal consideration of virtue.[16] On this point the analogy between the polity and the continent man does not hold because the intermediate of the middle class between the extremes of wealth and poverty simply abstracts from virtue; the analogy is rather to be

14. Thomas Aquinas, *Commentary on the Ethics of Aristotle*, I, 1.

15. This is one of the sources of confusion in the presentation of Aristotle's doctrine. Because the virtuous man is the measure and the rule of action, he is said to be above the law and not to rule according to law; at the same time, he is a constitutional ruler because he does not constitute a proximate measure and rule for anyone's actions. Hence, when Aristotle contrasts the rule of one most virtuous man with the rule of many, he does so by contrasting "rule of the best man" with "rule of law."

16. The consideration of virtue is not entirely absent, however, for property is for Aristotle a certain promise of virtue; and the many, in a situation where everyone may be assumed to be equal in virtue and natural disposition, will have more virtue than the few.

looked for in the fact that the rule by the middle classes prescinds from right appetite of the end, and the continent man does not live by virtue precisely but by something less, since right appetite of the end is also lacking in him. The measure and rule for the polity, as it is for the continent man, remains the virtuous man. Now the continent man imitates the perfect rule of law by moving in the direction of the abstemious man; he does indeed imitate the intermediate condition of virtue (intermediate between self-indulgence and complete abstention) by reason of the fact that, being himself inclined toward the extreme of self-indulgence, he devises to move to the other extreme of total abstention, thus imitating the intermediate condition by a somewhat precarious combination of both extremes. In a similar way Aristotle proposes that an imitation of the rule of law be contrived for the polity, which, not being constituted in terms of ends or virtue, provides no measure and role for human actions. And what Aristotle proposes is the institution of a regime of law that is an imitation as it is an approximation of the prudence of the truly virtuous man. Now what is this special and derivative sense of "rule according to law"? The prudence of the virtuous man is to be imitated in much the same way as the continent man imitates it, namely, by moving away from the passions altogether. And this, Aristotle suggests, is more or less successfully accomplished by having no man nor any group of men rule permanently, but having everyone rule by turns and in the same fixed manner.[17]

Aristotle's democracy supposes a people who are at least disposed to virtue; its chief feature is the imitative device of the "rule of law" by which the citizens may be guaranteed against themselves. It is a device intended to guarantee that political action be based upon right desire—a right desire which is not sufficiently eminent in any of the citizens. Those scholars who pretend to a reading of Aristotle that identifies absolutely the conception of rule of law with democracy seek to emancipate the intelligence from the condition of the appetite and thus to establish a proximate rule that will guarantee practical truth independently of the condition of right appetite. The consequence is the utter destruction of both democracy and the rule of law, for a political regime erected upon the negation of prudential truth becomes a proximate rule of action beyond which there is no other measure. There is no appeal be-

17. Aristotle, *Politics*, III, 16, 1287a17.

yond "the reaction of human preference to some state of social and physical fact," as Professor Sabine expresses this position. In effect this means that human preference is simply the ultimate measure—a proposition that Aristotle says would be true if man were the best thing in the world, which, he adds, he is obviously not.[18] The totalitarianism of this position is clear when we consider that if political science and political prudence are independent of the condition of right appetite, then human good and human society will be simply what we want to make them, and "we" will be whoever has power over us. "Following this hypothesis," writes Professor Charles de Koninck,

man will in truth be the measure of all things, and no other measure will be possible for him. But the proposition "Man is the measure of all things" remains abstract. In order that its consequence be made evident we must ask "What man?" or "What men?" Notice that we cannot ask "What man or what men have the right to impose themselves as a measure?" This will be the right of him who holds in his hands the power to impose himself. In good logic all that one can do is to await what events produce. . . . This is the consequence of the emancipation of man, *pur artifex*.[19]

If we have lost the truth in words then neither the words themselves nor institutions set up to preserve their substance will be of any avail. Professor Charles H. McIlwain sees the history of constitutionalism as showing a progress from the medieval intellectual and moral appreciation of the rule of law to the expression of this concept in formal documents and the imposition of sanctions to insure its maintenance.[20] He sees the modern problem of constitutionalism to be that of making government "within its legal limits, actually stronger than it is."[21] But what are we to say to the very corruption of the medieval intellectual and moral appreciation of the rule of law? Does it help to have the words in formal documents when the very substance has been repudiated and the very premises have become "simply irrelevant to the modern mind"?[22] Who will make government stronger if that very perversity in man on whose account the device of the rule of law was thought by Aristotle to be necessary, has divinized itself, and man has

18. Aristotle, *Nicomachean Ethics*, VI, 7, 1141a20.
19. Charles de Koninck, *De la primauté du bien commune* (Quebec, 1943), 88. [Author's translation]
20. McIlwain, *op, cit.*   21. *Ibid.*, 95 and *passim*.
22. See the "Introductory Essay" of George H. Sabine to the last work of Carl L. Becker, *Freedom and Responsibility in the American Way of Life* (New York, 1945).

emerged as the master of good and evil? It is not unlikely that this man is the most portentous of those mythical monsters that, as the late Ernst Cassirer said, return from out of the depths of human culture and "shake our cultural world and our social order to its very foundations." Unless we can take a humbler view of democracy and of human dignity—which, as every page of history attests, is so very precarious—we shall lose entirely the sight of the things that we ought to desire.

4. The Problem of the Origin of Political Authority*

[McCoy was well aware of the endeavor of modern political theory to cut all ties with classical reason and establish a political order independent of any reference to right and truth. Like democracy, political authority has had two different explanations, both related to the discussion of the rule of law and the relation of politics to speculative rectitude. McCoy in this essay analyzed the Transmission and Designation theories of the origins of political authority. He took care to note that the real origin of modern political philosophy might also lie with the Suarezian version of this Transmission theory. McCoy wished to show that the origin of political authority is man's social nature, so that it is reasonable and necessary that we have and establish a political form of rule over ourselves. But he also wished to argue that "democracy" is not the same as the civil multitude, so that we cannot argue that democracy is the natural and therefore best form of rule. This latter notion leads to various forms of contract theory which hold that man is not by nature a social being and that, in fact, society in some sense alienated him. This premise forms the main impetus to that phase of modern political theory which ends in man for himself, man presupposed to nothing but himself as the basis of political philosophy.]

There are two famous theories concerning the origin of political authority, both of them deriving from the tradition of Greek–medieval political philosophy—the Transmission theory and the Designation theory. Both accept the same basic conceptions of that tradition: the nature of man as a social and political animal, the existence of a natural law, and the establishment of political authority in response to the inclination of nature. The difference between them turns on the question: How does political authority

*This essay originally appeared in *The Thomist*, 16 (January 1953), 71–81.

originate? Or: In what manner is political authority in the people? Each of the theories contains a principle and a "corollary." The principle of the Transmission theory is that the whole people is the immediate or principle cause (though secondary or subordinate to the Primary Cause which is God) of political authority in whomever it is vested; its corollary is that there is one form of government by natural institution, namely direct democracy, that whether there be other forms is a matter left to the free choice of the people, and that other forms of government are instituted by a transference of political authority by the people to one or to several. There is by force of natural law no obligation on the members of the body politic to transfer political authority. Hence, it is the community itself, organizing into the body politic, that holds authority and continues to do so as long as it does not transfer it to an individual or group. There is, then, only one constitution which exists by natural law, viz., direct democracy. The Designation theory has for its principle that God is the immediate cause of political authority in whomever the people designate as having it, and the people in designating their rulers are merely acting as instrumental cause. The part that man plays in constituting authority is restricted to designation, when what is caused by man is simply the union of a particular person with a power which is not derived from man in any sense whatever. The corollary of this theory is that the whole people are not constituted as a form of government by natural law.

The Transmission theory, as least its principle, is the older one by far. It is found in some form in the writings of the Church Fathers. After the death of St. Thomas Aquinas it was distinctly formulated by his famous disciple, Giles of Rome. Names of renown are counted among its defenders: Cajetan, Francis of Vittoria, De Soto, Medina, St. Robert Bellarmine, Molina, Billuart and Francis Suarez. "There seems to be little doubt," says Professor Rommen, "that the translation theory is the most time-honored and that the great majority of the eminent doctors followed it."[1] The Designation theory was formulated as a reaction to the social contract theories of the eighteenth century; for there was a suspicion of doctrinal affinity between the Transmission theory (especially in the elaborate form of it given by Suarez) and the theory of the social contract.

1. Heinrich Rommen, *The State in Catholic Thought* (St. Louis, 1945), 446–47.

Now the corollary of the Transmission theory is known as the Suarezian form of the theory; for Suarez, the famous sixteenth-century theologian, is commonly thought to have given the clearest expression of the Transmission theory by adding the corollary. I should like to show in this note that the principle of the Transmission theory (that the whole people is the immediate cause of political authority) is entirely compatible with the corollary of the Designation theory (that there is no one form—direct democracy—of government by natural right); and that this position is in accord with the Greek–medieval tradition of political philosophy as represented in the works of St. Thomas Aquinas (who did not treat explicitly of this problem), and of St. Robert Bellarmine (d. 1604) who is credited with supporting the Transmission theory, but who, as will be made clear, most certainly did not support what came to be known as the Suarezian form of that theory, although it is commonly held that he did.

The Suarezian form of the Transmission theory assumes an identification of the multitude as a body politic with democracy as a form of government. That direct democracy is not a form of government by natural institution is clear from the texts of Bellarmine and St. Thomas Aquinas. By way of *praenotanda* we may note that, among the Greeks, government by the many did not signify government by the whole people, but by the mass of freemen *"who neither are rich nor have any merit of virtue."*[2] St. Thomas Aquinas distinguishes between the whole people sharing in government, and democracy as a form of government. "Two points are to be observed," he says, "concerning the right ordering of rulers in a state or nation. One is that all should take some share in the government . . . The other point is to be observed in respect of the kinds of government, or the different ways in which the constitutions are established."[3] The participation of the whole people in government is thus clearly not a matter which is dependent upon the forms of government, whether monarchy, aristocracy, or democracy.

It is in the light of these points, namely, that the whole people ought to share in government and that this sharing is or should be achieved in any of the kinds of government, that we ought to read St. Thomas's statement that the ordering to the common good

2. Aristotle, *Politics*, III, 2, 1281b16–26; 1282a28.
3. Thomas Aquinas, *Summa Theologiae*, I–II, 105, 7.

"belongs either to the whole people, or to someone who is the vicegerent of the whole people."[4] It is the intention of nature that the whole people make their laws according to some constitutional form; and then, whether that be one, few, or many, all the people ought to have some share in the government. This understanding of the above-cited text is borne out by what St. Thomas says concerning the various kinds of political prudence. In arguing that there is a species of prudence that belongs to kings, he considers the following objection:

[L]awgiving belongs not only to kings, but also to certain others placed in authority and even to the people. . . . Now the Philosopher (Ethics VI) reckons a part of prudence to be *legislative*. Therefore it is not becoming to substitute regnative prudence in its place.[5]

He replies, quoting Aristotle (*Politics* III) that "prudence is a virtue which is proper to the prince," as follows:

The Philosopher names regnative after the principle act of a king which is to make laws, and although this applies to the other forms of government, this is only insofar as they have a share of kingly government.[6]

We must notice that although he says that regnative "prudence should be denominated . . . so as to comprehend under regnative all other rightful forms of government," he explicitly allows three species of good government, and with none of these is the whole people identical, although he has said lawgiving belongs to the people. The same doctrine is manifest in the treatment of custom in relation to law. Here again the same two points are observed: the kind of government, and the sharing of the whole people in any kind. A whole people which is free and can make its own law can, under its constitution, introduce a custom which has "the force of law, abolishes law, and is the interpreter of law."[7] This custom has the force of, abolishes, and interprets law—What law? The law of the duly-constituted government which represents the people. We shall see below that according to the Roman and medieval legal tradition the constitution does not belong to positive law, but to the *jus gentium*, which is partly positive and partly natural. Can the whole people acting as a body politic never directly enact positive law? In answering this question we must keep in mind Aristotle's definition of the natural as that which happens

4. *Ibid.*, I–II, 90, 3.
6. *Ibid.*, ad 3.

5. *Ibid.*, II–II, 50, 1, Obj. 3.
7. *Ibid.*, I–II, 97, 3, ad 3.

always or for the most part.[8] Always, or for the most part, the whole people acts through one or few or many. It is conceivable, of course, that the whole people manages political power for itself; this is simply the unnatural but possible case. Always, or for the most part, the whole people acts through one, few, or many; and since the whole people is the principal cause of political authority, all the people ought, as St. Thomas points out, to have some share in the government, whatever kind it may be.

In treating the problem of the origin of political power, St. Robert Bellarmine makes it clear that the multitude as a body politic is not a form of government.[9] It is in its universal essence, he says, that political power is in the multitude as a body politic. "And since," he goes on, "the *respublica* cannot exercise (political power considered in its universal essence) . . . it is bound to transfer it to one person or to a few. Thus the power of the princes, considered in its genius, is also of natural and divine right, and the human race could not, even if all men were gathered, make a decree to the contrary."[10]

What is the signification of the word "bound" in "bound to transfer"? The whole people is said to be "bound" to transfer political power because the transference is done *"by the same law of nature"* by which it is originally, in its universal essence, in the whole people. Thus, clearly, political power as residing immediately in the whole people does not constitute a form of government.[11] Here we may observe that something is said to be derived

---

8. Aristotle, *Physics*, II, 2, 198b33–199a8.

9. Robert Bellarmine, *Controversiarum de Membris Ecclesiae*, Lib. III, *De Laicis sive Secularibus*, Chap. VI, *Opera* (Paris, 1870), III, 10–12.

10. *Ibid.*

11. It is interesting that Professor Yves Simon presented Bellarmine's theory as allowing that the *respublica* can manage political power for itself. The opposite opinion, he said, "does not seem to be borne out by (his) text"—this despite the explicit statement that "since the *respublica* cannot exercise this power for itself, it is bound to transfer it to one person or to a few." At the same time, Professor Simon admitted that "in all cases of which Bellarmine can think . . . the duty to pursue the common good . . . entails also the duty to put it in the hands of a distinct governing personnel . . ." [*The Philosophy of Democratic Government* (Chicago, 1951), 168].

If Bellarmine could not, as Simon acknowledged, think of any case in which the *respublica* can exercise political power for itself, how does Simon conclude that Bellarmine's theory allows for precisely that? It is, he told us, because "all that Bellarmine demonstrates is that the transmission of political power from the multitude to the distinct governing personnel is not a matter delivered to the free choice of the multitude *when*, as he put it, 'the republic cannot exercise such power for

from the natural law in two ways. In one way, a thing is derived from the natural law by a determination of common principles; for example, the law of nature has it that the evil-doer should be punished, but that he be punished in this or that way is a determination of the common principle. Things that are derived from the law of nature in this way, St. Thomas points out, "have no other force than that of human law."[12] These are the things which, Aristotle observes, are originally a matter of indifference, but when once laid down are not matters of indifference.[13] It is not in this way that political power is transferred from the whole people: the transference is not a matter of indifference; the people are "bound." Secondly, a thing is derived from the natural law in such a manner that it is "contained in human law not as emanating therefrom exclusively," but as having "some force from the natural law also."[14] Thus, St. Thomas points out, that *one must not kill* is derived from the principle that *one should do harm to no man* as having the force of the natural law itself. The transference of political power from the whole people is of the natural law in this latter sense. "The same law of nature" by which political power is in its universal essence in the multitude also establishes the forms of government *considered in their genus*:

> Notice, thirdly, that this power is transferred from the multitude . . . by the same law of nature. . . . Thus the power of the princes, considered in its genus, is also of natural and divine right, and the human genus could not, even if all men were gathered, make a decree to the contrary.[15]

That being the understanding of the word "bound" in "bound to transfer," what is the understanding of the word "transfer"? In what sense may the whole people be said to transfer political authority? The meaning becomes clear if we consider that the genus exists only as specified. The specification of the genus by the whole

---

itself'" (*ibid.*, 168; italics mine). But did Bellarmine put it quite that way? He said not *"when"* but *"since* the republic, etc." "Since" it cannot, Bellarmine, of course, did not treat of the conceivable case when it could: Science does not treat of the accidental as such. Certainly it may be said that there is some conceivable case in which the *respublica* can exercise political power for itself—this is simply the unnatural but possible case. Again we might recall Aristotle's definition of the natural as that which happens always or for the most part. That it is natural for the *respublica* to exercise political power for itself is explicitly denied by Bellarmine.

12. Thomas Aquinas, *Summa Theologiae*, I–II, 95, 2.
13. Aristotle, *Nicomachean Ethics*, V, 7, 1134b18–25.
14. Thomas Aquinas, *Summa Theologiae*, I–II, 95, 2.
15. Bellarmine, *Controversiarum*.

people in forming a constitution justifies the word "transfer." The people act as a principal cause with respect to the species of authority, and not merely with respect to the designation of the one holding it. Similarly, in this same philosophical tradition, a universal cause was said to concur with a particular cause in the generation of man. Socrates is the progenitor not of the universal man, but of his son, this *particular* man. But of this particular man the universal "man" is truly predicated, so that clearly he is produced not without the concurrence of a universal cause. Taken with respect to its particular cause, authority may fittingly be said to be transmitted by the community; but with respect to its universal cause, authority is in the person designated as having it. Because the act of instituting a particular government bears with it something of the force of natural law itself, it is an act which belongs not simply to positive law (it is not a matter of indifference) but to the *jus gentium*, which is partly natural, partly positive.[16] Bellarmine says:

Notice, fourthly, that distinct kinds of government, taken in their peculiarity, concern the law of nations, not the law of nature.[17]

All of these steps show clearly that the role of the people is more than one of designation, for the role of man in constituting authority is limited to designation, when that which is caused by man is simply the union of a particular person with a power which does not come from man in any sense whatever—as, for example, the papal power. But as Bellarmine makes clear—and Cajetan points out—whether a king be given by God, like David, or created by the people, like Saul, his function and power are those of the people: "The royal power, by natural law, resides primarily in the people, and from the people is transferred (*derivatur*) to the king."[18]

Two important texts of St. Thomas Aquinas are indispensable for a full understanding of this problem. St. Thomas distinguishes natural law from the "law of nations" in the following way:

The natural right is that which by its very nature is adjusted to or commensurate with another person. Now this may happen in two ways; first, according as it is considered absolutely: thus a male by its very nature

---

16. Thomas Aquinas, *Summa Theologiae*, II–II, 57, 3.
17. *Ibid.*
18. Thomas de Vio Cardinalis Caietanus, Scripta Theologica, I: *De Comparatione Auctoritatis Papae et Concilii cum Apologia eiusdem Tractatus*, V. Pollet, Editor (Rome, 1936), paragraphs 562–64.

is commensurate with the female to beget offspring by her, and a parent is commensurate with the offspring to nourish it. Secondly, a thing is naturally commensurate with another person, not according as it is considered absolutely, but according to something resultant from it, for instance, the possession of property. For if a particular piece of land be considered absolutely, it contains no reason why it should belong to one man more than to another, but if it be considered in respect of its adaptability to cultivation, and the unmolested use of the land, it has a certain commensuration to be the property of one and not of another man. Now it belongs not only to man but also to other animals to apprehend a thing absolutely; wherefore the right which we call natural, is common to us and other animals according to the first kind of commensuration. But the right of nations falls short of natural right in this sense, as the lawyer says [*Digest* of Justinian, I, 1 *Juri operam* (KR 1, 29a)] *because the latter is common to all animals, while the former is common to men only.* On the other hand, to consider a thing by comparing it with what results from it, is proper to reason, wherefore this same is natural to man in respect of natural reason which dictates it. Hence the lawyer Gaius says: '. . . Whatever natural reason decrees among all men, is observed by all equally, and is called the right of nations.'[19]

The second important text is as follows:

A thing is said to belong to the natural law in two ways. First, because nature inclines thereto: e.g., that one should not do harm to another.

Secondly, because nature did not bring with it the contrary: thus we might say that for man to be naked is of the natural law, because nature did not give him clothes, but art invented them. In this sense, the possession of all things in common and universal freedom are said to be of the natural law, because, to wit, the distinction of possessions [was] not brought in by nature, but devised by human reason for the benefit of human life.[20]

In order to understand the application of these texts to the problem we are discussing, it is necessary to recall the underlying principle of Aristotle's *Politics* and of the political philosophy of that tradition. St. Thomas announces this underlying principle in the Prologue to the *Commentary on the Politics*: that political science, like all practical sciences, proceeds by way of imitating nature. Nature proceeds from the simple to the composite. And

[i]n whatever things are constituted of many parts there is found a ruling and a subject element. But a multitude of men is constituted from a number of individuals; and therefore among men it is natural that one should rule and another be subject. . . . He [Aristotle] says therefore . . . that whatever things are constituted from many in such a way that from this

19. Thomas Aquinas, *Summa Theologiae*, II–II, 57, 3.
20. *Ibid.*, I–II, 94, 5, ad 3.

many a community results, whether the parts are continuous, as are the members of the body which are joined in the constitution of the whole, or whether they are discrete, as from many soldiers one army is constituted, in all of these there is found a ruling and a subject element. And this is both natural and expedient, as will be apparent from any example.[21]

Now in a natural composite, the ruling part and the subject part are brought in by nature itself, and the commensuration of one with respect to the other is natural by an absolute commensuration. Thus, St. Thomas says, the intellect is by its very nature, considered absolutely, commensurate to be the ruling principle of the sense appetites; and the male by its very nature is commensurate with the female to beget offspring by her, and the parent with the child to nourish it. Thus, in the household, the rule of the parent over the child is natural by an absolute natural commensuration. But in the political community, which is composed of freemen and equals, the ruling part is not brought in by nature itself. Thus it is that because nature does not itself bring in political authority, the condition of universal freedom is said to be natural in the sense of that whose contrary is introduced by human reason; by the same token, since human reason proceeds in imitation of nature, the contrary of universal freedom—that is, rulership of some over others—is said to be natural according to the inclination of nature. Therefore, although unlike the case of completely natural composites, there is no reason why, absolutely considered, any one or few should rule over others in the whole which is the civil multitude, there is a *relative* natural commensuration between some ruling part and some subject part; for it is fitting that among men the diversity of knowledge and virtue should issue to the benefit of all. "Wherefore," quoting St. Augustine, St. Thomas observes, " 'Just men command not by the love of domineering, but by the service of counsel. The natural order of things requires this; and thus did God make man.' "[22]

In the Suarezian form of the Transmission theory, the natural reason is made to introduce the rule of the whole over itself. Since nothing like that happens in nature either always or for the most part, the introduction of it as a principle of the political community makes political authority something outside the intention of nature—*praeter intentionem naturae.* We may observe, too, that in the Suarezian doctrine any form of government other than direct

21. Thomas Aquinas, *Commentary on I Politics of Aristotle,* Lect. 3
22. Thomas Aquinas, *Summa Theologiae,* I, 96, 4.

democracy becomes substitutional—a consequence palpably opposed to the whole political doctrine of both Aristotle and St. Thomas. It is precisely this consequence that prompted the elaboration of the opposite theory, the Designation theory. That theory was motivated by the failure of the Transmission theory in its Suarezian form to safeguard the natural order at the root of political society. In its Suarezian form—the commonly accepted form—the Transmission theory is not only defective on this score, but it begets a sophistical absurdity. It bears a strange affinity with the theory of Social Contract; the former begins with man by nature a social and political animal, and ends with a concept of political authority as *praeter intentionem naturae*; the latter takes as its first principle the thesis that political authority is something that arises outside of the intention of nature.

A study of the relevant texts of the Greek–medieval tradition shows that the Transmission theory carries with it as a corollary the introduction of political authority by the people according to that inclination of nature by which a ruling part (one, few, or many) is differentiated from a subject part. And the whole people, as the cause of whatever form of government is instituted, ought to have some share in it. The commonly accepted form of the Transmission theory is unfaithful to the tradition on these points. Bellarmine's exposition, on the contrary, upholds the tradition: it preserves the whole heritage of Western culture at its roots by safeguarding the natural order.

11. Modern Political Philosophy

5. The Meaning of Jean-Jacques Rousseau in Political Theory*

[In this essay McCoy was concerned with the relation, within modern political philosophy, of Rousseau to Marx in the light of Kant. A number of ideas frequently found in McCoy appear here in a clearly defined fashion. He speaks of the pure autonomy of nature and of the autonomy of intellect. McCoy was seeking to understand why modern political theory had become "revolutionary." That is, against what was it revolting and why? What McCoy noted was the possibility of a human being "formed" by nature to be a sort of revolutionary being and rationally obliged to see himself this way. The importance of Rousseau and the thought based on his position became clear when the notion of man as an intrinsically "malleable" being appeared. This notion meant that human nature as such was not something that defined what man ought to be from the fact that it was given in nature, itself formed by the Divine art. The intellectual effort to remove from nature any notion of a discovered intelligence not placed there by man is a necessary prerequisite for the transformation of politics into a revolutionary metaphysics in which what man is, is what he determines himself to be.]

In *Rousseau, Kant and Goethe,* and more fully in *The Question of Jean-Jacques Rousseau,* the late Ernst Cassirer has given a very profound reading of Rousseau by expanding upon Kant's appreciation of him.[1] This method of understanding Rousseau has not only the advantage that is always to be had, as Santayana once observed, from a grasp of tradition—for it is "conducive to mutual under-

---

*This essay originally appeared in the *Proceedings of the American Catholic Philosophical Association,* 50 (1956), 50–62.

1. Ernst Cassirer, *Rousseau, Kant and Goethe,* trans. J. Gutmann and others (Princeton, 1947); *The Question of Jean-Jacques Rousseau,* trans. and an Introduction by Peter Gay (New York, 1954). See also, Charles N. R. McCoy, *The Structure of Political Thought,* (New York, 1963), 212–22.

standing, to maturity and to progress"; it has, in this case, a very peculiar advantage, for it permits the reconciliation of Rousseau's apparent inconsistencies—not, indeed, as Cassirer believed, on the level of Rousseau's own perception or apprehension, but on the deeper level of meaning and significance.[2] If "the desperate absurdities of the assumptions of the Social Contract"[3] may seem at first to make questionable the value of demonstrating Rousseau's self-consistency, a careful examination of that demonstration shows that it has the unquestioned merit of suggesting a more intelligible "solution" at a deeper level of meaning. As Professor Gay observes in the concluding remarks of his Introduction to *The Question of Jean-Jacques Rousseau*, "For Cassirer's reader the problem of Rousseau's political theory emerges in its true dimensions only after the fundamental unity of his philosophy has been firmly established. . . . The relation of Rousseau's political theory to the historical process raises important questions which Cassirer's essay helps us to state properly but does not answer."[4] If this is indeed the case—as I believe it is—then it would appear that Kant's appreciation of Rousseau's "one great principle" did not reach the intelligible roots of Rousseau's thought—indeed, that Rousseau himself did not. And I would like to suggest that the critical method of *Verstehen* that Cassirer employs (in which the meaning of a philosopher's work is to be sought in a "dynamic centre of thought" related to the historical process) be extended from Kant to include Marx at the one extreme of the historical process and the Greek–medieval tradition at the other; then, I be-

2. As Professor Leo Strauss has well observed: "There is an obvious tension between the return to the city and the return to the state of nature. This tension is the substance of Rousseau's thought. . . . Today most serious students of Rousseau incline to the view that he eventually succeeded in overcoming what they regard as a temporary vacillation. . . . This interpretation is exposed to a decisive objection. Rousseau believed to the end that even the right kind of society is a form of bondage. . . . To return to the state of nature remains therefore for him a legitimate possibility. The question is, then, not how he solved the conflict between the individual and society, but rather how he conceived of that insoluble conflict." *Natural Right and History* (Chicago, 1953), 254–55. The position I shall develop in this paper agrees indeed that (contrary to Cassirer's view) Rousseau "believed to the end that even the right kind of society is a form of bondage," but will argue (in agreement with Cassirer) that a return to the state of nature was not, for Rousseau, a legitimate possibility.

3. John Morley, *Rousseau* (London, 1873), II, 134. Cited by Peter Gay in his Introduction to Cassirer's *The Question of Jean-Jacques Rousseau*, 9.

4. Peter Gay, in his Introduction to Cassirer's *The Question of Jean-Jacques Rousseau*, 27.

lieve, the true bearing of Rousseau's thought on the structure of political theory will become clearer, and that the questions which Cassirer's essay helps us to state properly may find an answer.

"Kant," says Cassirer, "regarded Rousseau not as the founder of a new 'system,' but as the thinker who possessed a new conception of the nature and function of philosophy, of its vocation and dignity"; he could "greet Rousseau as a philosophical liberator."[5] In what precisely did this function of philosophical liberator consist? It involved, Cassirer assures us, quoting Kant, 'a great discovery of our age,' a point of view "totally unknown to the ancients."[6] This discovery consisted in attributing an "ethical" and "teleological" sense not (as had always been done) to the man of reason and civilization (*homme de l'homme*) but to man as he comes from nature (*homme de la nature*).[7] Now it is indeed true that these terms "ethical" and "teleological" are here given a profoundly novel application. And I suggest that the originality and breadth of this conception can be understood only in the light of the transformation that had occurred, throughout the whole of eighteenth-century thought, in the meaning of *nature* and *reason*.[8] It was Rousseau's sensitivity to this transformation that Kant—alone, it seems, among students of Rousseau—detected in the apparent inconsistency of the appeal to reason in the *Social Contract* and the attack on reason in the *Discourse on the Origin of Inequality*.

"We can scarcely use the word [reason] any longer without being conscious of its history. . . . The general concept is vague, and it becomes clear and distinct only when the right 'differentia specifica' is added. Where are we to look for this specific difference in the eighteenth century?"[9] The answer, Cassirer amply demonstrates from his great erudition, lies in this, that "the whole eighteenth century understands reason . . . not as a sound body of knowledge, principles, and truths, but as a kind of energy, a force which is fully comprehensive in its agency and effects."[10] Speaking of Condillac's *Treatise on Sensation*, Cassirer finds the new sense of "reason" in the reduction of "the material and mental spheres . . . to a common denominator; they are composed of the same elements and are combined according to the same laws."[11] The phi-

5. Cassirer, *Rousseau, Kant and Goethe*, 1, 18.
6. *Ibid.*, 21.   7. *Ibid.*, 20.
8. *Ibid.*
9. Ernst Cassirer, *The Philosophy of the Enlightenment* (Boston, 1951), 6.
10. *Ibid.*, 13.   11. *Ibid.*, 18.

losophy of the Enlightenment moves toward an understanding of "reason" as identical with the elemental force in nature: "The dualism between creator and creation is . . . abolished. Nature as that which is moved is no longer set over against the divine mover; it is now an original formative principle which moves from within. . . . Nature is elevated to the sphere of the divine. . . . And from this characteristic force . . . is derived . . . the inalienable worth which belongs to [every object] in the totality of being."[12] Reason is no longer "the realm of the 'eternal verities,' of those truths held in common by the human and divine mind."[13] On the contrary, the intellect of man is, as it were, the theoretical form of the total being of nature, not in the sense that this intellect gives access to the intelligible world, but in the more modest sense that, as "the original intellectual force which guides the discovery and determination of truth" it reflects a nature now freed from the divine mover and considered instead "an original formative principle which moves from within. By its universal functions of comparing and counting, of combining and differentiating . . . the autonomy of the intellect corresponds to the pure autonomy of nature. . . . Both are now recognized as elemental and to be firmly connected with one another. Nature in man, as it were, meets nature in the cosmos half-way, and finds its own essence there."[14]

All past philosophy, in the eyes of the Enlightenment, had labored under the delusion, spawned by the fecundity of thought, that the theoretic mind existed independently of mundane reality—that "truth was something held in common by the human and divine mind." The relation of man to nature became, under this delusion, something other than man's relation to himself, and the relation of nature to man became something other than his own relation to the origin of his own natural determination. It was in this way that man (*homme de l'homme*) *first cut himself off from l'homme naturel*, from the real world, and proceeded to build up "pure" theory, theology, philosophy, ethics. This is the essential burden of the *Discourse on the Origin of Inequality*. This alienation of man (*homme de l'homme*) from himself (*homme de la nature*) took the *political* form of a ruling class, ruling first and foremost as "thinkers," as producers of "ideas": the first step toward degeneracy occurred when "the first man, who having enclosed a piece of ground, bethought himself of saying 'This is mine,' and found

12. *Ibid.*, 41.   13. *Ibid.*, 13.
14. *Ibid.*, 44–45.

people simple enough to believe him."[15] The distinctions constituted by birth, wealth, position, education, destroyed man's "essentiality" because they made some men dependent on others,
thus severing the individual from his original generic capacities by
making his life have its reason outside itself. As Cassirer observes,
"for Rousseau the real 'social bond' consists in the fact that particular individuals and groups are not called upon to rule over
others."[16]

Now as I have said, this profound tendency of the Enlightenment philosophy to identify "reason" with the intrinsic principle
of nature serves very well to render Rousseau's superficial inconsistencies intelligible; for we are able to perceive that the "reason"
which Rousseau opposes is the reason of the theoretical mind *considered as existing independently of nature*. We can see why it was
that "under the impression of Rousseau's writings, Kant's attitude
toward the world and toward man begins to change. His naive
confidence that the cultivation of the mind and its steady progress
would suffice to make men better, freer, and happier, is shaken."[17]
We begin to see that Rousseau's insistence that the real social bond
consists in the fact that particular individuals are not called upon
to rule over others is the political expression of a liberation effected
at a deeper level: the liberation from a theoretic intellect considered
as existing independently of nature and proceeding to form "pure"
theory, philosophy, theology, ethics, etc.

But Rousseau did not see the revolutionary implications of this
development at a level deeper than the political; he did not see it
at what Marx will call the "human" level; and this accounts for
the arbitrariness, the abstractness and sophistry of the "solution"
of the "General Will." In "the fully-developed political state"
where men are no longer, it is true, subject to the ideas of a ruling
class, the political community—Marx will point out—is allowed to
substitute for the true life of man. For "where the political state
has reached its full development, man leads, not only in his
thought, in conscience, but in reality in life, a double existence,
celestial and terrestrial, the existence in the political community,
where he considers himself a general being, and the existence in
civil society, where he works as a mere part, sees in other men

15. Jean-Jacques Rousseau, *Discourse on the Origin of Inequality*, in *Great Books of
the Western World*, ed. R. Hutchins (New York, 1952), 348.
16. Cassirer, *Rousseau, Kant and Goethe*, 30.
17. *Ibid.*, 6.

simply means, is himself swallowed up in the role of a simple means, and becomes the plaything of forces extraneous to himself."[18] If in the fully developed political state it is only "politically" and not "humanly" that man considers himself a "general being," this is because all the suppositions of the egoistic life continue to subsist in civil society where the individual, "separated from the community, folded back upon himself [is] uniquely occupied with his own private interests."[19] Thus the "ethical" intent of nature is still in reality frustrated; on the plane of the merely political the step forward remains on the false plane of the "theoretical"; for man's "general being" is established only in conscience, in the abstract, in the "general will"; "The generic life itself, Society, appears as a frame external to the individual."[20] However indispensable a step it may be toward the realization of man's original and proper vocation (and Marx insists that it is) in reality it is the old story of civilizing the individual and ruining the species. What Marx sees is this: The insoluble conflict between the individual and society—which is the substance of Rousseau's thought—is found to be at a deeper level the "old antagonism between man and nature, the individual and species"; this conflict cannot be resolved within the framework of even the right kind of state since the perfection of the state is in no way opposed to all the suppositions of the egoistic life; it is through itself as "intermediary" that the State "restores" to man his generic life—at an abstract level, thus perpetuating the separation of man's individual self from his generic self. Rousseau's solution is "a great step forward," but it remains inevitably abstract and sophistical.

Now if we address ourselves to the task of determining what in all this development is the "dynamic centre of thought" which seems to demand the profoundest dissolution of society before man's proper and original vocation can be realized, we are compelled to look more deeply into that "differentia specifica" which defines the Enlightenment understanding of "reason," We have observed that the whole of eighteenth-century thought moves toward an understanding of "reason" as being identical with the intrinsic principle of motion in nature: "the autonomy of the intellect corresponds to the pure autonomy of nature." If this is the "specific difference," *from what*—we must now inquire—does it

18. Karl Marx, *Die Judenfrage* (Marx-Engels, *Gesamtausgabe*), Sec. I, I, 1, 582–84.
19. *Ibid.*, 595.   20. *Ibid.*

differ. The answer to that question will, I believe, throw an entirely new light on the problem and serve to relate Rousseau's political theory more faithfully to the historical process. For by one of those curious turns in intellectual history, we discover in the Greek–medieval tradition a series of conceptions which seem to offer themselves today in the form of "hypotheses" if you will, for explaining phenomena occurring centuries after these "hypotheses" were formulated.

For the Greek–medieval tradition in philosophy, the "pure autonomy of nature" was not thought of as simply corresponding with the autonomy of intellect. There was a good reason for this, and it is easily shown by a reading of the second book of Aristotle's *Physics*. At the beginning of the second book, Aristotle defines nature as "the principle and cause of movement and rest in that to which it belongs primarily, in virtue of itself and not in virtue of a concomitant attribute."[21] In the course of this same work Aristotle demonstrates in many ways that nature acts for an end, but that in so doing it is not directed by an intellectual principle intrinsic to itself. In the light of this demonstration, St. Thomas, in his *Commentary on the Physics*, defines nature as a "reason put in things by the Divine art so that they are able to act for an end."[22] Nature then, is a "substitute intelligence," acting indeed for an end but without knowledge of the end. It is because nature is a substitute intelligence that it operates "always or for the most part in the same way," not varying its artefacts. Spiders make their webs always in the same way; swallows build their nests always in the same way. And this would not be the case if they operated by intelligence and art. Thus the uniformity of nature as well as its chance deviations are equally signs of its having no intellectual principle for itself. But architects do not all build the same kind of house; for being capable of judging about the form of artefacts the architect can vary them. Thus it is evident that it is not in the line of the "pure autonomy" of nature that art proceeds; the "autonomy of the intellect" does not simply correspond to the "pure autonomy of nature."

It is these considerations whose precise bearing on the structure of political theory will, I believe, serve to illuminate the meaning of Rousseau. If the kind of teleology that is attributable to nature

21. Aristotle, *Physics*, II, 1, 192b22.
22. Thomas Aquinas, *Commentary on II Physics of Aristotle*, 14, 8.

in the line of its autonomy were to be attributed to man, the intellect of man would move toward the condition of "creator" by
moving toward the condition of the "substitute intelligence" which
is nature. That nature acts always or for the most part in the same
way means that the teleology of nature in its pure autonomy does
not intend any *particular* individual, but intends individuals only
so far as the species cannot be maintained without them. Aristotle
remarks that if nature intended *this* individual, she would be like
the man who takes a bath so that the sun might be eclipsed.[23] And
St. Thomas explains this point by saying, "*Natura enim intendit
generare hominem, non hunc hominem; nisi inquantum homo non potest
esse, nisi sit hic homo.*"[24] Nature, to be sure, produces *this* individual;
but "originally he was no more intended than was the fact that
this particular fragment of birdshot should down the duck—in fact
considerably less so. Although the generation of Socrates Jr. is
ultimately a natural event, his already very tenuous possibility
could only materialize owing to a strictly fortuitous event. It was
quite by chance that Socrates first met Xanthippe."[25] By attempting
to assimilate the "autonomy of the intellect to the pure autonomy
of nature," man moves toward the condition of substitute intelligence in the line of nature's simple intention to generate and preserve the species. This assimilation of the individual to the species,
by which "the inequality that is not ordained by nature"[26] is overcome, takes place with Rousseau on the political level, where the
difference between ruler and subject is "overcome" in the "General Will." This is that nature ("interpreted in an unusual way,"
as E. H. Wright remarks) in accordance with which man "must be
perfected by his reason."[27] But since, as Marx will point out, the
ideas of a ruling class are simply the *ideal* expression of the dominant material relationships, the emancipation through the General
Will from the ideas of a ruling class is only "the last form of human
emancipation within the framework of the actual social order."[28]
With Rousseau's solution the theoretical mind remains critical from
the outside; it perpetuates a radical opposition between itself and
nature. A transformation at a deeper level must be effected before

---

23. Aristotle, *Physics*, II, 6, 197b25.
24. Thomas Aquinas, *Quaestio Disputata de Anima*, 18.
25. Charles de Koninck, "The Nature of Man and His Historical Being," *Laval
Théologique et Philosophique*, 5 (#2, 1949), 276, n. 2.
26. Gay, in Introduction to Cassirer's *The Question of Jean-Jacques Rousseau*, 18.
27. *Ibid.*, 20.
28. Marx, *Die Judenfrage*, 585–86.

the conflict between man and nature, individual and species, individual and society can be resolved; for it must be resolved in the
"real" life, and not merely in the abstract, in "thought" and in
"conscience."

The "real" life, Marx saw, had come to be identified with the
teleology of nature in its pure autonomy, and this was seen to
imply the negation of "all the forms and products of consciousness"—including the abstract overcoming (the General Will) of
abstract alienations (the State). If indeed, then, the autonomy of
intellect corresponds simply to the pure autonomy of nature, both
now to be "recognized as elemental and to be firmly connected
with one another"; if this means that "nature in man . . . meets
nature in the cosmos half-way and finds its own essence there,"
does it not follow—as Marx insisted—that "Society is the achieved
consubstantiality of man with nature . . . the realization of the
naturalism of man and the humanism of nature"?[29] Does it not
then follow that nature, taken as the sufficient principle of all that
is, and not intending the individual except for the species, intends
each individual as both individual and species?—that man "overcomes" the limitations of his individual self by a not merely theoretical, but also a practical and concrete recognition of his universal
potentiality as a species?[30] This is what Marx calls "the generic
natural relation," in which "the relation of man with nature is
directly his relation with man," by which man sees himself "a
being [related] to the species as to his own proper being, [and
related] to himself as a generic being."[31] Society, then, must be
understood in a manner hitherto unthought of; it must take its
"departure from the fact of the *substantiality* of man . . . from the
theoretically and practically sensible conscience of man in nature, considered as *being.*"[32] In Rousseau's doctrine of the General Will,
man's generic being is separated from his individual being: "There
where the political state has reached its full development," Marx
observes, "man leads, not only in thought, in conscience, but in
reality in life, a double existence . . . the existence in the political
community where he considers himself a general being, and the

29. Karl Marx, *Oekonomische-philosophische Manuskript*, 1844 (Marx-Engels *Gesamtausgabe*), Sec. I, III, 115.

30. See Footnote 8, above.

31. Karl Marx, *Manuscrit economico-philosophique*, XXIV. Cited in *De Marx au
Marxisme*, ed. by Robert Aron (Paris, 1948), 95.

32. *Ibid.*

existence in civil society, where he works as a mere part, sees in other men simply means, is himself swallowed up in the role of a simple means, and becomes the plaything of forces extraneous to himself."[33] The *practical* recognition of man's universal potentiality as a species demands the overthrow of all the "egoistic presuppositions" which continue to subsist in the "real" life of civil society. And since "the substantiality of man" (Rousseau's *homme de la nature*) is not an "abstract essence" but on the contrary, the product "of the total living sensuous activity of the individuals composing the sensuous world," it follows that "all the pretended history of the world is nothing but the production of man by human work . . . the *birth* of himself, or his *origin*."[34] It is precisely in this "real" life, in "the ensemble of social relations" (the context of *homme de l'homme*) that the concrete forms of the alienation of the natural man (*homme de la nature*) subsist and need to be overcome before man can be restored to his original birthright.[35] The "historical being" of man must be dissolved: As Marx, speaking of Hegel, clearly put it: "Our conception of history comes to the conclusion that all forms and products of consciousness cannot be dissolved by mental criticism . . . but only by the practical overthrow of the actual social relations . . . that not criticism but revolution is the driving force of history."[36]

The "ethical" and "teleological" sense of nature is not fully comprehended then until "all forms and products of consciousness" are overthrown by revolutionary action. We must see the full consequence of this imperative in Marx's view of man as a generic being. If in the line of its pure autonomy nature—as Marx points out—"works only within the limits and following the needs of the species," nature is not then the sufficient cause of the species itself, nor of the diversity of species. Indeed, for both Aristotle and St. Thomas nothing is done in nature without the cooperation of a separate intelligence.[37] Nature, then, in the line of its pure autonomy is reducible to a simple indeterminateness with respect to some possible form. And thus it is that the individual who relates himself to the species as to his own proper being must relate him-

33. Marx, *Oekonomische-philosophische Manuskript*, 125.
34. Marx, *Die Judenfrage*, 584.
35. Marx, *Oekonomische-philosophische Manuskript*, 125.
36. Karl Marx and Friedrich Engels, *The German Ideology* (New York, 1939), 28–29.
37. Thomas Aquinas, *Summa Contra Gentiles*, III, 65.

self to himself as a being of generic potentiality. And because this is his original and proper vocation, all the forms and products of consciousness must needs be destroyed. The whole of the political art becomes revolutionary.

These considerations bring us, I think, to see why it is that the basic questions pertaining to the relation of Rousseau's political theory to the historical process have their source in the dilemma inherent not in the inconsistencies but in the fundamental unity of Rousseau's political theory. For that dilemma is this: that the reduction of the "autonomous" intellect to the pure autonomy of nature confines science to nature as substitute intelligence in the line of its simple "formability": all "the forms and products of consciousness," both in the physical universe and in the moral and political world, are erased. This appears to be the intelligible root of Rousseau's thought: the conception of man not as specifically rational animal but as "specifically" infinitely malleable.

It was precisely the considerations we have been exploring that led Aristotle to seek to assure the limited nature of political rule by comparing the ends of political life not with the final causes in nature but with mathematical axioms.[38] Even though moral reasoning proceeds from final causes and not from antecedent hypotheses, the method of politics is compared to that of mathematics in the role played by its principles. For the aspect of nature in its pure autonomy should make it clear why it is that a comparison between the final causes in nature and in human action is unsuitable: it is because the necessity that is in the world of nature is there ultimately *ex suppositione finis*; the necessity that is found on the part of matter in all of nature has its reason *ex arte divina*. It is precisely because Aristotle wants to show that the ends of political life are unchangeable starting points for all judgments of political prudence that he compares them with the antecedent hypotheses of mathematics; he does not compare them to the final causes in nature because "as with productions of art, so . . . is it with the productions of nature"—the artist is free to choose the end. But the ends in human life do not depend on our simple will, as in the things of nature the end depends on the simple will of God ultimately, and in the things of art on the simple will of the artist. It is, then, with respect to the fixedness of mathematical

38. "For virtue and vice respectively preserve and destroy the first principle, and in actions the final cause is the first principle as the hypotheses are in mathematics." Aristotle, *Nicomachean Ethics*, VII, 8, 1151a16–17.

hypotheses as antecedent that Aristotle compares the final causes in human life, and thus withdraws such matters from the political art. But all those matters that Aristotle had reserved to the theoretic intellect are brought by Rousseau, the "philosophical liberator," within the sphere of human art. And since this is achieved by projecting the teleology of nature in the line of its pure autonomy onto the nature of man, the heightened sense of freedom comes not from the side of self-knowledge and self-government, but from a "substitute intelligence," indeed from the element of indetermination in nature: Man is infinitely malleable even to the point of washing his brain. The world is ready to be "made" according to the arbitrary whim of anyone who has sufficient force; reason is force, "and from this . . . force is derived . . . the inalienable worth which belongs [to every object] in the totality of being." We see why it is that Rousseau's "one great principle," the "point of view totally unknown to the ancients," opens the way for myth and magic into the very structure of the secular world. We see, indeed, that when "God is dead" (to use Zarathustra's celebrated announcement) the world does really collapse.

6. The Dilemma of Liberalism*

[The establishment and success of general liberalism became for McCoy a basic reflection about the direction of modern political philosophy. Rousseau's position on the general malleability of human nature is the key to understanding liberalism's newly formulated freedom. The intellectual problem for modern liberalism was to remove what were called artificial barriers from nature. The crucial removal in terms of political philosophy was the elimination of the Prime Intellect from nature, so that nature was presupposed to no intelligence but open only to human artistic and technical reconstruction. In this chapter, we encounter the fundamental position that Grotius played for McCoy's theoretical analysis. He carefully considers what it might mean to affirm that the natural law would remain the natural law even if God did not exist. As McCoy argues, this position leads to a nature that, contrary to the view of Aristotle or Aquinas, has no reason for being itself. McCoy outlines the direction and nature of later modern political thought as it logically works its way to the extreme but necessary and intelligible position of Marx. Here McCoy analyzes the liberal opposition to indefectible principles and the subsequent openness to totalitarian substitutes.]

Lionel Trilling, in a thoughtful and provocative series of essays on literature and society, has remarked that it has seemed to him "that a criticism which has at heart the interests of liberalism might find its most useful work not in confirming liberalism in its sense of general rightness but rather in putting under some degree of pressure the liberal ideas and assumptions of the present time."[1] If, to be sure, all must applaud liberalism's "vision of a general enlargement and freedom and rational direction of human life," there is reason for concern that the "characteristic paradox of liberalism is that in the very interests of its great primal act of imag-

---

*This essay originally appeared in *Laval Théologique et Philosophique*, 16 (#1, 1960), 9–19.

1. Lionel Trilling, *The Liberal Imagination* (Garden City, N.Y., 1957), viii.

ination by which it establishes its essence and existence . . . it inclines to constrict and make mechanical its conception of the nature of mind."[2] Speaking of the Kinsey Report, Mr. Trilling observes that "the preponderant weight of its argument is that a fact is a physical fact, to be considered only in its physical aspect and apart from any idea or ideal that might make it a social fact, as having no ascertainable personal or cultural meaning and no possible consequences—as being indeed, not available to social interpretation at all."[3] The tendency of liberalism to constrict its conception of the nature of mind was observed in a remarkable study by the late Ernst Cassirer, whom all must recognize as having been a scholar of great profundity and an ardent apologist of the liberal tradition of the West.[4] Speaking of those philosophers who, inspired by the theory of Evolution, made great contributions—in Cassirer's opinion—to the development of anthropological philosophy, Cassirer enters a caveat: "All these philosophers were determined empiricists; they would show us nothing but the facts."[5] And these facts have lent themselves to an interpretation that intends to "prove that the cultural world, the world of human civilization, is reducible to . . . causes which are the same for the physical as for the so-called spiritual phenomena. . . . Owing to this development our modern theory of man lost its intellectual center. We acquired instead a complete anarchy of thought."[6] Liberalism's aversion from making intellectual distinctions perceptive of values and consequences thus curiously constricts its "vision of a general enlargement and freedom and rational direction of human life."

How this paradox of liberalism is to be accounted for may very well be, as Mr. Trilling suggests, "the most important, the most fully challenging question in culture that at this moment we can ask." It is indeed the most important political question, for "it is no longer possible to think of politics except as the politics of culture, the organization of human life toward some end or other, toward the modification of sentiments, which is to say the quality of human life."[7] An inquiry into the matter will reveal not only the reason for the paradox that Trilling speaks of; it will reveal a

2. *Ibid.*, xi.   3. *Ibid.*, 235.
4. Ernst Cassirer, *An Essay on Man* (New Haven, 1944).
5. *Ibid.*, 21.   6. *Ibid.*, 20–21.
7. Trilling, *The Liberal Imagination*, 292, ix.

dilemma for liberalism that is not immediately suggested by the paradox itself.

Liberalism took its rise in the seventeenth century with the appearance of the modern scientific spirit, and the first postulate of that spirit was, as Cassirer has put it, "the removal of all the artificial barriers that had hitherto separated the human world from the rest of nature."[8] These barriers were chiefly the notion of a Prime Intellect, "on whom depend the heavens and the world of nature"[9] and the notion of human intellect as "separable indeed" although not existing apart from matter.[10] Nature was no longer understood, as it had been by the classical tradition, as "a reason put in things by the divine art so that they may act for an end."[11] All communication is severed between what traditionally had been thought of as the reason that is nature, the reason which is the cause of nature, and the human reason. This excision of reason from nature enhanced man's sense of freedom: Nature was no longer set against the Divine Mover; it no longer meant the created finite physical universe in which man is imprisoned. Nature was now equated with the inexhaustible and immeasurable abundance of reality. The new sense of "reason" is found in the reduction of "the material and mental spheres . . . to a common denominator; they are composed of the same elements and are combined according to the same laws."[12] And this meant that "the autonomy of intellect corresponds to the pure autonomy of nature. . . . Both are recognized as elemental and to be firmly connected to one another. Nature in man, as it were, meets nature in the cosmos half-way, and finds its own essence there."[13]

This theory of the autonomy of nature was expressed in classical fashion for political philosophy in the celebrated hypothesis of Hugo Grotius. In the *De Jure Belli ac Pacis* Grotius maintained that the natural law would be what it is even if, *per impossibile*, there were no God. How much Grotius intended by this hypothesis does not matter. What matters is that as it was subsequently interpreted and became the cornerstone of modern political philosophy it meant that nature, "hypothetically" cut from its dependence on

8. Cassirer, *An Essay on Man*, 13.
9. Aristotle, *Metaphysics*, XII, 7, 1072b13.
10. Aristotle, *Physics*, II, 2, 194b10–15.
11. Thomas Aquinas, *Commentary on II Physics of Aristotle*, 14, 8.
12. Ernst Cassirer, *The Philosophy of the Enlightenment* (Boston, 1951), 18.
13. *Ibid.*, 44–45.

the Prime Intellect, would be considered the sufficient and original formative principle of all that is. The meaning and implications of this hypothesis, both for the enlarged sense of freedom that it suggests and for its tendency to constrict the concept of mind, can be grasped only if we see how it meant a truncating of the traditional idea of nature and the law of nature.

In the classical and medieval understanding of natural law, law as an *ordinatio rationis ad bonum commune* (an ordination of reason to the common good) was taken to be an inclination toward the good conceived as consisting essentially in (*a*) the efficient and material principles presupposed to some form, (*b*) the form by which a thing is what it is, and (*c*) an inclination to action in accordance with the form.[14] Now this whole teleology, resting, as it did, on the concept of law as *ordinatio rationis,* was essentially dependent on the Prime Intellect. Law being something that pertains to the reason and not to nature (unless it be a rational nature) there can be no natural law for nonrational beings except by way of similitude.[15] If then law, as an inclination toward the good, consisted in material and efficient principles for the sake of some form, and form for the sake of action, the elimination of the Prime Intellect upon which the order of things depends leaves the "substitute intelligence" of nature and removes the element of *order to an end as such* from the law of nature. Henceforth the "teleology" of nature will be truncated in such fashion that it will terminate where natural movement would terminate in the line of its hypothetical autonomy. The structure of liberal political thought is based on the conception of material and efficient principles "manipulable" indeed but no longer presupposed to any form or end.

The political and social consequences of this hypothesis of the autonomy of nature were fully and clearly perceived by David Hume, the father of modern liberalism.[16] Liberal political and social

14. Thomas Aquinas, *Summa Theologiae,* I, 5, 5.

15. *Ibid.,* I–II, 91, 2, ad 3.

16. We may note that modern conservatism also has its roots in the principle of the autonomy of nature, but it emphasizes a different facet of this principle. If identifies the principle of action in political society with nature's action always or for the most part in the same way and for the best and without knowledge of the end. This is the way that Aristotle defined nature in the *Physics* but not in the *Politics.* Burke, for example, conceives the art of politics in a way that is proper to what tradition had distinguished as "operable" sciences that are classed under physics—as operating in conjunction simply with a purely natural principle, as medicine and engineering do. Burke is untrue to the classical and medieval tradition

philosophy is founded on the celebrated Humean principle that the contrary of every matter of fact is possible: There is no reason in nature why anything should be what it is or should not be what it is not. "The contrary of every matter of fact is . . . possible; because it can never imply a contradiction, and is conceived by the mind with the same facility and distinctness as if ever so conformable to reality."[17] This stretch of the liberal imagination was indeed proper enough: Nature, as signifying the inexhaustible and immeasurable abundance of reality must be taken to include the deflections from the regularity of its own actions as being ever so conformable to reality. This is the origin of liberalism's sense of "variousness and possibility," its "primal act of imagination whereby it establishes its essence and existence." It suggests to us why Mr. Trilling observes that "those who explicitly assert and wish to practise the democratic virtues have taken it as their assumption that all social facts . . . must be accepted, . . . and why Professor George Sabine says of Hume that his critique of human understanding has made it impossible to describe values with even so loose a word as utility.

But precisely by contributing in this way to what Mr. David Riesman has called the "increased possibilities of being and becoming," Hume's principle that the contrary of every matter of fact is possible has the effect of constricting and making mechanical its conception of mind. We must notice a curious thing. In the *Physics* of Aristotle variation from the norm in natural operation is ascribed to a defect on the part of matter and not to the play of intelligence; the ground for this is that what happens always or

---

here. The emphasis on natural properties and elemental force not subject to the command of reason places the ends of human life on the same plane with the final causes in nature—something Aristotle explicitly warned against (*Ethics*, VII, 8, 1151a15–20). The result is to leave political matters free from the scrutiny of reason as ordering and directing. The explanation of this lies in the fact that the final causes in nature have no necessity in them except *ex hypothesi*, that is, they depend ultimately on the simple will of God. *A pari*, then, the ends of human life in conservative political philosophy are made dependent on the equally inscrutable human will—on the will of Carlyle's "Able-Hero," of Hegel's *sacro-egoismo*, of the Duce and the Fuehrer. The facet of autonomous nature emphasized by nineteenth-century conservatism issued in an obscurantist spiritualism that opened the way to Hitler's "community homogeneous in nature and feeling"—*die Einheit Deutscher Seelen*—based on the primordial nature of race and blood. [This important note of McCoy indicates how he considered modern conservatism and liberalism to be rooted in the same intellectual system.]

17. David Hume, *An Enquiry Concerning Human Understanding*, in The English Philosophers from Bacon to Mill (New York, 1939), 598.

for the most part seems to be in accordance with some intention. On the other hand, the varying of human artefacts is ascribed to an intention proceeding directly from an intellectual principle, on the ground that it seems to be characteristic of man to vary his artefacts. This indeed was the basis in Aristotle's teaching of man's capacity for self-government. Now if we accept nature as the original formative principle of all that is, then the "aberrations" in nature become just as "intelligent" as its apparent "intentions"; indeed—and it is what we most particularly should notice—they become—by the law that reduces the material and mental spheres to a common denominator—the exemplar for freedom in the world of culture and civilization. The traditional idea of a free nature, namely, one that moves itself by an idea "conceived, and in a way contrived by it,"[18] gives way to a concept of liberty based on the element of indetermination in nature. This is why Mr. Trilling observes that the democratic virtues require the acceptance of all social facts "in the sense that no judgment must be passed on them, that any conclusion drawn from them which perceives values and consequences will turn out to be 'undemocratic.'"[19]

How free indeed this nature is may best be seen by examining its status as it appears to modern physics where the proper exigencies of its method justify its special view of nature. The situation in modern physics is excellently brought out by Eddington in the following paragraphs:

I have settled down to the task of writing . . . and have drawn up my chairs to my two tables. Two tables! Yes, there are duplicates of every object about me—two tables, two chairs, two pens. . . .

One of [my two tables] has been familiar to me from earliest years. . . . How shall I describe it? It has extension; it is comparatively permanent; it is coloured; above all it is *substantial*. . . .

Table No. 2 is my scientific table. It is a more recent acquaintance, and I do not feel so familiar with it. It does not belong to the world previously mentioned. . . . My scientific table is mostly emptiness. Sparsely scattered in that emptiness are numerous electric charges rushing about with great speed; but their combined bulk amounts to less than a billionth of the bulk of the table itself.

I need not tell you that modern physics has by delicate test and remorseless logic assured me that my second scientific table is the only one which is really there—wherever 'there' may be.[20]

18. Thomas Aquinas, *Summa Contra Gentiles*, II, 47.
19. Trilling, *The Liberal Imagination*, 234.
20. A. S. Eddington, *The Nature of the Physical World* (New York, 1946), ix–xvi.

This is what the "teleology" of nature looks like when nature in the line of its hypothetical autonomy is cut from dependence on the Prime Intellect: when nature is no longer a "reason put in things . . . so that they may act for an end." The new scientific developments have been marked by a scrupulous indifference to the "familiar world," the world of intelligible forms. In many respects this procedure is proper enough; it reflects, indeed, an exigency of experimental natural science, namely, that it get away from the world as "formed" or "given" and approach the cosmos from the point of view of the possibilities of its material and efficient principles. Thus the physical world appears to be bereft of specific natures and recognized "intentions." Liberty of contrariety seems indeed to be the very essence of liberty.

This certainly appears to be the meaning of liberty outlined for us by Judge Learned Hand in an address entitled "A Fanfare for Prometheus."[21] Judge Hand begins his inquiry into the notion of liberty by remarking indeed that it is "a naive opinion" that holds "that [liberty] means no more than that each individual shall be allowed to pursue his own desires without let or hindrance."[22] For this—he says somewhat surprisingly—is what characterizes those who believe in "indefectible principles": "Human nature is malleable *especially* if you can indoctrinate the disciple with indefectible principles."[23] What Judge Hand apparently means in these obscure and cryptic passages is that if there were some definite shape to human nature itself (human nature would be especially malleable) one could then without "let or hindrance" pursue the work of its formation. But there is no such definite shape at all, Hand thinks. Human nature is indeed malleable, but it is properly such not— Hand tells us—because of the infinite variability of prudential judgments in attaining the mean of reason which is the appointed end of the natural reason, but rather because of the absence of any end appointed by the natural reason. Disciples of indefectible principles are compared to the bee or the ant who "appears to be, and no doubt in fact, is, accomplishing his own purpose."[24] Judge Hand sees in the regularity of the bee's and the ant's action for an end a rudimentary "liberty" the perfection of which is in proportion to the possibilities of deflecting from any fixed end. Since the

21. Learned Hand, "A Fanfare for Prometheus," *The Freedom Reader* (New York, 1955), 22–26.
22. *Ibid.*, 22.   23. *Ibid.*, 23. Italics added.
24. *Ibid.*, 22–23.

possibility of deflection from a "natural intention" is notably greater in the case of human behavior, Judge Hand seems to think that the specific difference between human liberty and animal "liberty" lies in the absence in human affairs of any indefectible principles. And this absence of indefectible principles is the very essence of liberty—a liberty based on the element of indetermination in nature. As Judge Hand says, human nature is malleable *especially* if you can indoctrinate the disciple with indefectible principles; it is freer and not so malleable if it cannot be definitely shaped. But what human nature is if it has no recognizable shape at all is something for which it would appear to be hard to find a word: It is like Eddington's "scientific table"—it is "there—wherever 'there' may be." It is as Mr. David Riesman says: in our other-directed society we find ourselves by "radar." And Mr. Trilling— to refer to him again—says that the American critic in his liberal and progressive character, prefers Theodore Dreiser to Henry James because Dreiser's books "have the awkwardness, the chaos . . . which we associate with 'reality.' In the American metaphysic, reality is always material reality . . . unformed, impenetrable."[25] No more than does physics have anything to say about the "familiar table" that "lies visible to my eyes and tangible to my grasp" does liberalism have anything to say about the familiar world of moral, aesthetic, and political ends.

But we must notice what it is that prevents man, in Judge Hand's view, from pursuing his desires without let or hindrance. It is not "indefectible principles"; it is the delicate test and remorseless logic of facts: "In any event my thesis is that the best answer (to indefectible principles) is . . . that they are at war with our only trustworthy way of living in accord with the facts."[26]

What are these facts in accord with which we must live if we want to be free? In regard to them we must take notice of an important difference between the physical world and the world of human culture and civilization. After telling us that modern physics has by delicate test and remorseless logic assured us that the "scientific table" is the only one which is really "there," Eddington quickly adds:

On the other hand I need not tell you that modern physics will never succeed in exorcising that first (familiar) table . . . which lies visible to my

25. Trilling, *The Liberal Imagination*, 10–11.
26. Hand, "A Fanfare for Prometheus," 24.

eyes and tangible to my grasp. . . . No doubt they are ultimately to be identified in some fashion. But the process by which the external world of physics is transformed into a world of familiar acquaintance . . . is outside the scope of physics. . . . The frank realization that physical science is concerned with a world of shadows is one of the most significant of recent advances.[27]

The physicist is not disturbed by his inability to account for the "familiar world": it is there "without let or hindrance." The electric charges, sparsely scattered in emptiness and rushing about with great speed—these are undeniably, if mysteriously, directed to the forming of the "familiar table"—the coloured, hard, shaped table of a certain magnitude, "visible to my eyes and tangible to my grasp"—the table of Aristotle's "proper sensibles" and "common sensibles." The physical world is something "given" and something "governed." And because this is so the hypotheses employed by physicists to "save the appearances" are not unlimited in number: they must "increasingly explain the domain understood by the sensible impressions."[28] But the world of human culture and civilization is, on the contrary, a world that has to be constructed—not from nothing, but, unlike the familiar table, there is nothing there that cannot be exorcised. What is there are the ends of human life appointed by the natural reason (including truth, which is the end of the theoretic intellect) and the natural associations (the family, the state) which guarantee the ends of living. These are indeed indefectible principles in the sense that the liberty of contrariety whereby they can be exorcised is not a mark of the perfection of human nature. Indeed, as Aristotle says, it is vice that exorcises them. "Virtue and vice respectively preserve and destroy the first principles, and in actions the final cause is the first principle as the hypotheses are in mathematics."[29] The self-liberation envisaged by liberalism is precisely that man may experience very tangibly the material infinity experienced theoretically by the modern physicist and free himself from the world of common experience—the world from which, as we have noticed Eddington and Einstein attest, the physicist never succeeds in freeing himself. If modern physics is taken to mean, indeed, that "the human intellect becomes aware of its own infinity through

27. Eddington, *The Nature of the Physical World*, xvi.
28. Albert Einstein and Leopold Infeld, *L'Evolution des idées en physique* (Paris, n.d.), 286. See also *ibid*, 35–36.
29. Aristotle, *Nicomachean Ethics*, VII, 8, 1151a15–20.

measuring its powers by the infinite universe,"[30] modern social science means that in the world produced by "human sensuous activity" man is freed from the imaginary boundaries of "indefectible principles" and "natural associations" so that he may experience practically and not merely theoretically the generic nature of his being: The Kinsey Report offers a "democratic pluralism of sexuality" and Mr. Riesman says that "the Bill of Rights requires permitting pornography and even *Confidential* to circulate,"[31] and Erich Fromm traces the genesis of "authoritarian ethics" to the family, where the individual is first separated from himself by the authority of his parents and where obedience is the first virtue and disobedience the first sin.[32] The "facts" which liberalism recognizes as providing the "only trustworthy way of living" must never be thought of as "explaining" the domain of that common moral experience which holds the same relation to the field of human behavior as common sensible experience holds in relation to physics. Pornography, *Confidential*, a democratic pluralism of sexuality, the radar-controlled, other-directed society of peers, the disappearance—not of a ruling class but of what Mr. Walter Lippmann calls "the functional (arrangement) of the relationships between the mass of people and the government" (the substitution of veto-groups, Gallup-pollsters and inside-dopesters for genuine rule)—these things mean nothing less than what Judge Hand avows, namely, that "(indefectible principles) are at war with our only trustworthy way of living in accord with the facts."[33] Indefectible principles are not among the facts in accord with which we must live if we want to be free. The only facts are material and efficient principles, "manipulable" indeed, but no longer presupposed to

30. Ernst Cassirer, *An Essay on Man*, 15. In classical metaphysics, the human intellect was considered to be relatively infinite but to be simply speaking finite. See Aristotle, *De Anima*, III.

31. David Riesman, "The Supreme Court and Its New Critics," *The New Republic*, July 29, 1957, 12, n. 6.

32. Erich Fromm, *Man for Himself* (New York, 1947), 10–13. Fromm even traces "authoritarian ethics" back to the teaching concerning the first parents, Adam and Eve, whose chief sin, he says (contrary to the formal teaching of theologians on this point), was disobedience. It is interesting indeed that theologians in fact maintain on the contrary that the first sin was not disobedience but pride—meaning thereby what Fromm means by "humanistic ethics," namely, the inordinate desire for a spiritual good, which good desired was the "science of good and evil" and the inordinateness consisted in wanting to determine good and evil for themselves. [This note is a key observation for McCoy's understanding of the relation of reason and revelation.]

33. Hand, "A Fanfare for Prometheus."

any intelligible form or end. As Mr. Trilling says, ideas perceptive of values and consequences "are held to be mere 'details,' and what is more, to be details which, if attended to, have the effect of diminishing reality."[34] They have less relation to the world of morals and politics than does the "familiar table" to the world of physics; for the "scientific table" saves the appearances of the familiar one.

The growing awareness of liberalism that such ideas are not among the facts in accord with which we must live marks the transition of liberalism from what Mr. Riesman calls the phase of "other-direction" to what he calls "autonomy." It marks the effort of liberalism to overcome its paradox, to "humanize" nature and to restore to mind its role of causality, its effectiveness as a governing instrument. It marks also its dilemma. For if liberalism's phase of anomy and other-direction is characterized by the "facts" arising from indetermination of material and efficient principles in human behavior, its phase of autonomy is marked by the conscious overthrow of that common experience of moral ends and purposes that opposes its "free constructs." This is liberalism's necessary direction. As Judge Hand observes, "[Indefectible principles] are at *war* with our only trustworthy way of living in accord with the facts." And Professor Arnold Brecht, speaking of the liberal methodology ("Scientific Value Relativism,") observes that this method does not doom us to indifference and apathy, for "it can often demonstrate that some type of political actions give the people a better guaranty than do alternative actions for getting what they actually desire and avoiding results that they actually do not desire."[35] It is exactly at this point that the devastating effects of liberalism appear. A people that has moved to autonomy by way of other-direction (and more remotely from inner-direction and tradition-direction) can only desire the overthrow of everything that stands in the way of their "free constructs."

Liberalism's path from anomy to autonomy can only be what it is indeed for Marx—the destruction of every hitherto-existing social form so that man himself may become "the totality . . . the subjective existence of society thought and felt for itself."[36] There

---

34. Trilling, *The Liberal Imagination*, 19.

35. Arnold Brecht, *Political Theory: The Foundations of Twentieth-Century Political Thought* (Princeton, 1959).

36. Karl Marx, *Oekonomische-philosophische Manuskript, 1844* (Marx-Engels, Gesamatausgabe), Sec. I, III, 117.

is more than a striking parallel between Mr. Riesman's description of autonomy as implying "a heightened self-consciousness" by which man realizes "increased possibilities of being and becoming" and Marx's final emancipation of man's "generic being"—a "being which relates itself to the species as to his own proper being or relates itself to itself as a generic being."[37] Is this not the meaning of Riesman's "heightened self-consciousness" which, he tells us, "is not a quantitative matter but in part an awareness of the problem of self-consciousness itself, *an achievement of a higher order of abstraction.*"?[38] The separating of man's individual self from his generic self is expressly attributed by Erich Fromm, the distinguished defender of liberal humanism, to the institution of the family; man can be returned to himself (obviously by a "higher order of abstraction") only when the primordial relationship of the family community is rationalized and exorcised.[39] The title of Mr. Fromm's book on humanistic ethics—*Man for Himself*—epitomizes this demand and is curiously reminiscent of Marx's italicized emphasis on a "complete, conscious return, accomplished within the interior of the whole wealth of past development, of *man for himself.*"[40]

In short, liberalism's primal act of imagination whereby it established its essence and existence in the enhanced sense of freedom consequent upon the Humean principle that the aberrations in nature are ever so conformable to reality as its apparent intentions issued in anomy and other-direction. This condition is overcome by the profounder insight that, as we have noted, by the law that reduces the material and mental spheres to a common denominator the aberrations in nature become the exemplar for freedom in the world of culture and civilization. The way to autonomy then must lie, as Marx most clearly perceived, in destroying all the "intentions" of nature—the "forms and products of consciousness" represented by "'pure' theory, theology, philosophy, ethics, etc." These are the presuppositions of Riesman's "tradition directed" and "inner directed" societies and of Fromm's authoritarian ethics—"religion, the family, state, law, morals, science, spirit,

37. *Manuscrit economico-philosohique*, XXIV, cited in *De Marx au Marxisme*, ed. Robert Aron (Paris, 1948), 95.
38. David Riesman, *The Lonely Crowd* (Garden City, N.Y., 1955), 143. Italics added.
39. Fromm, *Man for Himself*, Chapter I.
40. Marx, *Oekonomische-philosophische Manuskript*, 114. Italics in original.

etc."[41] These are the indefectible principles and natural associations, and they are not among the facts in accord with which we must live—in a people's democracy. But they are precisely the things upon which, in the classical tradition of the West, all free government has depended. And the reason for this is that all of these things are nothing but participations of that intellect that is "separable indeed but [does] not exist apart from matter" in the life of that Prime Intellect upon whose perfect freedom, indeed— as Aristotle well understood—"depend the heavens and the world of nature."[42]

41. *Ibid.*, 114–115.   42. See above, footnotes 9 and 10.

7. The Historical Position of Man Himself*

[This essay is a study of Heidegger. It takes up the progress of the argument about political philosophy where it left off in *The Structure of Political Thought* and analyzes the importance of existentialism in political philosophy. McCoy understood Heidegger to have penetrated more deeply than Marx in his analysis of being. But this analysis still lies within the position of Aristotle and Aquinas on the relation of being and action, in the understanding of the good. Heidegger's notion of the destruction of ontology meant the endeavor to think out of existence the metaphysical structure of reality, to arrive at a formlessness which would oblige man to nothing but himself. McCoy analyzes the existentialists' continuation of intellectual argument based on the premises of modern philosophy. McCoy sees that the sort of "being" which Heidegger pursued was that being presupposed to no hypothetical possibility from the First Mover or Divine Being. Thus, neither nature nor man had any discoverable meaning or unity.. In this sense, Heidegger represented something of an intellectual extreme which, paradoxically, enabled the order of true being to become evident.]

And when he was now coming near the descent of mount Olivet, the whole multitude of his disciples began with joy to praise God with a loud voice, for all the mighty works they had seen.

Saying: Blessed be the king who cometh in the name of the Lord, peace in heaven, and glory on high!

And some of the Pharisees, from amongst the multitude, said to him:. Master, rebuke thy disciples.

To whom he said: I say to you, that if these shall hold their peace, the stones will cry out.

Luke 19, 37–40.

"[I]n whatever direction we may look today, it is hard to escape the conclusion that we have entered upon what Christians might

*This essay originally appeared in *Mélanges à la Mémoire de Charles de Koninck* (Quebec: Presses de l'Université Laval, 1968), 219–31.

describe as an eschatological age. This does not necessarily mean that the end of the world is chronologically imminent. . . . But what is clear is that men today . . . know that they have it in their power to destroy the universe. Moreover, one would have to be blind not to see that, at every level of being, a clearly traceable process of self-destruction is taking place; . . ."[1] In these sentences, Gabriel Marcel speaks of self-destruction at every level of being, and he joins this observation with the demurrer concerning the chronological imminence of the end of the world. It seems that the suggestion is being made that the bomb is only the terrible external sign of that "darkening of the world, the flight of the gods, the destruction of the earth"[2] whose prototype is an intensity of defect in the very heart of man's being. Marcel's phrasing suggests a link with the Heideggerian proposal of the destruction of the history of ontology; for Heidegger's proposal, of which (although he has not yet carried it out) we have valuable clues, opens to man a most curious experience: an experience wherein the transceucny and pure exteriority of the cosmos in its initial state—separated from itself, wrapped in its own obscurity—is interiorized in such a way that—and this is the particularly curious and important element—it is as if the cosmos itself were imaginatively projecting a "consciousness" of pure exteriority and irrelationality *to man*: a paradox of empathy by which man stands outside of himself and communicates total irrelationality to himself. This is the more remarkable in view of the fact that in the theory of the expansion of the universe, physics unveils to us a world first arising from the explosion of an immense atom: The energy amassed within is dispersed, and, before the appearance of life, the fragmentation of space and the diffusion of time dominate all things: time and space are, as it were—indeed, as Heidegger says of human existence—their substance and being. The intellectual destruction of the history of ontology has induced in the region of intellect a consciousness of primeval being such as the primeval atom and the atom bomb alike establish in the region of reality. We shall inquire into this apocalyptic philosophy to discover in it a clue to where man himself stands historically.

1. Gabriel Marcel, *The Philosophy of Existence* (New York, 1949), 32.
2. Martin Heidegger, *An Introduction to Metaphysics* (Garden City, N.Y., 1961), 31. Heidegger ascribes these dire happenings to the forgetfulness of "being" and a preoccupation with technics, but I will argue that they attach most fundamentally to his notion of "homecoming" or return to origins by way of getting behind both metaphysics and technics to the "poverty of existence."

With his usual perspicacity, M. de Koninck advised us that

[t]he philosophical doctrine that properly concerns the opinions advanced by Existentialism is not the doctrine of being; rather, it is the doctrine of the good. Nor do we mean by "good" the transcendental property which is convertible with being; we are referring, more particularly, to the good that divides being.[3]

To be a man and to be a good man are not the same thing. "The good man is 'good, absolutely' (bonus simpliciter) not by reason of his 'absolute being' (esse simpliciter)—this, in fact, is not good except in a certain respect (bonum secundum quid),—but by reason of a superadditive or ultimate perfection, which derives from an accidental being (esse secundum quid), and in itself is separable from his absolute being."[4] The reason for this, as St. Thomas makes clear, is that

[a] thing is called a being inasmuch as it is considered absolutely, but good . . . in relation to other things. Now it is by its essential principles that a thing is fully constituted in itself so that it subsists; but it is not so perfectly constituted as to stand as it should in relation to everything outside itself except by means of accidents added to the essence, because the operations by which one thing is in some sense joined to another proceed from the essence through powers distinct from it. Consequently nothing achieves goodness absolutely unless it is complete in both its essential and its accidental principles.[5]

It is only in God that what is being in the absolute sense is also good in the absolute sense; the esse simpliciter which encloses all perfection of being is the proper being of God, Whose essence is His being. Now then, in making the point that it is only in the human intelligence that the cosmos becomes a universe in the full sense, St. Thomas describes the perfection of man in the following manner:

[T]he perfection of each individual thing considered in itself is imperfect, being a part of the perfection of the entire universe, which arises from the sum total of the perfections of all individual things.

As if to compensate for this imperfection, another kind of perfection is to be found in created things. It consists in this, that the perfection belonging to one thing is found in another. This is the perfection of a knower

---

3. Charles de Koninck, "The Nature of Man and His Historical Being," *Laval Théologique et Philosophique*, 5 (#2, 1949), 275. See Thomas Aquinas, *Quaestiones Disputatae de Veritate*, 21, 2, ad 6; *Summa Theologiae*, I, 5, 1, ad 1.

4. De Koninck, "The Nature of Man,", 275.

5. Thomas Aquinas, *De Veritate*, 21, 5.

in so far as he knows; for something is known by a knower by reason of the fact that the thing known is, in some fashion, in the possession of the knower. Hence, it is said in *The Soul* that the soul is, "in some manner, all things," since its nature is such that it can know all things. In this way it is possible for the perfection of the entire universe to exist in one thing. The ultimate perfection which the soul can attain, therefore, is, according to the philosophers, to have delineated in it the entire order and causes of the universe.[6]

Now the reason M. de Koninck felt it necessary to say that it is the doctrine of the good and not the doctrine of being that properly concerns the opinions advanced by Existentialism is that these opinions are indeed ostensibly concerned with the doctrine of being. And the reason why the Existentialists are ostensibly concerned with the doctrine of being is that they are preoccupied with viewing man as fully constituted in his simple act of being so as to stand as he should in relation to everything outside himself. This "ontologized ethics" arises out of the wish to make the very power of man the rule and measure of his acts.[7] We may notice as a sign of this preoccupation the saying of Kierkegaard that the opposite of sin is not virtue but faith: Adherence by the "leap" of faith to the being of God, in Whom what is being in the absolute sense is also good in the absolute sense is offered as the alternative to what otherwise is all sin. Kierkegaard has man stand out, in pure subjectivity, from the world of moral law and find himself simply "there" with God, in Whom is every perfection of being. We may profitably notice the parallel between this Kierkegaardian notion and Heidegger's notion of "guilt" as connoting not a consciousness of any special fault or wrong, but rather a failure to attain "authentic" existence in the absolute "ecstasy" of standing out from being and making a "homecoming," a return to origins in the "poverty of existence." In Kierkegaard's case there is an extraordinary keenness about what theologians call the first inordinateness in man's will—which inordinateness could not have been the choosing of anything evil in itself but could only have been by way of a simple and total turning toward one's own excellence and away from God as the measure and rule of all things.[8] In Heidegger's case, on the other hand, there is an extraordinary sensitivity to the beginning of things as described in the opening

6. *Ibid.*, 2, 2.
7. Thomas Aquinas, *Summa Theologiae*, I, 63, 3 and ad 4.
8. *Ibid.*, II–II, *163*, *1*, *ad* 1.

passages of Genesis[9]—to the abyss of division, solitariness, and exteriority that mark the minimum of immediacy and intrinsicness of the cosmos in its initial state and long before the eventuality of the human intelligence through which the corporal world is brought back to its first Principle. In each case—that of Kierkegaard and that of Heidegger—we find evidence of that process of self-destruction that Marcel speaks of as going on at every level of being.

How does it come about that the effort to see man as fully constituted in his simple act of being so as to stand as he should in relation to everything outside himself has led to the "poverty of existence" manifested both in Kierkegaard's radically contingent and gratuitous "decisiveness" of the "leap" to God, and in Heidegger's "absolute ecstasy" of "presence" (*Anwesenheit*) by which man's existence is said to be his substance?[10] To find an answer to this question it will be illuminating to approach Heidegger's notion of *Dasein* ("being-there," "thereness," human existence) by way of an examination of the salient differences between the realm of the inorganic and the biosphere as the latter makes its appearance in the cosmos. The adumbration, as it were, of existentialist themes in the being of the cosmos in its initial state will have its shadow removed by evidence from modern art—since, indeed, Heidegger has argued that it is through the intuitions of art that man comes closest to the sources of being. And indeed, since we are involved—as will become clear—with a certain *manner of viewing* the experience of the world rather than with an expression of "facts" about the world, it is with very good reason that Heidegger has appealed to art as a vehicle for expressing his philosophy. Finally, we shall look at the notion of *Dasein* itself for confirmation of the thesis that its "ontology" is "borrowed" from the understructure of the levels of being.

We alluded above to the fact that before the appearance of life on the planet, the fragmentation of space and the diffusion of time dominated all things. With the appearance of life we find an element that works against the diffusion of time. De Koninck has described this phenomenon in the following text:

9. Werner Brock in his commentary on Heidegger's essay "What Is Metaphysics?" remarks that Heidegger's "vision and outlook" in delineating man's experience of "nothingness" has in its favor its evocation of the beginning of *Genesis*. *Existence and Being* by Martin Heidegger, with an Introduction by Werner Brock (Chicago, 1949), 215.
10. *Ibid.*, 111.

[Life] is a kind of triumph over the diffusion of time. . . . We find the most manifest sign of this in the knowledge of animals and men, and especially in the memory. In the measure that a being lives, it rises above the conditions of space and time. . . . A knowing being is present to itself and assimilates to itself intentionally its surroundings, while there where space dominates, things are separated one from another and lost in the night. . . .

It is understood, of course, that the different durations of natural beings are all of them truly temporal, that is to say, successive and continuous. But some are less so than others. And when we consider the hierarchy of durations in the sense of their lower limit where they become experimentally measurable, we notice that they tend to lose their identity and to disappear in physical time to the point of the obliteration of all distinctions between *beings*. If the principle of the conservation of energy is true, and if the mass of the universe is constant, physical time is, under this aspect, absolutely one; in this perspective, which abstracts from the real breaks or incisions dividing the world in individuals, the different physical times proper to beings—the life of a cat, for example—are only local condensations of an identical time which goes back to the origin of things. . . .

In assimilating the other in sensible knowledge, the animal already breaks the barriers of space which separates; it extends to that which is not itself—extends to it intentionally. . . . In the measure that animals are perfect, the field of their knowledge becomes vaster: that is to say, the world more and more compenetrates itself, becomes, in this way, more and more present to itself, more and more interior. This increasing interiorization culminates in true simplicity in the human soul whose intelligence embraces and transcends space without being mixed in it.[11]

Further, in the realm of the inorganic, motion is wholly transeunt; the effects on this level of being always terminate outside the causes. There being no self-motion, no life, inorganic things move only by being moved; the subject and the object of an action are external to each other. There where space dominates, things are separated one from another and lost in the night.

If we turn now to the "ontology" of *Dasein* as it is brought before us in modern literature, it will become apparent that human life has a minimum of intrinsicness, is rendered mute by the barriers of space and dispersed by time. The interiority proper to the human intelligence is "exploited" by lending itself, as it were, to the cosmos in its initial exteriority, so that the cosmos, as it were again, imaginatively projects in us a "consciousness" of pure exteriority. It is through this consciousness that all the modes or structures of *Dasein* become intelligible. This paradox of empathy finds an ex-

11. Charles de Koninck, "Le cosmos comme tendance vers la pensée," in *Itinéraires*, N. 66 (September–October, 1962), 174, 191.

cellent portrayal in lines from Alexander Trocchi's *The Outsiders*—lines appositely selected by Fernando Molina at the beginning of a chapter on Heidegger[12]:

And now suddenly, as soon as I left the others, I was conscious of being coerced no longer, and the world came to exist for me again, not as a foreign element to be looked at, but as a climate in which I could become immersed, whose parts were merely an extension of myself, or, the same thing, were continuous with me and I with them.

It is understandable that Existentialism should be taken as engaging the person in the world to the point of having him follow all its sinuosities.[13] In the near-naught of undifferentiated otherness, engagement reaches the point of obliteration of the distinction between beings. Alluding to Heidegger's concept of *Dasein*, William Barrett speaks of "the flattening out of all planes and climaxes" in modern art as testifying to the existentialist view of man, and he speaks of Faulkner's novel, *The Sound and the Fury*, as effectively reproducing the sense of *Dasein*:

In the course of the brute random flow of detail that is that last day of his life, Quentin Compson breaks the crystal of his watch. He twists off the two hands and thereafter, throughout the day, the watch continues to tick loudly but cannot, with its faceless dial, indicate the time. Faulkner could not have hit on a better image to convey the sense of time which permeates the whole book. . . . Time is no longer a reckonable sequence, then, for him, but an inexhaustible inescapable presence. . . . Real time, the time that makes up the dramatic substance of our life, is something deeper and more primordial than watches, clocks, and calendars. Time is the dense medium in which Faulkner's characters move about as if dragging their feet through water; it is their substance or Being. . . . The abolition of clock time does not mean a retreat into the world of the timeless; quite the contrary: the timeless world, the eternal, has disappeared from the horizon of the modern writer; . . . and time thereby becomes all the more inexorable and absolute a reality.[14]

In the perspective of the "temporality" of *Dasein*, which abstracts from the real breaks or incisions dividing the world in individuals, the different physical times proper to beings—the life of Quentin Compson, for example—are only local condensations of an identical time which goes back to the origin of things.

---

12. Fernando Molina, *Existentialism as Philosophy* (Englewood Cliffs, N.J., 1962), 53.

13. See Maurice Merleau-Ponty, *The Primacy of Perception and Other Essays*, ed. by James M. Edie (Evanston, Ill., 1964), 28.

14. William Barrett, *Irrational Man* (Garden City, N.Y., 1962), 53.

The intuitions of art reach the modes or structures of *Dasein* in a more penetrating way than does philosophical exposition, and this is because the concept of *Dasein* derives, as I have said, from *a certain manner of viewing* the experience of the world. Although the aim is to give a "fundamental ontology," to elucidate the meaning of Being, the instrument of this task is a so-called existential experience of the way the person finds himself being in the world. The fundamental ontological characteristics of human existence (*Dasein*) are *Befindlichkeit* (self-encountering, with its special reference to the fact that *Dasein* is "there," in the state of "thrownness"), Existentiality (with its reference to the potentiality of Being, "project" and "understanding"), and *Verfallensein* (Fallenness—a movement into inauthenticity, although, with its reference to the present, it is found in some respects in every *Dasein*). Now then, we may observe that the difference between a "natural entity," called an "object" as signifying "thrown against," and *Dasein*, lies in the phenomenon of "self-encounter": finding himself "there," the person is said not to be "thrown against," but to be "thrown" or "thrown into" and in the movement of the "throw." This "thrownness" is experienced without any comprehension of the *why this place,* and is unaccompanied by any evidence of where-from or where-to. The experience is made agonizingly real in the novels of Franz Kafka: With a minimum of self-affirmation and intrinsicness, the hero is in the "throw" of obscure and inscrutable agents. He has the sense of living on the margin of the world, a world rapidly losing its intelligibility and becoming increasingly dense and opaque. "Thrownness" is indeed nothing else than *the experience of* being "thrown against": that is to say, it is an interiorizing of the wholly transeunt motion that is found in the inorganic realm of the primeval cosmos.

Now it is important to take account here of Karl Jasper's observation that "extreme situations" have become the commonplace thing in our world; we seem increasingly to be brought whither we would not go, victims of chance and circumstance and violence. It is important to notice this because in Heidegger's philosophy of being, the commonplace, everyday world of the "one-among-many"—the world in which the prevailing dimension, as Heidegger says, is that of extension and number—finds its paradigm in the world of Kafka's hero who is wholly in the movement of the "throw." Life is tuned to the high key of extreme situations. The one-among-many, who sets his watch by the public clocks, soon finds that clock time is an inauthentic telling of the real, dense, primordial time into which we are all "thrown." The "sense" of this, the "meaning" of this being in the world is in the awareness of Kafka and the Faulkner hero more sharply: He is out in the world, standing out from it, in the mode of "*Befindlichkeit*" and finding himself "there." And standing out in this "ecstasy of temporality," he sees that he is not a center of determination, of immanent movement—that he is not "self," but is estranged from himself, alienated in the world of one-among-many, whose parts are continuous with him and he with them. This is the mode of *Dasein* called *Verfallensein*: the mode of inauthenticity and guilt, in which the prevailing dimension is extension and number.

The two modes of Being-in-the-world, *Befindlichkeit* and *Verfallensein*, with their references to the past and present respectively, contribute to defining the "ontology" of the Being of *Dasein* and are part of what is called "the ecstatic (standing out from) unity of Temporality." But the guiding and dominant mode of Temporality is that of the "future" understood in the existentialistic sense and not as a "now" which has not yet become "real" and has yet to "be." Future is understood as the movement of *Dasein* from the "thrownness" of *Befindlichkeit* and from the dependence of unresolved *Verfallen* back toward the "self" of *Dasein* in its "innermost" and "eminent" potentiality of Being. In this "projection" of himself toward his innermost potentiality, the person finds himself, in the ecstatic unity of Temporality, away from the condition of the one-among-many; he finds himself alone in his power-to-be authentically. Nonetheless, Heidegger tells us, "this existential solipsism is so far from being an isolated subject-thing, that it indeed brings the person into an extreme sense before his world as world."[15]

What is this "extreme sense" into which a person is brought before the world as world by the movement of *Dasein* toward itself in its own potentiality? The meaning is contained in the notion of Temporality as the ontological "meaning" of the Being of *Dasein*, and the significance of that notion itself will become clear if we consider that

when we were saying that the biosphere rises more and more above time, this was not said merely metaphorically. Beings are perfect in the measure in which they are not temporal; transcendence over the diffusion of time is a condition of life, of knowledge, of thought. If the vegetable species

15. Martin Heidegger, *Sein und Zeit* (9th ed.; Tübingen, 1960), 27.

are hierarchized according to their approach to animal species, and these in turn according as they approach man, it is necessary to say that the vital drive with which the cosmos is animated from outside since the beginning, extracts from the power of matter composites whose form emerges more and more from matter; that is to say, substances that are more and more simple. *Quanto forma magis vincit materiam, tanto ex ea et materia magis efficitur unum.* But, since existence is proportionate to essence, the duration of cosmic beings is more and more one and simple as it is less and less temporal. As we have said, they are specifically hierarchized in their existence as well as in their essence. The animal is less temporal than the plant.[16]

Now for Heidegger, on the contrary, Temporality is the ontological "meaning" of human existence. If indeed the guiding mode is the "future" which defines the "existentiality" of *Dasein*, the past and the present define the ontology of *Dasein* in the line of its "there-ness" and transeuncy. In the "Being-guilty" of *Verfallensein*, the prevailing dimension, as we saw, is that of extension and number. Now in the perspective of the "future" mode of Temporality, the Being of *Dasein* is said to be "in-advance-of-itself" because it is "itself-moving-toward-itself," that is, toward its own innermost, extreme, and eminent potentiality. In this mode of *Dasein*, the "self" will emerge from the *Verfallen* of the one-among-many, from the prevailing dimension of extension and number. What is the nature of the "authenticity" into which it moves and which brings it into an extreme sense before the world as world?

The answer to this question lies in Heidegger's relation to Marx. Hailing Marx's doctrine of alienation as the greatest boon to modern philosophy, Heidegger has his metaphysical inquiries take their point of departure from the "*Zuhandene*" (the instruments of production) rather than the "*Vorhandene*" (the world of nature). Since existence for Heidegger is peculiarly human existence—*Dasein*—the notion of "being" must be approached through the things "at hand"—the complexus of tools and the relations of production which first give significance, Heidegger insists, to the world of nature. But Marx failed to understand "the crux of the matter" of authenticity, which, Heidegger tells us, is the masquerading of spirit as intelligence: "The crux of the matter is the reinterpretation of the spirit as *intelligence*. . . . The spirit falsified into intelligence . . . falls to the level of a tool in the service of others."[17] Marx himself fell prey to the fecundity of thought. In Marx's doctrine of

16. De Koninck, "Le cosmos," 175–76.
17. Heidegger, *An Introduction to Metaphysics*, 38.

the "generic being" of man, the individual realizes the "general mode" of his generic being in the activity of the generic conscience, and this general mode is the "theoretical form of that of which the living form is the real community," the product of "the total living sensuous activity of all the individuals composing the sensuous world."[18] Thus, "Socialism takes its departure from the theoretically and practically sensible conscience of man in nature, considered as being. . . . The objective reality becomes for man the reality of human forces . . . the object of himself."[19] For Marx, all that is "natural" (Vorhandene)—the forms and products of a consciousness that has separated itself from the "real" world and gone off into "pure" theory, theology, philosophy, ethics, etc.—must be overthrown by revolutionary action. But their surrogate—work, considered as the first need of life because by work man makes himself specifically human—is, in Heidegger's view, a perpetuation of man's self-estrangement; he is alienated in the products of his labor. Spirit is to be found neither in "the regulation and domination of the material conditions of production" nor in "the intelligent ordering and explanation of everything that is present and already posited at any time."[20] Spirit is anterior to the division of knowledge into theoretical and practical, as well as to the distinction between subject and object. Heidegger wants from the Zuhandene the ground of their being, the principle of exterior activity. One must get behind both metaphysics and technics; a "homecoming" must be made to the origins, to the "poverty of existence."

Now if Temporality is the ontological meaning of Dasein and if the "future" is the mode of Temporality that guides one toward authenticity in overcoming the prevailing dimension of extension and number, then the "projection" of existentiality toward Dasein's innermost, eminent, and extreme potentiality must in some way reduce the quantitative aspect of time in favor of a "simple duration."[21] Now we must consider that

[i]n our idea of evolution, the beings below man are essentially a function of man, and, as such, transitory; these natures are by reason of this func-

18. Karl Marx, Oekonomische-Philosophische Manuskript, 1844 (Marx-Engels, Gesamtausgabe), Sec. I, 3, 125–26; Marx and Engels, The German Ideology (New York, 1939), 37–38, and see The Structure of Political Thought, Chapter X.
19. Marx, Oekonomische-Philosophische Manuskript, 119.
20. Heidegger, An Introduction to Metaphysics, 38–39.
21. See de Koninck, "Le cosmos," 177–78.

tion open one to another, constituting in their ascension toward man an *élan* more and more determinate and powerful. . . . If evolution were able to accomplish itself in one leap, it would realize by a single stroke an immortal cosmic being whose duration would be at once quantitatively indefinite and yet simple in reality. Submitted to the resistance of matter, the world achieves this end in projecting a whole hierarchy of intermediary composite beings in which it has not yet succeeded in establishing that equivalence of quantity with an intensity of duration. The natural species below man ought to be considered as attempts, more and more audacious, to detach themselves from the dispersion of time, and to dominate it. This ascension accomplishes itself in sacrificing time from the point of view of quantity, just as, with man, life is sometimes sacrificed in an heroic act which renders him worthy of immortality.[22]

In the ascension toward man there is a sacrifice of time from the point of view of quantity—the animal is less temporal than the plant—just as, de Koninck points out, with man life is sometimes sacrificed in an heroic act which renders him worthy of immortality. For Heidegger, for whom existence is peculiarly human existence, "experienced" in the exteriority and transeuncy of the primeval cosmos, there is, in the movement of *Dasein* toward its innermost potentiality a like sacrifice of time from the point of view of quantity: The projection toward "authenticity," Heidegger tells us, is a "Being-toward-Death," which, because it discloses all the potentialities that precede it, is called the "whole" of *Dasein*. Quantity of time is a sign of slackened existence.[23] In the perspective of Heidegger's Temporality as the ontological meaning of *Dasein*, the dimension of extension and number which prevails in the mode of *Verfallensein* (in the everydayness of the one-among-many) is overcome by the emergence of the "self-alone" through a reduction of the quantitative measurability of being: The projection of *Dasein* toward its innermost potentialities in *itself-moving-toward-itself* is accomplished not by intensifying the duration but by shortening it. Death is the *"whole" of Dasein*. The world of the Kafka hero is indeed a paradigm of the slackened everyday world of the one-among-many; so much in the movement of the "throw," it is always near its end.

It is here, finally, that a curious turn brings us in view of the historical position of man himself today. How is it that the "existential solipsism" of the Being-toward-Death as the "whole" of the Being of *Dasein* "is so little an isolated subject-thing that, on the contrary, it brings the person into an extreme sense before his

22. *Ibid.*, 183, 179.   23. *Ibid.*, 177–78.

world as world"?[24] We must recall that with Marx the reappro-
priation of man's substantial forces—forces that in the whole history of philosophy had become foreign objects—is accomplished
by revolutionary action: The forms and products of consciousness
represented by "pure theory, theology, philosophy, ethics, etc.,"
are to be won not in the purely speculative fashion of Hegel, but
in the "real" life of sensuous, practical activity. Heidegger contends that while Hegel's metaphysics represents indeed the perfection of all metaphysics, Marx rightly subjected this metaphysics
to the humanist critique that brought it down to the "real" life.
But, as we saw, Heidegger proposes the destruction of the history
of ontology—an ontology which was brought to perfection by Hegel and was brought down to earth by Marx. Hence, it is not the
winning—whether speculatively or practically— of the world of
that-which-is that engages Heidegger. Rather, he wishes to go
behind both metaphysics and technics to the "origins," to the
"poverty of existence"—to lay being bare by denuding the world
of that-which-is. If, with Marx, philosophy passes into practice by
transposing to the practical intellect all that Aristotle had reserved
to the speculative intellect, Heidegger brings us to a simple contemplation of the nudity of the world that is subject to the total
power of man.

The "being" that is laid bare by Heidegger—the "poverty of
existence" that is anterior to Metaphysics—is the purely passive
principle that is anterior logically to the activity of nature—the
"essential need" as de Koninck puts it, "that calls upon the spiritual world for the constitution itself of active nature. . . . It is
precisely this essential lack that opens the inorganic world as such
to life and intelligence, without which the inorganic would be deprived of its natural end and contradictory."[25] This "essential lack
that opens the . . . world" is what Heidegger speaks of when he
says that possibility is higher than actuality. It is the "call" of this
"essential need" itself that Heidegger would identify with "every
word-creating impulse of the spirit." Werner Brock has pointed
out the sequence in Heidegger's analysis of, "on the one hand,
the experience of Nothingness as the ground of being, and, on the
other, the resulting genuine meditation on the coming into their
own of the things in the world."[26] The evocation of the Book of

24. Heidegger, *Sein und Zeit*, 188.
25. De Koninck, "Le cosmos," 183–84.
26. Brock, Introduction to Heidegger's *Existence*, 210.

Genesis by Heidegger's meditation on Nothingness shows the kinship of his position with Kierkegaard's "leap" of faith. Indeed, the Heideggerian experience of Nothingness as a preparation for the coming into their own of the things in the world has its counterpart in the individual's Being-toward-Death as awakening him to the formlessness, as it were, of his substantial being by comparison with the accidental being which renders him good in the absolute sense—which being, if we consider the order of things themselves, is what man principally is, and which—as we saw at the beginning of our considerations—consists ultimately in man's bringing the corporeal world back to its first Principle:

In the human intelligence the corporeal universe not only becomes present to itself: this presence opens it to the whole of being, and thereby it can then realize a return, explicitly lived, to the first principle of being—God, who draws the world to himself with the purpose of having it "speak" to him through man, in whom he thus establishes an abode for the dwelling of the divinity.[27]

The intensity of defect at the heart of man's being has grown so great that man's recession from the first Principle of the universe is experienced by the primeval cosmos itself—"I say to you, that if these shall hold their peace, the stones will cry out."[28] *Aggiornamento*, in its emphasis upon return to sources and to the sense of mystery, seems unerringly to have perceived how dumbly the world waits for God.

27. De Koninck, "Le cosmos," 188.   28. *Luke*, 19:40.

8. The "Value-Free" Aristotle and the Behavioral Sciences*

[Here McCoy addresses the dominant philosophic position within professional political science circles in the United States during his lifetime. McCoy is insistent in relating political ideas to Aristotle and Aquinas, here the famous "value-free" problem. Paradoxically, he held that it was Aristotle who was in fact "value-free" while that word, "value," has taken on overtones in modern thought that are by no means philosophically neutral. This essay is essential in understanding the distinction between political life and trans-political reality. The relation of these two areas has become a most confused one, particularly in religious circles. McCoy provided a way to justify the behavioral sciences but only if they could be seen in the light of the original Aristotelian distinctions between art and prudence, between the speculative and the practical sciences. The unity of ideas in the history of political philosophy, beginning with the relation of Plato and Aristotle and reaching to contemporary controversies about the study of politics, is quite evident in this chapter.]

In the controversy on facts versus values in political science the assumption seems generally to be made that classical political philosophy is the bastion of the "value approach" and that modern political philosophy has freed itself for a "scientific" study of "facts." I would like to suggest that there is a very real and profound sense in which classical political philosophy—and that of Aristotle in particular—is value-free—value-free but not ethically neutral; and that modern theory, while ethically neutral, is distinguished indeed by a preoccupation with value such as was quite absent from the classical treatment of politics. My suggestion may

*This essay originally appeared in the *Western Political Quarterly*, 23 (March 1970), 57–74.

serve, I would hope, to narrow the "unbridgeable intellectual gulf [which separates] today as in the past . . . the noumenalist political philosophers and the exponents of naturalist behavioral political science."[1]

I

A preliminary observation will serve to suggest the general thesis which I wish to develop. After Aristotle had delineated his absolutely best form of government—the Royal polity—he noted a curious defect of this "best" regime: there is no participation by the citizens who have turned the care of the polity over to the most virtuous man; and the ruler himself "can no longer be regarded as part of a state."[2] This paradoxical outcome led Aristotle to conclude that "legislation is necessarily concerned only with those who are equal in birth and capacity; and that for men of preeminent virtue there is no law."[3] In his *Commentary on the Politics* at this point, St. Thomas Aquinas observes that Aristotle's best regime is supra-political or meta-political. And he adds that the assumption that no one but a citizen should rule is an assumption that simply does not hold in the Royal polity, which is above both law and citizenship: "Just as he who rules by the excellence of his virtue is not a citizen but above citizenship, so in the same way members of the best polity are above citizenship by reason of the excellence of their conduct."[4] It would thus appear that the law and the polity do not concern themselves directly and by their proper structure with the excellence of virtue.

This brief consideration reveals two underlying principles of classical political philosophy: First, that the quality of human life is the ultimate concern of politics; second, that this concern goes hand in hand with freedom for the spirit—a freedom so essential to the very notion of "polity" that it prohibits the state from directly regulating by law the quality of human life. With great precision Aristotle withdrew from the determination of the politician all matters of speculative truth: neither in what precisely "the good" consists, nor the interior truth of theoretic science is a matter

1. William T. Bluhm, *Theories of the Political System* (Englewood Cliffs, N.J., 1965), 483.
2. Aristotle, *Politics*, III, 13, 1284a5.
3. *Ibid.*, 5–12.
4. Thomas Aquinas, *Commentary on the Politics of Aristotle*, III, 12.

for human determination. "Political" rule is defined indeed precisely in terms of the free man's immunity from compulsion to the true "good": if this immunity did not mark the rule, then the rule would be the opposite of "political," namely, "despotic." Following Aristotle's teaching on this matter, St. Thomas writes that although virtue is the end at which every lawmaker aims, it does not itself come under the precept of law. "Political" refers to the man who is *"causa sui,"* cause of himself, and as such he enjoys the liberty of contrariety with respect to good and evil. The state is absolutely required to protect those who, without being good men, obey the penal laws. If, to be sure, the true good is the motivating principle of all human conduct, it does not constitute the structure itself of political life but is a meta-political principle that sustains the structure as a hidden dynamic force.

In Aristotle's teaching the dynamic role played by the idea of good is set forth in the *Ethics* and the *Metaphysics*. Inquiring into the worthwhileness of political life, Aristotle offers two different lines of consideration: The first is proper to what I have called the structure of politics and consists in analyzing the nature of the political community as one of free men having the freedom of "moral action," that is, action which depends not on a natural power determined to its act, but on a power that is indifferently disposed to many different things contained under the notion of the good, whether true good or having the appearance of good. The second approach to the ground of the goodness of political life is meta-political; it is to be found in considerations that lie beyond the directly pertinent ones of structure. In the opening chapters of the *Ethics* Aristotle maintains that the ultimate end of all the things we do is the first principle or first reason for doing all the lesser things: whether building a ship or curing the body or engaging in politics; and in the Tenth Book this ultimate end of all the things we do turns out to be contemplation of the order of the universe and of that principle upon which order depends.[5] For man is "a little world," Aristotle points out, not only in the sense that he contains all the degrees of natural being within himself, but more profoundly in that he uses the resources of art to draw to himself all the richness of the world diffused in space and time. The goodness of political life is said to consist ultimately in the political order being an imitation of the order of the universe in

---

5. Aristotle, *Nicomachean Ethics*, X, 8, 1178b25; see *Metaphysics*, XII, 10, 1075a12.

which—together with God upon whom the order depends—consists the highest good. This is why Aristotle says in the *Ethics* that if the good is the same for a single man and for a whole community, that of the whole community of men is "more divine"; he calls it more divine because it is a more perfect likeness of the good of the universe and of the ultimate essential goodness which draws all things to itself. Thus man is thought of as sharing proportionately in the activity of God by being the cause of goodness in the whole community as God is the cause of goodness in all that is. There is, then, in the thought of Aristotle a meta-political dynamic that sustains and perfects the structure of political life; but none of this is required for citizenship, nor does it come under any law; it is not part of the structure of politics.

The relation between what I have called the "structure" of politics and its "dynamics" is grounded in two considerations. First, there is no analytical connection between metaphysics and moral science, nor between moral science and concrete conduct—that is, no connection such that in order to conduct oneself well one must be a sound moralist, or that a sound moralist will conduct himself well. It cannot be required of the citizen that he subscribe to any moral science or to any metaphysics. Indeed, if that were necessary where would the political community be? It does not belong to the authority of civil law to determine exactly in what the goodness of the good man consists. Indeed, as Aristotle observes, such as a man is, so the end in life appears to him to be.[6] In all this we see that Aristotle's political science is quite value-free. Exercising his liberty of contrariety, the free man may seek power, wealth, honor, pleasure—even therapy for neuroses. Aristotle would consider motives of this kind to be very active and indeed contributing forces in political life. This suggests the great need for "insight" in the study of political phenomena because the variousness of these phenomena is from the fact that, as Aristotle states it, they are related to a power that is indifferently disposed to many different things under the most general concept of good. Without this freedom political life and citizenship would be impossible: the public power would be not political but its opposite, despotic. The dynamics of the structure is thus a mixture of meta-political and infra-political forces. As de Jouvenel has remarked, "Observation . . . suggests that the sport of moving men is enjoyed in itself,

6. See Aristotle, *Ethics*, III, 4, 1113a22; a30; 5, 1114b23.

even when the operation is not inspired by a high purpose, or addressed to a salutary end."[7] Transactional analysis in psychotherapy has given us valuable insights into the game aspect of social behavior.[8] The "awareness," "spontaneity," and "intimacy" required for autonomy, for a "game-free" candidness in living in the "here and now" is remarkably infrequent, as Eric Berne has demonstrated.[9] The vision of the game-free life is reserved for the eyes of "the eidetically perceptive, uncorrupted Child in all its naïveté living in the here and now."[10] Or, as St. Thomas Aquinas remarked of Aristotle's best regime—it is supra-political.

Second, we must observe why it is that if classical political philosophy was value-free it was nonetheless ethically oriented. This was so because while there is no analytic connection between concrete conduct and moral science nor between metaphysics and moral science, there is —so it was held—a connection between them in the order of things themselves; and it is this connection that provides what I have called the meta-political dynamics of the structure. If law preserves the liberty of contrariety by excluding virtue itself from its precept, we may observe that the acts that are in fact prescribed and forbidden by law are, nonetheless, acts that pertain respectively to virtue and vice: a man is free to be quite intemperate, but he will not be permitted to be publicly drunk; he is free to be truly a coward, but he will be restrained from panicking in battle. This is why, as we have observed St. Thomas remark, every lawmaker aims at virtue although virtue does not itself come under the precept of law. The lawmaker aims at virtue because it redounds to the preservation of the structure, which is built on the severely minimal lines of a liberty of contrariety restricted only by the imposition of those external acts without which living together at all would be impossible. Thus the idea of "the good" acts as a dynamic force sustaining and perfecting the political structure.[11] The ultimate political significance of Aristotle's exclusion of virtue itself from the precept of law may be seen in the consideration of the fact that the good which the truly good man

7. Bertrand de Jouvenel, *The Pure Theory of Politics*, (New Haven, 1963), 9.

8. Transactional game analysis would appear to be a more useful tool for the behavioral sciences than its sister science of mathematical game analysis. See de Jouvenel, "Political Science and Prevision," *American Political Science Review*, 59 (March 1965), 37.

9. Eric Berne, *Games People Play* (New York, 1964).

10. *Ibid.*

11. See Bernard Crick, *The American Science of Politics* (Berkeley, 1959), 203.

chooses, and which augments political life, is not itself determined by a political rule; again, if it were so determined, if an attempt were made to "overcome" the meta-political principles by finding their source and reason in the political order, the political structure itself would be destroyed. In short, if there is indeed no analytical connection between moral science and politics, there is, in the order of things themselves a profound connection—it is the very dynamism (hidden, if you will, and seen only after a long effort) that keeps the political structure intact.

The "ideal" polity is not, then, something built into the structure of politics; otherwise we would have to say that political society achieves existence only with the attainment of moral and intellectual unity. But since the pluralism that is humanly ineluctable is so essential to the nature of political life that political life cannot be understood without it, the "ideal" society must rather be conceived as not more real than the ideal gas of physics. This is not to say that the true and the good are to be denied or ignored; on the contrary, from the errors and evils that must inevitably arise, we ought to draw lessons for acting with greater prudence and wisdom. That is the meaning of "ideal" in classical politics, its meaning from the point of view of action. Aristotle observed that the best regime—that supra-political regime we have alluded to—lent itself more readily than less ideal regimes to the destruction of the very nature of the political community. The notion of "ideal" society is thus in Aristotle's view a perilous one: to paraphrase the celebrated epigram on Bergonsian ethics, it preserves all of politics except politics itself. This is the force, I think, of one of the Schaar-Wolin criticisms of *Essays on the Scientific Study of Politics,* which alleges that the authors show "a blunted sensitivity to what is political. . . . [T]he lack of political relevance stems from an exaggerated moralism which converts all political issues and analyzes political phenomena by means of moral categories."[12] Nonetheless, however perilous it be, the notion of "ideal" society can not be abandoned without—in the sense of the epigram just mentioned—losing all of politics including politics itself. For where there is an attempt to ignore the meta-political dynamics, to "overcome" these higher principles by concretizing them in the political order, the liberty of contrariety proper to the political structure is itself

12. John H. Schaar and Sheldon S. Wolin, "Essays on the Scientific Study of Politics," *American Political Science Review,* 57 (March 1963), 136.

also destroyed. If we assume that those political scientists whom Schaar and Wolin criticize do in fact hold that political society has no life unless it is living at the height of its principles, we must not fail to notice that those who would altogether abandon these higher principles deprive the body politic of the very principle of life. This is, then, a more radically antipolitical position, and it is exactly this consequence that Christian Bay perceives in speaking of the "anti-political dimension" of the "liberal-democratic bias" of contemporary studies in political science.[13]

It is here, too, I think that we will find the clue to a political science that in its ethical neutrality is value-dominated: value is built into the structure. The distinguished political sociologist Seymour Lipset has, for example, suggested that, as Bay has pointed out, "The age-old search for the good society can be terminated, for we have got it now."[14] Such a view of political life is obviously not ethically oriented (the search for the good society can be terminated), but it is as obviously not value-free ("for we have got it now"). Or if not quite now, very presently: "[I]n a visible future," Herbert Simon tells us, "the range of problems [machines] can handle will be coextensive with the range to which the human mind has been applied."[15] It has been suggested that the theory of democracy in which *Voting* culminates may be stated as follows: "Our institutions do not do what they are supposed to do according to the older understanding of politics, our citizens lack the qualities they are supposed to have, but we have a healthy democracy nevertheless: we move and we cohere."[16] It has been remarked that the "group approach" to political studies assumes "that all activity is 'by very definition' ordered or systematic."[17] It is this "built-in" value that Bay must have in mind when he speaks of the anti-political dimension of much of the literature in the behavioral sciences. I would like to show that the dimension is not so much anti-political as, in a new and curious way, supra-political.

13. Christian Bay, "Politics and Pseudopolitics: A Critical Evaluation of Some Behavioral Literature," *American Political Science Review*, 59 (March 1965), 39, 44.
14. Cited, *ibid.*, 44.
15. Herbert A. Simon and Allen Newell, "Heuristic Problem Solving: The Next Advance in Operations Research," *Operations Research* (January–February 1958), 8–10.
16. Herbert Storing, (ed.) *Essays on the Scientific Study of Politics* (New York, 1962), 54.
17. *Ibid.*, 218.

II

The genesis and exact nature of the ethically neutral but not value-free stance of the avant-garde Behavioralists may best be understood, I believe, by noting the underlying direction of all political theory in modern times. I have elsewhere tried to show[18] that all of the great modern theories of politics reveal a growing lack of interest in the contingent and difficult thing that political liberty is, and a growing preoccupation with a kind of causality and a kind of being that are absolute and universal in efficacy. Marx's first principle of socialism—"socialism takes its departure from the *theoretically and practically sensible conscience of man*, in nature, considered as *being*"[19]—is the paradigm of many notable efforts in the history of political thought to find a "system" and a "method" that would allow us to surmount the contrarieties of existence by imposing itself as the sufficient reason for all that happens in the world. "What irks and infuriates us," wrote Hegel, "is not what is, but the fact that it is not as it should be; once we know that it is as it must be—that is to say, not arbitrary or contingent—we also recognize that it should be as it is."[20] And Marx taught that all the absurdities and frustrations in life are traceable to the fact that existing social relations have come into contradiction with existing forces of production. Hegel and Marx had brought to culmination a long effort in modern political theory to overcome by means of art the difficulties of right action in morals and politics. The bringing together of the whole of reality under human power had its beginnings in Machiavelli's attempt to overcome the contingency and difficulty of moral action by giving to prudence the kind of domination and freedom enjoyed by art over its materials—with the result that success in the realization of the end chosen became the only criterion of good and bad in politics. It was not so much a disdain for the classical political virtues that inspired Machiavelli as it was an impatience with the age-old search for the good society: an ethically neutral political science would allow man to define the good simply in terms of the achievements of political power. The only respect in which the

---

18. Charles N. R. McCoy, *The Structure of Political Thought* (New York, 1963).

19. Cited in *ibid.*, 293. (*Oekonomische-Philosophische Manuskript*, 125).

20. Georg W. F. Hegel, *Schriften zur Politik und Rechtsphilosophie*, ed. by George Lasson, *Sämmtliche Werke*, VII (Leipzig, 1913; 2d edition, 1923).

freedom of art is like the freedom of moral action is that both are concerned with things that can be other than they are—both involve a kind of "making." The freedom of art differs profoundly from that of moral action in that it is concerned with the excellence of things made, not with the interior disposition of man himself; concerned with things outside of man, art succeeds more easily than moral action: it enjoys the benefit of fixed and determinate rules. Success in moral action depends primarily on a right desire—for the proper human good; and this desire is notoriously unstable.

The attempt to make the power of human agency the very measure and rule of human acts by bringing the moral good and bad under the liberty of art was raised to a new level in the "natural rights" philosophies. For in these philosophies it is the freedom by which science is said to be free that is the objective. We say that science is "free" in the sense that science is above that which can both be and not be; in this, it differs both from the freedom of art and that of the moral order, though in its simple concern with the disposition of objects it resembles art rather than the moral habits. In speaking of Hobbes, Maréchal has pertinently summed up the moral problem in all the natural rights philosophies:

> The good is defined in relation to the "ontological" perfection of each "nature"; *the moral problem is a problem of maximum being*. This "maximum being" must not be imagined to be an *end* pursued; it has nothing to do with ends pursued, but only with necessary effects. . . .
> In each "rational nature," the moral problem, the problem of the intensification of the *power of existence*, will be resolved without any liberty of choice, by the progressive substitution of action for passion, by means of the correcting of inadequate ideas.[21]

Locke, the apostle of laissez-faire individualism, achieves this "maximum being" by the simple device of identifying the power of individual well-being, the independent operation of ultimate units, with the realization of the public good. The device is made practical by rules of mutual security which define "limited" government. Limited government—as Locke made clear—is exactly a device for correcting the inadequate ideas held by man in the condition of nature. With Rousseau, "maximum being" is expressed

21. Joseph Maréchal, *Précis d'histoire de la philosophie moderne* (Brussels, 1951), I. 137, n. 77.

in terms of that peculiar "perfectibility" which, denied the brute and yet not resting on the quality of free agency, is understood not as an accidental perfection (in the classical manner) but as completely comprised within man, belonging to human nature itself. Rousseau's "science of simple souls" is a science that supposes (as theologians say is true of God) that in man intellect and will are one with his essence. In place of the inequality of class and modes of existence which befell historical man, a true "public right" must effect a union of each with all so that each "may obey himself alone, and remain free as before." By means of the General Will the dependence of each of us upon others is overcome in a kind of generic being whereby man is returned, on the political plane, to the primitive feeling for existence.

These efforts of the Enlightenment philosophers bore—as Marx pointed out—an "idealist" character; they achieved an "ideal" generic being for man through the intermediary of the state, but they left the individual isolated and helpless in real life. "There where the political state has reached its full development, man leads . . . a double existence, heavenly and earthly, the existence in the political community where he considers himself as a generic being, and the existence in civil society where he works as a mere part . . . and becomes the plaything of forces extraneous to himself."[22] Marx did not indeed destroy the "divine science"; what he did— as Heidegger has pointed out—was to bring metaphysics down to earth. What precisely he did was to carry through the conversion of politics into a pseudo-metaphysics via the productive sciences: The contrarieties of existence find their explanation in the fecund principle of contradiction in matter and the motion of matter; the absurdities and frustrations in life are traceable to the contradiction between existing social relations and existing forces of production. There is still the same effort to solve the moral problem not by liberty of choice, not in terms of moral action and of Aristotle's "right appetite," but by "correcting of inadequate ideas." The ideas are now indeed more down-to-earth: they have become, with Marx, "the theoretical form of that of which the living form is the real community"—the correspondence of existing social relations with existing forces of production.

22. Cited in McCoy, *The Structure of Political Thought*, 204. (Marx, *Die Judenfrage*, 583–84).

III

Now the Behavioralists are the heirs of the modern tradition in political philosophy from Machiavelli to Marx, but the prevailing "scientific outlook" among them is dominated by Hume whose critique of nature, order, and causality did not affect science as a tool. Now it is science not in the Aristotelian sense of demonstration (in the case of the speculative sciences) of properties from definable natures and (in the case of the practical sciences) of reasoning from ends as first principles to means that interest the Behavioralists; it is as a tool that science concerns them. The implication of this for the preoccupation with value that characterizes contemporary theory will become evident from an examination of this aspect of science.

The difference between the Aristotelian concept of science and that of the Behavioralists may be grasped from a remark of Hermann Weyle concerning the new mathematics: "For the mathematician it is irrelevant what circles are. It is of importance only in what manner a circle may be given."[23] The mathematician, as Weyle presents him, is not at all concerned with definable natures. "It is as if," de Koninck observes, "we said that it is irrelevant for us what man is; it is of importance only to know in what manner we can meet one."[24] Or, it is irrelevant for us what length is; it is of importance only to know how its measurement is actually made. And this is the case because as a tool, science is almost entirely identified with a process of mensuration which results in a measure-number. It is precisely this indeed that accounts for the rigor of the technique. It is clear, for example, that while computing, say, with 2, we need not trouble ourselves as to whether 2 is in fact one two having a *per se* unity or whether 2 is simply two ones, a class, or a collection—so that $1 + 1 = 2$ is nothing other than $1 + 1 = 1 + 1$. Bertrand Russell's appreciation of this distinction is cited by de Koninck:

There is no doubt about the class of couples; it is indubitable and not difficult to define, whereas the number 2, in any other sense, is a metaphysical entity about which we can never feel sure that it exists or that

23. Cited in Charles de Koninck, *The Hollow Universe* (Quebec, 1954), 13. I have found these lectures (of de Koninck) on the state of the new mathematics, physics, and biology to be of inestimable value in appraising the condition of the behavioral sciences.
24. *Ibid.*

we have tracked it down. . . . Accordingly we set up the following definition:

> *The number of a class is the class of all those classes that are similar to it.*

. . . In fact, the class of all couples will *be* the number 2, according to
our definition.[25]

It should be noted that if 2 were taken as something other than
1 + 1—if 2 were taken to enjoy its own irreducible unity so that
by taking one of its units away the new thing which is 2 would
be destroyed (if "animal" were taken out of the definition of man
as "rational animal," Socrates would cease to be what he is—a
man); this number would not be just 1 + 1. Now this aspect of
number—the two that is once two and not twice one will have to
be ignored by any computer, machine or man; for the computer
must be indifferent to *what* things are, apart from their being collections: "as a highway policeman who checks the weight of trucks
is indifferent as to whether the loads are potatoes, cement, horses,
or men. From the computer's point of view, the only thing found
in 2 which is not found in 1 + 1 is the symbol, and who is responsible for that?"[26] We notice, then, that the art of calculation
enjoys a peculiar freedom which is not that of science as such: it
is manifest in the fact that when carried on there is no concern
involved with what those things are which we calculate about, but
only with how we can operate upon them. The mathematical physicist, for example, must define his terms by a description of his
manner of attaining them, i.e., by a process of mensuration which
will give him a measure-number. If held to Aristotle's definition
of length, which tells or pretends to tell "what" a thing is absolutely ("length is what is extended in one dimension"), the physicist can make no progress (even though he need not reject such
a definition). But allow the physicist his own kind of definition
and he will do astonishing things with it. "Let us notice, however," de Koninck observes, "that if this type of definition were
the only valid one at all levels of science, the definition of man
would have to be something like this: 'when I bump into something and it produces a series of sounds like "Where do you think
you're going" this *is* man'—which would be a possible enough
interpretation of the name."[27] We may note, for the moment, that
A. F. Bentley's careful empirical definition of "interest" as the

25. *Ibid.*, 13–14.
26. *Ibid.*, 12.   27. *Ibid.*, 53.

"manner of stating the value of the group activity"[28] is similarly a possible enough interpretation of the word: "when I bump into something and it produces a series of sounds like 'Where do you think you're going?'"—this *is* interest. However useful and necessary this mode of defining may be, it obviously does leave something out. It is as if someone were to ask "what is a book?" and receive a reply telling him how to obtain a book.

The prevailing tendency among the extreme Behavioralists is to take their world of measured activity for the substance of the political world. "If we can get our social life stated in terms of activity, and of nothing else," Bentley advised:

We have not indeed succeeded in measuring it, but we have at least reached a foundation upon which a coherent system of measurement can be built up. . . [W]e shall cease to be blocked by the intrusion of immeasurable elements, which claim to be themselves the real causes of all that is happening, and which by their spook-like arbitrariness make impossible any progress towards dependable knowledge.[29]

The extrusion from the world of politics of what Russell called "the metaphysical, . . . about which we can never feel sure that it exists or that we have tracked it down" means that observable behavior patterns and actions alone remain, and from these a measure-number results. "Conduct," T. V. Smith wrote, "is, in a word, the plotted curve of behavior."[30] In the rigor and simplicity of number taken as the class of all classes that are similar to it, irreconcilable differences are surmounted; as Bentley says, measure conquers chaos: "It is of the very definition of activity that it is systematized. . . . All the actions that enter into the behavior of an idiot are correlated."[31]

We must not permit such a statement to mislead us on the important point. "It is surely a mistake," de Jouvenel writes, "to regard the validity of [the scientific method] applied to [man's] case, as dependent upon the ontological assumption [of man as a 'mere thing']. The method is not, in consequence, valueless: though we find in a number of men different conducts in the same circumstances, if we note the distribution of such conducts and its mode, and if we can find that over time this distribution and its

28. A. F. Bentley, *The Process of Government* (San Antonio, 1949), 215.

29. Cited in Crick, *The American Science of Politics*, 121.

30. T. V. Smith, "Conduct," in *Encyclopedia of the Social Sciences* (New York, 1937), IV, 177.

31. Bentley, *The Process of Government*, 285.

mode change but little or shift but slowly, we have therefrom a predictive tool."[32] Bentley is obviously not concerned, in *The Process of Government*, with idiots. He is concerned with "mentally competent persons" whose actions, he says, are "more correlated." Apparently they are more correlated because they proceed from some purpose. Now it is precisely here that the notion of activity as of very definition systemized reveals the essential note of behavioral science—its character of tool. The *per accidens* purpose represented by the erratic, ignorant voter (the *political* idiot) cannot be handled by science concerned with definable natures and *per se* purposes; it can be handled by science as tool. The distinction between *per se* and *per accidens* purposes in view of action for an end is transcended by science as tool, which is indifferent to this distinction in purposeful activity.

Were it not for the tool concept of activity of very definition systematized we should not likely have subjected to rigorous test the hypothesis that, as *Voting* expresses it, "an individual 'inadequacy' provides a positive service for the [democratic] system," that the combination of motivated, knowledgeable voters and marginal, erratic, and ignorant voters "makes for enough consensus to hold the system together and enough cleavage to make it move."[33] I am not saying, then, that the kind of study represented by *Voting* is without value. On the contrary, as I said earlier of Aristotle's value-free attitude: all kinds of character enter into the

32. De Jouvenel, "Political Science and Prevision," 35–36.
33. Bernard Berelson *et al., Voting* (Chicago, 1954), 322; 316; 318. This seems to verify the point earlier made concerning the trend of all modern political theory toward making the moral problem a problem of maximum being. (See also previous chapter). This maximum being must not be imagined to be an *end* pursued; it has nothing to do with ends pursued but only with *necessary effects*. The effect here in question is societal equilibrium or stability of the system. In *The Structure of Political Thought*, I have traced the steps by which the classical notion of *telos* was increasingly truncated; from the *good* understood as that which things seek in so far as they seek their perfection (the political virtues) to the *good* that is simply convertible with being (the principle of self-preservation in the "natural rights" philosophies, the contemporary concern with equilibrium and stability of systems) to the *good* as comprising the material and efficient principles that are presupposed to no end— neither to the good which things seek in so far as they seek their perfection nor to the good that is convertible with being. The inconsequence of behavioral science's preoccupation with stability as a "good" has been called attention to in a recent article by Willmoore Kendall and George W. Carey: "Though apparently determined to remain ethically neutral, they (the Behavioralists) are still forced back upon stability or 'system persistence' for justification of their enterprises." "The 'Intensity' Problem and Democratic Theory," *American Political Science Review*, 62 (March 1968), 9, n. 8.

makeup of the free polity. What I am saying is that if we were to use exclusively this method for the sake of defining the substantive problems of concept formation and theory construction, the world of politics would indeed become a "hollow universe." Indifference to the distinction between *per se* and *per accidens* purposes means that the infinity of purpose that may be prior or concomitant to voting must either (a) be resolved by transfiguring the field of human action (where what transpires is often so painfully irrational) with the simplicity and rigor of the mathematical disciplines, or (b) compel us to vindicate that extreme form of sophistry which exploits the kind of non-being found in the infinite *per accidens* and so deprive us of any insight into the substantive issues of politics.

Nor may we neglect the implications of behavioral science for the idiot in the Greek sense of the word, the non-participant, the solitary, imprisoned within himself; or indeed the idiocy of the "mindless activist." It will be instructive to attend to the comparison made in William Barrett's *Irrational Man* between the world of Shakespeare and the world of William Faulkner and James Joyce. After remarking that the Aristotelian canon of intelligible literary structure—that a literary work must have a beginning, a middle and an end—reflected a universe that was itself believed to be an ordered structure, Barrett observes that the dissolution of "definable natures" is manifest in all of modern art. Speaking of Faulkner's *The Sound and the Fury*, he remarks:

The brute, irrational, given quality of the world comes through so strongly in Faulkner's peculiar technique that he actually shows, and does not merely state, the meaning of the quotation from which his title is derived:

[Life] is a tale,
Told by an idiot, full of sound and fury
Signifying nothing.

Shakespeare places these lines in the context of a fairly-well-made tragedy; . . . but Faulkner shows us the world of which Shakespeare's statement would be true: a world opaque, dense, and irrational, that could not have existed for Shakespeare.[34]

There is "a flattening out of all planes and climaxes" in modern art: Man sees himself immersed in a universe whose parts are an extension of himself, continuous with him and he with them: time

34. William Barrett, *Irrational Man* (Garden City, N.Y., 1962), 52.

and space dominate all things and are the very substance of man's being.

Aristotelian philosophy had held, on the contrary, that life is a kind of triumph over the diffusion of time and space:

[W]e find the most manifest sign of this in the knowledge of animals and men, and especially in the memory. In the measure that a being lives, it rises above the conditions of space and time. . . . A knowing being is present to itself and assimilates to itself its surroundings, while there where space dominates, things are separated one from another and lost in the night. . . . A living being that were to exist but an instant would have a duration infinitely more rich, if infinitely shorter, than that of the stars; it is infinitely closer to eternity than anything of the oldest inorganic world. . . . It is the notion of physical time, first in the experimental order, that leads us to suppose that quantity is an essential property of duration. . . .

It is understood, of course, that the different durations of natural beings are all of them truly temporal, that is to say, successive and continuous. But some are less so than others. And when we consider the hierarchy of durations in the sense of their lower limit where they become experimentally measurable, we notice that they tend to lose their identity and to disappear in physical time to the point of the obliteration of all distinctions between *beings*. If the principle of the conservation of energy is true, and if the mass of the universe is constant, physical time is, under this aspect, absolutely one; in this perspective, which abstracts from the real breaks or incisions dividing the world in individuals, the different physical times proper to beings—the life of a cat, for example, are only local condensations of an identical time which goes back to the origin of things.[35]

In the reduction of conduct to "the plotted curve of behavior," to the activity that is of very definition systematized, to—indeed—"homologus processes" that abstract from the real, heterogeneous order of sociopolitical life and go back to those "particles" out of which, David Easton says, "all social behavior is formed,"[36] behavioral science would appear to be seeking to reduce the heterogeneous whole of society in the way in which durations can be reduced to their lower limit where they become experimentally measurable. The "stable units of analysis" that behavioral science strives to locate are, it is said, "ubiquitous, uniform, and repetitious."[37] Despite the claim of behavioral science to take its depar-

35. I have translated these passages from Charles de Koninck, "Le cosmos comme tendance vers la pensée," *Itinéraires*, N. 66 (September–October, 1962), 174, 176, 178, 181.

36. David Easton, "The Current Meaning of Behavioralism," in James C. Charlesworth (ed.), *Contemporary Political Analysis* (New York, 1967), 24.

37. *Ibid.*

ture from the individual actor, it brings us to a sense of unity of man with man that, unlike Aristotle's moral unity based on the liberty of contrariety (and therefore perfectly free in its inner structure) abstracts from the real breaks and incisions dividing the world in individuals; they become only local condensations of an identical "stuff" that goes back to the origin of things. The heterogeneous whole of society is reduced to the point of the obliteration of distinctions between *beings.* The activity of an idiot and that of a mentally competent person are correlated.

Now Aristotle has also begun his study of politics with the individual actor, in protest against the simple, generic unity of Plato's conception of the ideal state: By reducing differences to a common genus, Plato's generic thinking had absorbed the real individual in a way similar to the way in which the physico-mathematical methodology of Behavioralism transfigures the diverse and complex world of politics with the simplicity and rigor of the mathematical disciplines. It is curious and noteworthy that both generic and mathematical thought are at one in producing this kind of rationality: There are, to be sure, homologous processes in all animals, but they don't serve to distinguish an ant from a rattlesnake (an important distinction if you are sitting on one); and is it incidental that two tons should be two tons of elephant rather than of coal? Homologous processes—whether these are thought-processes or quasi-mechanical processes—that offer the stable units of analysis in decision-making must be as indifferent to *what* the decision is about as the highway policeman who checks the weight of trucks is indifferent as to whether the loads are coal or elephants.

Behavioral science reduces individual action to such processes as "the mutual modification of images through . . . feedback and communication," "control of non-leaders by leaders . . . , control of leaders by other leaders . . . ; control of leaders by non-leaders"; "thought processes and quasi-mechanical processes."[38] It should be noted that this "typology" of the decision-making process is exclusively engaged with singular, contingent happenings (including, to be sure, the singular act whereby the individual expresses his value-preferences). Now singular contingent events are potentially infinite. It is the recognition of this fact that forces Herbert

---

38. James A. Robinson and R. Roger Majak, "The Theory of Decision-Making," in Charlesworth, *Contemporary Political Analysis,* 180–81.

Simon to identify "rationality" in decision-making with infinite calculational capacity: In Simon's concept of "rationality" not only are singular contingent happenings potentially infinite, but ends (or "values") related to principles that are known in a universal way and carry the note of necessity (e.g., that man cannot live without suitable nourishment) are also considered to be potentially infinite:

> [T]he subject, in order to perform with perfect rationality . . . would have to have a complete description of the consequences following from each alternative strategy and would have to compare these consequences. He would have to know in every single respect how the world would be changed by his behaving one way instead of another, and he would have to follow the consequences of behavior through unlimited stretches of time, unlimited reaches of space, *and unlimited sets of values.* Under such conditions even an approach to rationality in real behavior would be in-conceivable.[39]

Now a mathematician may use as much infinity as he wants; but not an administrator. If, in order to act in a reasonable manner, we had to know *all* the objective circumstances of our action, we should never be able either to move or to refrain from moving, to think or not to think. We would be reduced to the non-participant, the *Idiotes* of the ancient Greeks, or to the "mindless activist."[40] Simon is forced—most incongruously within his own context, and most certainly unwittingly—to resort to a portion of the solution to the problem of human choice offered by St. Thomas Aquinas: to resort to *facts which may be taken as certain,* not absolutely, but for the time being, as far as they concern the work to be done. Asking whether the counsel of inquiry is without end, St. Thomas observes: "In contingent singulars, something may be taken for certain, not absolutely, indeed, but for the time being, as far as it concerns the work to be done. Thus, that Socrates is sitting is not necessary; but that he is sitting, as long as he continues to sit— *that* is necessary; and this can be known with certainty."[41] And Simon observes: "It is very *fortunate* that . . . human activities are so strictly segregated; if they were not, the problem of reaching rational decisions would be impossible."[42] Fortunate, to be sure—

---

39. Herbert Simon, *Administrative Behavior, A Study of Decision-Making Process in Administrative Organization* (New York, 1957), 69. Italics added.

40. See Bertrand de Jouvenel, "On the Nature of Political Science," *American Political Science Review,* 55 (December 1961), 777.

41. Thomas Aquinas, *Summa Theologiae,* I–II, 14, 6.

42. Simon, *Administrative Behavior,* 77.

but not for Simon's behavior alternative model which is wrecked by the fortunate facts.[43] Perhaps no other behavioral scientist demonstrates so clearly as Simon how science as tool, how the art of calculation seeks to put itself in the very place of the substantive problems of politics. What Simon does not, of course, realize is that truth in human behavior is not to be derived either from our speculative knowledge of facts or even from moral (or administrative) science as such, however elaborate. This particular issue need not be pursued further here; it will suffice to recall one of the relevant considerations—already made—that there is no analytical connection between moral science and concrete conduct.

It is the neglect of that principle, it seems to me, that accounts for the fact that behavioral science strives to build value into the structure of politics. The definitions employed by science as tool are made to take the place of the substantive problems to which they are applied. The Behavioralist tends to understand his science to be not simply the scientific method applied to the substantive problems of politics. On the contrary, as David Easton says, and as all the evidence indicates, behavioral science as tool would *determine* the substantive problems: ". . . Behavioralism is [the scientific method] with a shift in emphasis to the substantive problems of concept formation and theory construction."[44] Indeed, it is this theoretical tenet and not the "scientific method" that "gives the scientific enterprise in the social disciplines the special character implied in the idea of the behavioral sciences."[45]

This "shift" in emphasis "to the substantive problems of concept formation and theory construction" is evident in Harold Lasswell's "aim . . . to bring into being a democratic equilibrium in social relations in which deviations are promptly rectified."[46] It is precisely by this shift that value is built into the structure of politics—as, Lasswell says, in the constructing of a machine we might "build

43. The remark that Robert A. Dahl directs against traditional political philosophy—that an act of political evaluation can be performed (according to that philosophy) "in a sterile medium free from contamination by brute facts" ("The Behavioral Approach," *American Political Science Review*, 55 [December 1961], 771)—is precisely true of Simon's infinite calculational capacity, which is rendered sterile by being required and never able to attain all the facts. It is not at all true of the classical-medieval teaching on political decision-making. See Thomas Aquinas, *Summa*, I–II, 14, 6.

44. Easton, "The Current Meaning of Behavioralism," 27.

45. *Ibid.*

46. Harold D. Lasswell, *The Political Writings of Harold D. Lasswell* (New York, 1958), 513–14.

in a set of servo-mechanisms which perform [the] re-stabilizing operation."[47] This is more than scientific method: it is scientific method determining the problems of concept formation and theory construction. The profound difference between the value-free assurance of Aristotle's notion of "ideal" society and Lasswell's notion is quite perfectly brought out in a remark of Freud's:

The unworthiness of human beings, even of analysts, has always made a deep impression on me, but why should analyzed people be altogether better than others? Analysis makes for *unity*, but not necessarily for *goodness*. I do not agree . . . that all our faults arise from confusion and ignorance. I think that too heavy a burden is laid on analysis when one asks of it that it should be able to realize every precious ideal."[48]

Science as tool indeed provides a freedom that lies precisely in a unity of action that delivers us from the exigency of what Aristotle considered to be the first moving principle of politics—"the good . . . at which all things aim."[49] But even this—science as tool—could indeed be useful (as I have already remarked); rather, it is the shift in emphasis from science as tool to the tool as determining the substantive problems of politics that builds value into the structure of political life and gives us a new supra-political politics. By pursuing the rigor demanded by the activity-that-by-very-definition-is-systematized-and-computer-philosophy we are led to this utter impasse: No questions may now be asked or answered; no statement made which is not tautologous; no mental act performed which cannot be matched by machine. "The search for the good society can be terminated; for we have got it now."

Henry S. Kariel has suggested that the concept of total freedom in existential psychology might be used to contain the extreme determinism of behavioral psychology through the "strategy of constitutional proceduralism."[50] The term "strategy" is evidently used because Kariel realizes that there is no way of joining these

47. *Ibid.*
48. Cited by Ernest Jones, *The Life and Work of Sigmund Freud* (New York, 1958), 513–14. See also Maxwell Maltz, *Psychocybernetics* (New York, 1967), 18, 22.
49. Aristotle, *Nicomachean Ethics*, I, 1, 1094a2; *Politics*, I, 1, 1252a1.
50. Henry S. Kariel, "The Political Relevance of Behavioral and Existential Psychology," *American Political Science Review*, 61 (June 1967), 334. Although a number of political scientists have come to recognize the anti-political bias of behavioral science, there has not been any clear indication of its cause, which, as I have been arguing, lies in the shift of emphasis from Behavioralism as scientific method to Behavioralism as that method employed in determining the substantive problems of concept formation and theory construction. The fact of the anti-political bias of behavioral studies is well put by Professor Kariel, *ibid.*, 336–37.

extremes; there is possible only a policy of "containment" of one by the other. For as he clearly puts it, the existential commitment to freedom derives from the conviction that "by nature, man is obstinately in rebellion against social restraints."[51] The freedom that concerns existential psychology—certainly in its most profound presentation, which is that of Heidegger—is neither the freedom of the moral order, nor of art, nor of science nor of science as tool; it is a freedom that, as Werner Brock has acutely remarked, suggests the opening passages of the Book of Genesis: a freedom that goes behind all science and technique, back beyond the "knowable" and the "measurable" to the purely passive principle of nature that calls upon "the world-creating impulse of the spirit" and precedes what Heidegger calls "the dimension of extension and number."[52]

Professor Kariel's suggestion is interesting because it recalls the Aristotelian teaching (alluded to at the beginning of this paper) concerning the freedom of the Divine Intellect upon which the order of the universe depends, and how, Aristotle maintains, this Intellect is imitated by man in the ordering of the world of politics. Because the end of a practical science is truth sought not for its own sake but as a means of operation, the object of political science is "operable" by man; i.e., it is measured by and dependent upon the human intellect (as the order of the universe, Aristotle says, is measured and dependent upon the Divine Intellect).[53] And because the object of political science is an operable object its mode of proceeding is practical; i.e., it considers the political community not merely according to definition and properties but as to how it is actually to be made. But it is not from nothing that the political community comes into being: The ends we seek play the role of first principles in practical science; these are the dynamic forces, for it is these that move political intelligence to find the means through which the *raison d'être* of the political structure is ensured. This finding does not proceed *more geometrico*. The relation of ends to means, unlike that from essence to properties in mathematics (we see *equiangular* in the notion of equilateral triangle) is an extrinsic relation, a relation that can be discovered only through experience. The political scientist must be practical in his mode of

51. *Ibid.*
52. Werner Brock, "Introduction," in Martin Heidegger, *An Introduction to Metaphysics* (Garden City, N.Y., 1961), 38.
53. Aristotle, *Metaphysics*, XII, 7, 1072b12 ff.; 10, 1075a12ff.

knowing in just the way in which the architect will be practical (and, indeed, as in the ordering of the parts of the universe God's knowledge is said to be practical). For the architect must consider not simply the nature of a house but must know how houses are actually built—what sorts of materials are available and useful; at what angle the light can best be captured. The facts are the crucial matter here. As St. Thomas Aquinas puts it:

[I]n proportion as any science approaches to a consideration of singulars, as do the sciences of operation, such as medicine . . . and ethics [and politics], it is the less capable of possessing certitude because of the multitude of things that must be considered in such sciences; for errors frequently arise if any single fact is omitted, and also because of the variability of the facts themselves.[54]

The behavioral sciences can serve as a useful and necessary tool in the marshaling and ordering of the facts. But all the differences that have been here considered—the difference between theoretic science and practical science, between science as tool and science as dealing with the substantive issues of concept formation and theory construction, between art and morals, and the different kinds of freedom proper to each of these—all of these distinctions, which traditional political philosophy united in a subtle and comprehensive way, are dangerously undone by the extreme forms of the "scientific" study of politics.

54. Thomas Aquinas, *De Trinitate,* 6, 1, ad 2.

9. Man's Lost Intellectual Center*

[Throughout McCoy's work, the influence of Cassirer is constant. In this review-essay McCoy discusses the reservations he has with Cassirer's insightful work. McCoy again and again referred to Cassirer's notion that myth and magic have returned to political philosophy in the twentieth century. The understanding of how this came about and its relation to the hold of ideology in modern political theory rightly fascinated McCoy. He argues, following the lead of Cassirer, that this eventuality was part and parcel of the development of modern political philosophy. But it was the task of the political philosopher to spell out why this result took place. The rationalism that Cassirer attempted to elaborate, the goal of setting man free only to himself, is, in fact, in McCoy's view, the avenue by which myth has become active and artistic in the political world. McCoy traces how these ideas have deviated from the analysis of being and its causes in Aristotle and Aquinas. He argues that Cassirer made a correct analysis of what has happened. What Cassirer did not realize was the fact that on the basis of his rationalism, there was no proper being against which to correct rationalism's efforts to establish whatever man wants.]

For those who are acquainted with the works of the late Ernst Cassirer it is unnecessary to say that his last book, *The Myth of the State*, reveals a most profound and sharp intelligence as well as, of course, a tremendous scholarship. But I think that in this instance Professor Cassirer's insight and erudition have benefited his students with a light in the way of which, though it was his own, he himself stood. The wonderful and terrifying truth that his book contains was quite hidden from Professor Cassirer. I shall try to show this. But first it is necessary to see what it was that Professor Cassirer intended to do and in a measure did not fail to do.

*This originally appeared as a book review in *Modern Schoolman*, 25 (May 1948), 271–78.

The book is divided into three parts. Part one is entitled "What is Myth?"; part two, "The Struggle Against Myth in the History of Political Thought"; and part three, "The Myth of the Twentieth Century." In the first chapter, "The Structure of Mythical Thought," the point is made that primitive thought, despite its open contradiction to our sense experience, is nevertheless logical in its structure. The savage is not, to be sure, a philosopher or dialectician; but at the same time there is "scarcely anything that escapes [the primitive mind's] constant urge for classification."[1] The point is well substantiated by the researches of modern anthropologists and of Mr. Cassirer himself. The problem arises as to why men cling so obstinately and systematically to beliefs that are in such open contradiction to sense experience. Although, Professor Cassirer admits, a new way to answer this question was indicated by the progress made in modern anthropology and psychology, he feels that the new emphasis, valuable as it was, upon the physiological and pathological basis of myth provided only an explanation of the infinitely multiple objects of myth—"the mere substance of myth," not "its function in man's social and cultural life." "It is not," says Professor Cassirer,

a very satisfactory explanation of a fact that has put its indelible mark upon the whole life of mankind to reduce it to a special and single motive. Man's psychic and cultural life is not made of such simple and homogeneous stuff. Freud could not prove his point any more than Max Müller and all the other scholars of the Society for the Comparative Study of Myth.[2]

Rather, it is the all-important matter of the function of myth in man's social and cultural life that Professor Cassirer wishes to convey to us.

The subjects of myth and the ritual acts are of an infinite variety. . . . But the motives of mythical thought . . . are in a sense always the same. In all human activities and in all forms of human culture, we find a "unity in the manifold." Art gives us a unity of intuition; science gives us a unity of thought; religion and myth give us a unity of feeling. Art opens to us a universe of living forms; science shows us a universe of laws and principles; religion and myth begin with the awareness of the universality and fundamental identity of life.[3]

As with art and science, myth is a *symbolic* expression, but its

1. Ernst Cassirer, *The Myth of the State* (New Haven, 1946), 14. (See also Ernst Cassirer, *An Essay on Man* (Garden City, N.Y., 1944).

2. Cassirer, *Myth*, 35.   3. *Ibid.*, 37.

intellectual content stops short there; it is a symbolic expression of rites which dramatize the desire and the feeling for "the eternal unity of life."[4] This indeed is possible only "if man sacrifices his individuality; if he breaks down every barrier that lies between himself and the eternal unity of life."[5] In brief, myth is understood to be the symbolic expression of the irrational, and the irrational is understood as comprising whatever may be above as well as below the human reason.

Even if we were not aware of the reputation that Professor Cassirer enjoyed as the most distinguished of modern rationalists, we should readily perceive the rationalist premise to his analysis of the function of myth. In his article on rationalism in volume eighteen of the Encyclopaedia Britannica, Professor Cassirer gives it as "the fundamental idea of rationalism . . . that reason can recognize completely only that which it can produce according to its own design"; and he defines rationalism as

that trend of philosophy which intercedes for the rights of "natural reason," and sees in it the source of all truth. Common to all historical forms of rationalism is the belief in the "autonomy of thought," i.e., that view that thought can discover by its own strength, without support from a supernatural revelation and without appeal to sense perception, a system of "eternal truths," a system presented to thought within its own realm and comprehended by thought as necessary.[6]

It is, then, upon the Procrustean bed of this particular philosophy that the great writers in the field of political thought are laid, but the work is done in so gentle, scholarly, and persuasive a manner that one is scarcely aware of the deep discomfort arising from these Kantian distortions.

The struggle against myth in the history of political philosophy is traced in Plato, the medieval theologians, Machiavelli, and the Enlightenment. It is a winning struggle up to the time of the Enlightenment; with the romantic criticism of the Enlightenment, mythical thought rises once again and begins to rule the whole of man's social and cultural life.

The problem that Plato had to face and the solution that he offered bear a striking resemblance to St. Thomas Aquinas's handling of the same problem of myth. Plato saw that myth is fairly harmless and even of some benefit as long as it is not permitted

4. *Ibid.*, 43.   5. *Ibid.*
6. Cassirer, "Rationalism," *Encyclopaedia Britannica* (New York, 1947) v. 18, 991.

to enter into ethical and political life. He therefore relegated myth to his metaphysics and natural philosophy and made ample use of it in these fields. But he says that

if we tolerate myth in our political systems . . . all our hopes for a reconstruction and reformation of our political and social life are lost. . . . In the Legal State, the state of justice, there is no room left for the conceptions of mythology, for the gods of Homer and Hesiod.[7]

St. Thomas Aquinas was faced, we are told, with the challenge of an even more tremendous myth than Greek mythology, namely, that of Christian revelation. It is most interesting to see how Professor Cassirer develops this thesis, suggesting, unfortunately, that Etienne Gilson in his *The Spirit of Mediaeval Philosophy* has substantially shown that any true knowledge of God's essence and existence is beyond the light of natural reason. It belongs to the realm of myth; and St. Thomas, like Plato before him, saw clearly enough the necessity of relegating this myth to the region of dogmatic theology. "Of course Thomas Aquinas never doubted any dogma of the Christian Church"; but with all serious thinkers of the period, he was clearly up against "a mythical element that could not be openly attacked."[8] It is in the light of this attitude, from this point of view, that the solution of St. Thomas to the problem of the relation of reason and faith is given; and although when it is given it is quite correctly stated, the false understanding is already indelibly fixed. Thus St. Thomas is quite subtly reduced to a kind of Averroist himself, setting the human reason "free to create a world of its own." Another point is scored for human reason in the battle against myth.

The treatment of Machiavelli, which follows upon the above considerations, is equally skillful and original, but more just. Professor Cassirer was too serious a thinker and his intelligence was at once too profound and ordinary to have accepted the rather widespread contemporary view of Machiavelli as a lover of the people and the common good. If Machiavelli can be said to have had any interest in common good, then that common good must be interpreted, says Professor Cassirer, as a "common evil."[9] "It remains, however, one of the great puzzles in the history of human civilization how a man like Machiavelli, a great and noble mind, could become the advocate of 'splendid wickedness.'"[10] The an-

7. Cassirer, *Myth*, 72.   8. *Ibid.*, 110.
9. *Ibid.*, 143.   10. *Ibid.*, 145.

swer to this puzzle is to be found, it seems, if we see Machiavelli as standing "at the gateway of the modern world," pointing the direction away from "all traditional concepts and external authorities," setting the mind of man free, once more, to create a world of its own. Another point is scored for human dignity in the struggle against myth. Professor Cassirer admits that

this result [in the case of Machiavellianism] had to be bought dearly. The state is entirely independent: but at the same time it is completely isolated. The sharp knife of Machiavelli's thought has cut off all the threads by which in former generations the state was fastened to the organic whole of human existence. The political world has lost its connection not only with religion and metaphysics but also with all other forms of man's ethical and cultural life. It stands alone—in an empty space.[11]

Civilization precisely needed, however, this cutting of all the threads by which the state had been fastened to the organic whole of human existence if the seventeenth-century philosophers were to be in a position to reset mankind upon a moral basis, this time, however, perfectly independent of all traditional concepts and external authorities. The seventeenth century avoided Aristotle and the medieval tradition in ethics and politics and returned for its inspiration to the Roman Stoics. Why?

There is a double reason that may explain this fact. What matters here is not so much the content of Stoic theory as the function that this theory had to fulfill in the ethical and political conflicts of the modern world. . . . Neither the religious nor the ethical world seemed to possess a fixed control. . . . If there was to be a really universal system of ethics and religion, it had to be based upon such principles as could be admitted by every nation, every creed, and every sect. And Stoicism alone seemed to be equal to this task. It became the foundation of a natural religion—a system of natural laws. Stoic philosophy could not help man to solve the metaphysical riddles of the universe. But it contained a greater and more important promise—the promise to restore man to his ethical dignity. This dignity, it asserted, cannot be lost; for it does not depend on a dogmatic creed or any outward revelation. *It rests exclusively on the moral will—on the worth that man attributes to himself.*[12]

The conclusion is clear, and it was altogether clear, as Professor Cassirer points out, to Thomas Jefferson, whose Declaration of Independence was only a sign and symbol of the

intellectual Declaration of Independence that we find in the theoreticians of the Seventeenth Century. It was here that reason had first declared its

---

11. *Ibid.*, 140.   12. *Ibid.*, 169–70. Italics added.

power and its claim to rule the social life of man. It had emancipated itself from the guardianship of theological thought; it could stand on its own ground.[13]

But now, at the very moment that reason has come into its own, there takes place a most curious phenomenon, and one that ought considerably to have disquieted Professor Cassirer in the pursuit of his purpose. The significance of the modern development of myth can, I believe, scarcely be overstated. Human reason has won its autonomy, its freedom to "recognize completely only that which it can produce according to its own design"—the fundamental idea of rationalism and the true goal, according to Professor Cassirer, of human civilization. But now there begins, in the nineteenth and twentieth centuries, a series of perversions and conceits unmatched, as Professor Cassirer himself makes clear, by the myths of any primitive tribe and distinguished, be it most carefully observed, from all primitive myths precisely by the "rational," technical, and scientific precision of their manufacture and propagation. In the section entitled "The Myth of the Twentieth Century" Professor Cassirer considers in the preliminary chapters the seeds of the totalitarian myth; he finds them in Carlyle's theory of hero worship, Gobineau's theory of race, and most importantly in the philosophy of Hegel. In the elaboration of their mythical edifices all of these men were convinced in a way never possible to an Aristotle or St. Thomas Aquinas that the intellect of man was penetrating to a perfect comprehension of the ultimate reasons of the universe.

Professor Cassirer calls our attention to a remark of Pascal's that "there are certain words which suddenly and unexpectedly make clear the sense of a whole book."[14] Carlyle's mystic adulation of the "great man" and Gobineau's mad worship of race are one with what Professor Cassirer calls the Hegelian concept of *sacro egoismo;*

the power that puts all historical actions in operation and gives them determinate existence, is the need, instinct, inclination, and passion of man. This is the absolute right of personal existence, to find *itself* satisfied in its activity and labor.[15]

What is this exaltation of man but the outcome of a doctrine which insists that the dignity of man "rests exclusively on the worth that man attributes to himself," that the reason "recognize completely

13. *Ibid.,* 167.   14. *Ibid.,* 150.
15. *Ibid.,* 267–68.

only that which it can produce according to its own design," and that it make only those judgments that "depend upon a free act which creates a world of its own"? These are the elements of Professor Cassirer's definitions of rationalism. But they apply very perfectly to Hegel whom indeed Professor Cassirer has called "one of the great champions of rationalism."[16] Our trouble, Hegel had said, is that we lament that things are not what they ought to be; once we can be made to see that things as they are, are as they ought to be, we shall have a perfectly rational solution to the main problem of social existence.

The insight to which . . . philosophy is to lead us, is that the real world is as it ought to be—the truly good—the universal divine reason—is not a mere abstraction, but a vital principle capable of realizing itself. . . . Philosophy wishes to discover the substantial purport, the real side of the divine idea, and to justify the so much despised reality of things.[17]

How could Professor Cassirer have failed to see that here is at once the apotheosis and the nemesis of rationalism? What he does say is that with Hegel, "one of the great champions of rationalism," we have reached the apotheosis of myth.

The twentieth century adds a new dimension to myth, and one that deserves the most careful understanding. In primitive societies myth does, to be sure, pervade and govern the whole of man's social life; but as Professor Cassirer points out, citing the researches of Malinowski, myth is not operative in the same way or at the same strength in all aspects of primitive life. In those areas of activity in which man has a proper and adequate competence and where technical means are usable, the savage does not have recourse to magic; myth and magic appear only in those tasks that seem to lie beyond man's natural powers. How then does myth find a place in the twentieth century, a century of the greatest technological competence? It is indeed something of a mystery—at least to a rationalist. Professor Cassirer has no answer to this question; but he gives an account of what has happened, and in this account we may find the answer. He reminds us that historians of civilization record two great phases through which man has passed: "Man began as a *homo magus*; but from the age of magic he passed to the age of technics. The *homo magus* of former times and of primitive civilization became a *homo faber*, a craftsman and an artisan." Therefore, as Professor Cassirer frankly says,

16. *Ibid.*, 73.   17. *Ibid.*, cited p. 258.

our modern political myths appear indeed as a very strange and paradoxical thing. For what we find in them is a blending of two activities that seem to exclude each other. . . . [The modern politician] has to act, at the same time, as both a *homo magus* and a *homo faber*.[18]

In fact the paradoxical thing, the startling thing, is that myth in the twentieth century has lost precisely the social function which Professor Cassirer attributes to it in his early chapters, namely, that of expressing only and all that which lies beyond the proper competence of man. The contrary is now true: it is the everyday activities of man that are the special object of myth and magic. There is no longer anything that is *natural* to man: the modern politician is master and diviner in the most obscure and inscrutable way of men's ordinary daily lives.

It is now possible to find the ultimate force of Professor Cassirer's book. We have already adverted to the paradoxical character of the blending of the activities of *homo magus* and *homo faber*; in Professor Cassirer's words, it resembles squaring the circle.[19] But that we may understand the final significance of this phenomenon, it is necessary to recall that for Aristotle and St. Thomas the universe, while formable and formed by the practical knowledge of God, is for our human intellect something "given," whose ultimate reasons may be ever more closely approached through experimental science but never ultimately reached; furthermore, divine providence, for both Aristotle and St. Thomas, was seen as ordering all things in the most extraordinary fashion so that even chance events—indeterminate in their causes—fall nevertheless under the divine intelligence. Now the twentieth-century man is pre-eminently the *homo faber*, the man of technics; and he is set free—by Plato, by St. Thomas Aquinas (*sic*), by Machiavelli, by the Encyclopedists, by Kant—to create his own world. Is there any other possibility now but that the modern superman should assume the role of Providence, foreseeing, ordaining, ordering all things according to the free designs of his own mind? And Professor Cassirer very explicitly makes this point:

[The modern politician] . . . proceeds very methodically. Nothing is left to chance; every step is well prepared and premeditated. . . . Myth has always been described as the result of an unconscious activity and as a free product of imagination. But here we find myth made according to plan. The new political myths do not grow up freely; they are not wild

18. *Ibid.*, 281–82.   19. *Ibid.*, 281.

fruits of an exuberant imagination. They are artificial things fabricated by very skillful and cunning artisans. It has been reserved for the Twentieth Century, our own great technical age, to develop a new technique of myth. Henceforth myths can be manufactured in the same sense and according to the same methods as any other modern weapon. . . . That is a new thing—and a thing of crucial importance.[20]

In his brief "Conclusion" to this deeply provocative and erudite book, Professor Cassirer reminds us that "the mythical monsters" that have been fought down through human history are never entirely conquered, that from time to time chaos comes again, and "mythical thought starts to rise anew and to pervade the whole of man's social and cultural life." What it is, it seems to me, that Professor Cassirer has conclusively and brilliantly, if unwittingly, shown is that the most portentous of mythical monsters is that *sacro egoismo* which allows nothing except that which "reason can produce according to its own design"—the fundamental idea, the very badge of that rationalism in which Professor Cassirer had so learned and charming a faith.

20. *Ibid.*, 282.

10. On the Revival of Classical Political Philosophy*

[Here McCoy defines his position in relation to the work of Leo Strauss. Throughout the work of Strauss, there was a great admiration for the teachings of Thomas Aquinas in the light of Strauss's well-known endeavor to return to classical political philosophy. As the problem of reason and revelation was a central one for Strauss, McCoy's peculiarly Christian critique of Strauss is most telling. McCoy begins with Strauss on his own grounds: whether his interpretation of Aristotle on the nature of politics in relation to metaphysics is correct. Throughout McCoy's work, he argued that Aquinas did interpret Aristotle correctly on the crucial points so that the real battle in modern theory was not over reason and revelation but over the relation of politics to metaphysics, which issue needed to be addressed first. This entailed a renewed discussion of the relation of Plato and Aristotle, together with the relation of Plato's notion of myth or the ideal state and its subsequent relation to revelation and to ideology. Strauss's analysis of the philosophic life in relation to the life of politics and to the life of revelation is clarified in a way that illuminates both why Strauss seemed to prefer the philosophic life and why the position of Aristotle and Aquinas was capable of being precisely philosophical. McCoy discussed the perplexing question of Strauss's understanding of Aristotelian "natural right." McCoy found that Strauss's preference for Plato over Aristotle led him to a kind of disguised theology.]

In the "metaphysical squabbles" that Bertrand de Jouvenel has said characterize much of American political science, none has been more bitter and perplexing than the controversy surrounding the work of Leo Strauss. To the extent that one can speak of a revival of classical political philosophy in this country, the credit for it assuredly belongs to the influence of Strauss's profound

*This essay originally appeared in the *Review of Politics*, 35 (April 1973), 161–79.

scholarship. Nonetheless there is common agreement among fair-minded reviewers of Strauss's writings that a "calculated obscurity" hides his message. "He does not wish to tell us, in bold propositional terms, what is on his mind," says Robert McShea.[1] Granted that "Strauss indulges in the . . . game of esoteric silences," that his real views are often "camouflaged," we must see these devices for what Lee McDonald suggests they are: devices to persuade the reader to "a special way of reading the 'classics' "; they are not primarily concerned with "specific details of interpretation."[2]

"The character of classical political philosophy appears with greatest clarity," Strauss tells us, "not in Aristotle's work but in Plato's Laws,"[3] especially in the speech about wine which makes up the bulk of the first two books of the Laws. "The speech about wine appears to be the introduction to political philosophy."[4] What is the lesson that Strauss says is to be learned from the speech about wine? "The vicarious enjoyment of wine through conversation about wine . . . enlarges the horizon of the law-bred old citizens, [but] limits the horizon of the philosopher. . . . Plato likens philosophy to madness, the very opposite of sobriety and moderation"; philosophy is likened to the drinking of wine (not conversation about wine) because "moderation is not a virtue of thought."[5] Aristotle's name is not mentioned in these passages, but in Natural Right and History we learn that "Aristotle opposes the divine madness of Plato . . . in the spirit of his unrivaled sobriety."[6] We know that sobriety is not a virtue of thought: it is not a virtue of thought because, unhappily for the metaphor, moderation in thought induces "dimness of perception" and "obfuscation."[7] The political science of Aristotle—and he, not Plato, is the founder of that science, Strauss acknowledges[8]—is the product of sobriety of thought, of "dimness of perception" and is marred by "obfuscation." Plato's political philosophy is written in the light of the sun; Aristotle's is written in the shadows of the cave and

1. Robert McShea, "Leo Strauss on Machiavelli," Western Political Quarterly, XVI (December 1963), 782.

2. Lee McDonald, Western Political Theory from Its Origins to the Present (New York, 1968), 213, n. 72.

3. Leo Strauss, What Is Political Philosophy? (Glencoe, Il., 1959), 29.

4. Ibid., 31.   5. Ibid., 32.

6. Leo Strauss, Natural Right and History (Chicago, 1953), 156.

7. Strauss, What Is Political Philosophy?, ibid., 32.

8. Leo Strauss, The City and Man (Chicago, 1964), 21.

is, naturally, dim and obfuscated. "Aristotle's philosophizing has no longer to the same degree and in the same way as Socrates' philosophizing the character of ascent."[9] It treats "of each of the various levels of beings . . . on its own terms."[10]

From this contrast between Plato's virtuous, immoderate thought and Aristotle's less virtuous, sober thought we must infer that if in the thought of each we find "the essentially political character of natural right doctrine" affirmed, this affirmation will be less clearly presented in Aristotle's writings. And indeed Strauss says that though the essentially political character of natural right doctrine "appears most clearly in Plato's *Republic*," it is "hardly less revealing[ly]"[11] found in Aristotle's discussion of natural right. What, now, is this most clear way in which Plato presents the essentially political character of natural right? It has, of course, the character of "ascent" and it proceeds thus: "Plato eventually defines natural right with direct reference to the fact that the only life which is simply just is the life of the philosopher"[12]; for "the question as to what is by nature right or as to what is justice finds its complete answer only through the construction, in speech, of the best regime,"[13] This "best regime" is identical with "the perfect moral order."[14]

Unlike Plato, Aristotle does not define natural right with direct reference to the fact that the only life which is simply just is the life of the philosopher. Rather, "Aristotle . . . treats of each of the various levels of beings . . . on its own terms."[15] By treating politics on its own terms Aristotle dims the perception of natural right: he allows us to take "the justice that may be available in the cities [for] perfect justice and unquestionably good."[16] In Aristotle's view, in fact, "there is no need for the dilution of natural right. Aristotle says, then, simply that natural right is part of political right."[17] Since the justice that may be available in the cities is indeed not perfect, Aristotle's way of dimming our perception brings it about that the Platonic notion of the best regime ceases to be identical with the perfect moral order. Thus Aristotle takes the position that the end of civil society is no longer virtuous life as

9. *Ibid.*
10. Strauss, *Natural Right and History,* 156.
11. *Ibid.,* 144.   12. *Ibid.,* 156.
13. *Ibid.,* 144.   14. *Ibid.*
15. *Ibid.,* 156.   16. *Ibid.,* 157.
17. *Ibid.*

such, but only a certain segment of the virtuous life. The divine madness of Plato had held out a hope that is seriously compromised by Aristotle's sober second thoughts about human life as it can be managed by civil society. Strauss's innermost thought appears to be that Aristotle had sowed the seeds of destruction in the classical tradition; if that tradition is to be saved, we must read Aristotle in the light of Plato's sun.

Curiously enough, it is in the context of distinguishing classic natural right from its "crucial modification" by the biblical tradition of faith that Strauss makes the point about the essentially political character of classic natural right.[18] Curiously, I say, because it is sufficiently clear that Strauss has most certainly, if somewhat obliquely, found that crucial modification in Aristotle himself. Indeed, Strauss is compelled in all honesty, if surreptitiously, I am afraid, to enter a hint of his concealed teaching on this matter when he says: "Still, even this crucial modification of the classical teaching was in a way anticipated by the classics. According to the classics, political life as such is inferior to the philosophic life."[19] Who was responsible for the notion of "political life *as such*" but Aristotle, who treated of each of the various levels of beings on its own terms? The philosophic life, to which political life is inferior and to which political life is ordered, was referred by Aristotle to another level of being and to another science: to metaphysics and that part of metaphysics that is called natural theology. McDonald is right in his suspicion that "Strauss is more concerned to promote a special way of reading the 'classics' than in specific details of interpretation. . . ." It ought to be fruitful to pursue further the inquiry into that special way of reading the classics.

We may begin by trying to discover why Strauss says that thought ought to be drunk with boldness. Aristotle had taught that the good of anything consists in a mean, according to which it is conformed to a rule of measure which it is possible to overstep or to fail to reach. The good to which intellectual virtue is directed will consist in a mean insofar as it is subject to a measure. The good of intellectual virtue is *the true*; now, Aristotle tells us,[20] the truth apprehended by our intellect is as something measured by things, since things are the measure of our intellect; for, there is truth in what we think or say according as the thing is so or is

18. *Ibid.*, 144.   19. *Ibid.*, 145.
20. Aristotle, *Metaphysics*, X, 1, 1053a33.

not. Consequently, the good of speculative virtue consists in a certain mean by way of conformity with things themselves. There will be excess and "immoderation" if something false is affirmed (as though something were, which in reality is not); and there will be deficiency if something is falsely denied and declared not to be, whereas in reality it is.

Now in Strauss's understanding of Plato the mind does not stand in a relation of obedience of things as described by Aristotle. Strauss writes: "it appears that . . . man as man is the measure of truth and untruth, of the being or non-being of all things. . . . For the human faculty . . . that discovers nature is reason or understanding, and the relation of reason or understanding to its objects is fundamentally different from . . . obedience."[21] Nature is not to be taken as "the authority" by philosophers qua philosophers. Aristotle's sober manner of philosophizing did indeed take nature as "the authority": by treating each of the various levels of beings on its own terms he allowed the intellect to be measured by things; he found intellectual virtue to consist in a certain mean by way of conformity with things themselves.[22] In this way he came, unlike Plato, to understand moral virtue to be not merely "a kind of halfway house between political or vulgar virtue . . . and genuine virtue which . . . animates only the philosophers as philosophers"; he came to regard moral virtue as "an absolute" and thereby "closed" the "sphere ruled by prudence."[23] "Because Aristotle held that . . . prudence is inferior to theoretical wisdom . . . he could found political science as in independent discipline among a number of disciplines in such a way that political science preserves the perspective of the citizen or statesman. . . ." It was in this way, then, that Aristotle abandoned the divine madness that is a virtue of thought, and by conforming the intellect to things, permitted the justice of the cities to appear to be perfect justice and unquestionably good.

It will now be useful to consider two illustrations of the profoundly different ways in which Plato and Aristotle establish the essentially political character of natural right. Of the Platonic way of direct ascent to the construction, in speech, of the best regime Strauss gives two examples:

21. Strauss, *Natural Right and History*, 87, 92.
22. Aristotle, *Metaphysics*, X, 1, 1053a33.
23. Strauss, *The City and Man*, 278, 25.

Let us take the example of the big boy who has a small coat and the small boy who has a big coat. The big boy is the lawful owner of the small coat because he, or his father, has bought it. But it is not good for him; it does not fit him. The wise ruler will therefore take the big coat away from the small boy and give it to the big boy. . . . If there is to be justice, the wise rulers must assign to everyone what is truly due to him, or what is by nature good for him. . . . Justice is then incompatible with what is generally understood by private ownership. . . . Justice exists, then, only in a society in which everyone . . . has what he can use well. Justice is identical with membership in such a society—a society according to nature.[24]

And:

[C]ivil society in one way or another qualifies the principle or merit, i.e. the principle par excellence of justice, by the wholly unconnected principle of indigenousness. In order to be truly just, civil society would have to drop this qualification; civil society would have to be transformed into the "world state."[25]

We observe then that the direct ascent of Plato to what is right by nature "by-passes" two obfuscations of natural right—"indigenousness" and "private ownership." When now we turn to Aristotle for his views on these matters we find that he allows his vision of natural right to be "dimmed" by these two "obfuscations." Common possession of things under the dispensation of the "wise rulers" is not according to nature and is unreasonable, Aristotle argues, because it does not take account of the way things are in fact. Now it is in the nature of the thing, he says, that people who have their property in common would describe it "as belonging to them not severally but collectively. That all persons call the same thing mine in the sense in which each does so may be a fine thing, but it is an impracticable one; or if the words are taken in another sense, such a unity in no way conduces to harmony."[26]

Granted the disparity between that which is and that which ought to be, it would seem that the way things authoritatively are by nature should be the starting point for any change. If indeed truth is in the intellect as something measured by things, then, since law is a work of practical reason directing human actions, it must, being itself a rule and measure, be homogeneous with what it measures.[27] The legislator must take his matter as he finds it.

24. Strauss, *Natural Right and History*, 147–48.
25. *Ibid.*, 148–49.
26. Aristotle, *Politics*, II, 3, 1261b23–33.
27. Aristotle, *Metaphysics*, X, 1, 1053a24.

Civil law measures refractory material and is of necessity imperfect—*of necessity*, that is, by its proper structure human law falls short of natural justice. The law cannot be expected to do justice in every case. Speaking of this inherent defect in the law, Aristotle observes:

All law is universal but about some things it is not possible to make a universal statement which shall be correct. In those cases, then, in which it is necessary to speak universally, but not possible to do so correctly, the law takes the usual case, though it is not ignorant of the possibility of error. *And it is none the less correct: for the error is not in the law nor in the legislator, but in the nature of the thing, since the matter of practical affairs is of this kind from the start.*[28]

Aristotle brings the same sort of consideration to bear on the principle of indigenousness as a qualification for civil society. On the unnaturalness of an all-comprehensive society subject to one human government, he remarks:

[A] great city is not to be confounded with a populous one. Moreover, experience shows that a very populous city can rarely, if ever, be well-governed; since all cities which have a reputation for good government have a limit of population. We may argue on grounds of reason, and the same result will follow. For law is order, and good law is good order; but a very great multitude cannot be orderly: to introduce order into the unlimited is the work of a divine power—of such a power as holds together the universe.[29]

In Aristotle's view, to conceive of natural right as requiring civil society to forego the principle of indigenousness and to entrust to "wise rulers" the task of assigning to everyone what is by nature good for him would be to attempt "to introduce order into the unlimited"; it would be an act of "divine madness" on the part of man. Strauss acknowledges indeed that civil society "shows a specific recalcitrance" to the reasonableness of natural right as Plato conceives it.[30] Indeed, the civil society that Aristotle speaks of as natural is, in Strauss's view, a compromise of reason with unreason, of wisdom with folly.[31] We are led, then, to ask what it is more precisely that distinguishes what is right by nature for Plato from what is right by nature for Aristotle and to seek the reason for that "specific recalcitrance" that civil society, by Strauss's admission, shows for Plato's natural right.

28. Aristotle, *Nicomachean Ethics*, V, 5, 1137b12–19.
29. Aristotle, *Politics*, VII, 4, 1326a24–32.
30. Strauss, *The City and Man*, 22.
31. Strauss, *Natural Right and History*, 152.

The correct understanding of natural right is to be had, Strauss argues, by taking nature not as "the authority" but as "the standard."[32] We have already seen that the relation of human reason or understanding to its objects is not one of obedience. Moderation is not a virtue of thought. Nature as authority would deflect the mind from ascending to the good itself; the mind would be deflected into the various levels of being where the good itself is obfuscated. But if the several disciplines are achieved at the price of dimming our perception, there is yet further obfuscation to be suffered from accepting nature as "the authority": the world as it is simply given by the authority of nature is filled with irrationalities. The crucial text for understanding the import of treating nature as "the authority" rather than as "the standard" is, Strauss suggests, the saying of Heraclitus, "In God's view, all things are fair (noble) and good and just, but men have made the supposition that some things are just and others unjust."[33] Strauss then elaborates this:

God, or whatever one may call the first cause, is beyond good and evil and even beyond good and bad. God is not connected with justice in any sense that is relevant to human life as such: God does not reward justice and punish injustice. Justice has no superhuman support. That justice is good and injustice is bad is due exclusively to human agencies and ultimately to human decisions. No traces of divine justice are found except where just men reign; otherwise there is one event, as we see, to the righteous and to the wicked.[34]

The import of taking nature as "the authority" is precisely that, Strauss suggests, "all things [would be] fair and good and just, but [that] men have made the supposition that some things are just and others unjust."

32. *Ibid.*, 92.   33. *Ibid.*, 93.
34. *Ibid.*, 93–94. As an example of "camouflage" in Strauss's teaching, to which McShea calls attention, we have the following curious remarks of Strauss on the "world-state": "[W]hat is divined in speaking of the 'world-state' as an all-comprehensive human society subject to one human government is in truth the cosmos ruled by God, which is then the only true city, of the city that is simply according to nature because it is the only city which is simply just. Men are citizens of this city, or freemen in it, only if they are wise; their obedience to the law which orders the natural city, to the natural law, is the same thing as prudence" (*ibid.*, 149–50). Since, as we have just seen, the justice that has superhuman support is what is right according to nature as standard, the meaning of these sentences can only be that if God were to rule the "world-state" his rule would ignore the principles of indigenousness and private ownership. "God" is "camouflage" for "wise rule." Indeed, Strauss tells us that Plato's cosmology is not separable from the quest for the best political order (*The City and Man*, 21).

Strauss does not, of course, accept the proposition that justice is good and injustice bad simply because the decisions of human agencies have made them such; on the contrary, he believes that there is something that is right by nature and that this natural right indeed has superhuman support. The justice that has super-human support is that which is right by nature *as standard*: the giving of the small coat to the small boy, not of the principle of private ownership; the principle of merit, not the principle of in-digenousness. Now we have seen that Aristotle does not pro-pound this notion of natural right, a notion that would, he says, require introducing order into the unlimited, "a work of a divine power such as holds together the universe." Aristotle's position is that nature indeed is a kind of "reason" put into things so that they may act for determinate ends (*Physics* II), but that the ultimate reasons of things are not subjectified in the things themselves of the world. As one of the most distinguished students of Aristotle in our times, the late Charles de Koninck, has written: "As seen in the particular things and actions of which it is composed, the world reveals itself full of irrationality and absurdity. . . . It is Prof. Bummelklotz, of all people, who strikes oil in his backyard while digging for water."[35] Aristotle had observed that if nature intended a particular individual she would be like a man who takes a bath so that the sun might be eclipsed—that is to say, there is as much reason between the intention of nature and the production of Soc-rates, Jr., as there is between a man taking a bath and the eclipse of the sun.[36] After all, it was quite by accident that Socrates first met Xanthippe. Nature produces this man, to be sure, but she does not intend him as such: he is intended only inasmuch as man cannot be unless this man be. Much more happens in nature, Aristotle realized, than can be accounted for by nature as "the standard." The import of nature's indifference to the ultimate rea-sons of things may best be understood, de Koninck suggests, by considering that "the absolutely universal causality of God, as well as His properly divine wisdom, appears most strikingly in the intrinsic contingency and the inherent absurdity of the world: for only God is the determinate *per se* cause of that, too, which in itself is contingent. No creature can be the *per se* cause of what is either

35. Charles de Koninck, "The Nature of Man and His Historical Being," *Laval Théologique et Philosophique*, V (#2, 1949), 274.
36. Aristotle, *Physics*, II, 7, 197b25–27.

casual or fortuitous."[37] If we were to take nature as "the authority," the very notion of the best regime as identical with the perfect
moral order would be impossible; and, indeed, "philosophy, in
particular political philosophy, would lose," Strauss says, "its
character, it would undergo a . . . transformation into theology. . . ."[38]

Confronted by the incommensurability of the divine reason with
our own reason—and with the reason of nature as "the standard"
(the meaning of which will shortly become clear)—Strauss ignores
the obfuscations of the world and, as we have already noted, has
recourse to "man as man" as "the measure of the truth or untruth,
the being or non-being of all things."[39] The naturally right will be
defined with direct reference to the fact that the only life which is
simply just is that of the philosopher, and that it is he who gives
us the complete answers as to what is right by nature, in the
construction, in speech, of the best regime: the perfect moral order,
the good itself.

Now of the notion of "the good itself," Aristotle made two observations that throw light on the Platonic idea of the "best regime" constructed "in speech." First, if "the good itself" is taken
as a logical universal, predicable of many good things, it has no
existence as a universal except in the mind which abstracts it from
the things of which it is predicated; it exists as a universal in the
logical order only, "in speech." Thus, for example, there exists no
animal-in-general: "animal as such" exists only in speech. It has
no authority in nature. Second, if we take the "good itself" to be
an ontological principle, capable of separate and independent existence, the study of such a principle does not belong to political
science but to a science concerned with another level of being, to
metaphysics and theology.[40] All sciences show by their procedure,
says Aristotle, that "they aim at *some* good and seek to remove the
deficiency of it; but they all leave to one side the knowledge of *the*
good."[41] It would be madness, divine or other, he suggests, for a
weaver or a carpenter to suppose that he will be benefited in regard
to his own craft by knowing the good itself, or that a man "who
has viewed the Idea itself will be a better doctor or general

37. De Koninck, "The Nature of Man and His Historical Being," 274.
38. Strauss, *Natural Right and History*, 92.
39. *Ibid.*, 87.
40. Aristotle, *Nicomachean Ethics*, I, 6, 1096b8 ff.
41. *Ibid.*

thereby."[42] In a similar way, it would be madness to suppose that the common possession of things would lead to people's calling the same thing "mine" in the sense in which each does so: "they would say 'all' but not 'each.'" But indeed, it is that first "good itself," constructed in speech, that Strauss fastens upon and to which he wishes to give the status that the "good itself" as an ontological principle, capable of separate and independent existence, enjoys at a different level of being. This, again, is to wish to find the "sufficient reason" of the world somehow justified *in* the world. Community in general has no existence, but Strauss wishes us to find the standard of "family," "village," and "civil society" subjectified in the more common concepts of universal community and universal possession. Nature as standard is the generic nature that fails to express, as Aristotle puts it, "the peculiar nature of anything that *is*. . . ."[43]

Strauss is compelled to acknowledge, as we have noted, that civil society shows a specific recalcitrance to this kind of generic thought. There is, he says, a radical antagonism between philosophy and politics.[44] The root of this antagonism is not uncovered by Strauss. But it can be discovered by observing that the reason for a man who knows the "good itself," found in all good things, not being made a better weaver or carpenter thereby is that this "good itself" is not a universal cause in the order of causality but simply in the order of predication: "artisan" is universally predicable of and found in weaver, carpenter, shoemaker *et al.*, but "artisan" does not cause the differences among the crafts. Although indispensable to our knowledge of things, the universal of predication does not belong, as a universal, to the real world, to nature as "authority."[45] The same is true of "family," "village," and "civil

42. *Ibid.*
43. Aristotle, *De Anima*, II, 3, 414b20–25.
44. Strauss, *Natural Right and History*, 152.
45. One ought not to abandon the search for universal causes in the line of causality itself. Unlike the universal of predication which contains its subject parts indeterminately and confusedly (elephant and man are contained confusedly in "animal"; family and village are contained confusedly in "community"), the universal cause in the order of reality belongs to nature as "authority": it has real existence *as a universal* and is a universal cause by reason of extending to many different kinds of effects. When Aristotle says that the state is prior by nature to the family, his meaning is that the state is a more universal final cause of good, diffusive of itself by reason of its communicability and reaching to the various parts of the whole state in their very diversity. But this diversity comes from the order of parts in the whole; thus, the common good is the good of individuals as parts

society": in no way do they arise out of community in general; similarly the species "triangle" and "isosceles" are in no sense an elaboration of the genus "figure." But Strauss would have it that as weaver and carpenter disappear into "artisan," so statesman should disappear into philosopher, the political into the philosophical. To suggest this is to engage in that immoderation of thought which does not conform to the way things are. It is precisely this generic reason, the universal of predication, to which nature as "authority" is opposed. What then, we are led to ask, is Strauss's final thought on the question of classic natural right and the securing of its political character? How do the frustrations engendered by taking nature as standard bring Strauss to his final position on this matter?

Account must be taken of Strauss's persistent refusal to accept Aristotle's way of defining natural right. This is rejected because, as we have seen, by making natural right simply part of political right, Aristotle "absolutizes" that heterogeneity of social life that obfuscates what is right according to nature as standard. In Aristotle's view, "the nature of the state is to be a plurality and in tending to the greatest unity, from being a state it becomes a family, and from being a family, an individual; for the family may be said to be more one than the State, and the individual than the family. So that we ought not to attain this greatest unity even if we could, for it would be the destruction of the state."[46] The principles of indigenousness and of private ownership that belong to this concept of the nature of the state as a plurality make it necessary, in Strauss's view, to surrender the notion of the best regime as identical with the perfect moral order. Furthermore, in Aristotle's philosophy the ultimate reasons for things are not found subjectified *in* the things of which the world is composed. This Aristotelian position prepares the way, of course, for the Thomistic view of natural right, which is rooted in Aristotle's natural theology and brought to completion by revealed theology. This is a position and a consequence unacceptable to Strauss.[47]

The second consideration that dictates Strauss's final solution to

and members of society and is sought by them precisely as members of society and as being not all alike. Reaching thus to individuals in what is most determinate and actual in them, the common good is a universal cause in the order of causality: this common good of the community is, for each of the members, also the good of the others.

46. Aristotle, *Politics*, II, 1, 1261a18–23.
47. Strauss, *Natural Right and History*, 163–64, 144.

the problem of classic natural right turns on the modern solution to the question of natural right. Here we must take account of an argument that is set forth with that obscurity which has been alluded to. McShea has called attention to the fact that in Strauss's view "the failure of modern theorists to return to the classical idea of natural law followed from the fact that the mediaeval thinkers had so thoroughly welded the concept of natural law to revealed theology that the latter could not be discarded without loss of, or serious damage to the former."[48] Therefore, speaking of the contractualist doctrines of the seventeenth and eighteenth centuries, Strauss says: "In the modern era the notion that nature is the standard was abandoned.[49]

If modern natural law was based neither on theology nor on the classic concept of nature as standard, on what concept, then, of nature was it based? For we are nonetheless told that the revolutionists of the eighteenth century "resorted to nature," and we are further told that "what is true of the eighteenth century revolutionists is true, *mutatis mutandis,* of all philosophers *qua* philosophers."[50] Philosophers *qua* philosophers always appeal, Strauss insists, to nature as standard and not to nature as authority.[51] Thus it is clear that the eighteenth-century revolutionists indeed appealed to nature as standard, but *mutatis mutandis.* What is the *mutatis mutandis*?

All the renowned thinkers of the seventeenth and eighteenth centuries adopted a conception of nature that, as Cassirer puts it in conveying the general features of Enlightenment thought, "reduces the mental and material spheres to a common denominator; they are composed of the same elements and are combined according to the same laws."[52] Nature as standard meant for the Enlightenment philosophers and scientists that "nature in man . . . meets nature in the cosmos half-way and finds its own essence there."[53] For Plato, nature as standard had meant that the real world is, most perfectly, the world of immaterial archetypes of species and genera bearing the imprint of logical being and ultimately—since Plato's cosmology, Strauss tells us, is not separable from the quest for the best political order[54]—the construction, in

48. McShea, "Leo Strauss on Machiavelli," 786.
49. Strauss, *Natural Right and History,* 119.
50. *Ibid.,* 92–93.   51. *Ibid.*
52. Ernst Cassirer, *The Philosophy of the Enlightenment* (Boston, 1951), 18.
53. *Ibid.,* 144–45
54. Strauss, *The City and Man,* 21.

speech, of the best regime. For the eighteenth-century philosophers, nature as standard is found rather in the essential likeness
of the elements that compose the mental and physical worlds and
they are composed of the same elements and are combined according to the same laws: "The autonomy of intellect corresponds
to the pure autonomy of nature. . . . Both are recognized as elemental and to be firmly connected with one another."[55] It was no
longer necessary for the new science to consider the divine art as
the principle of the works of nature. There is no "authority" for
nature beyond nature's own properties.

Now, as can be gathered from the remark of Aristotle on the
fortuitousness of the production of Socrates, Jr., it is one of the
properties of nature, nature as standard, that she does not intend
any particular individual as such; she produces this individual, to
be sure, but intends him only inasmuch as without him the species
cannot be maintained. Another property of nature as standard is
that she does not herself account for the diversity of species; she
produces the different species, to be sure, but since, as Aristotle
argues in *Physics* II, the spider and the bee, while accomplishing
their specific ends accomplish them without knowledge of them
as such, it follows that their specific functions and the diversity of
these functions cannot be attributed to nature as to their ultimate
and sufficient cause. In the real world, nature as standard, Aristotle suggests, is a kind of "substitute intelligence."

In this new sense of nature, the idea of "law" in nature as Aristotle had understood it is radically changed, but the new sense
of nature retains the idea of "law" as Plato had understood it.
While for both Plato and Aristotle the notion of law implied the
presence of intelligence, the role of intelligence was very different
for each. For Aristotle, law, as a work of the practical intellect, is
something ordained to the good as an end of action.[56] Now in the
eighteenth-century's reduction of the mental and material spheres
to a common denominator, the "reason" that is imputed to nature
acts, of course, without knowledge of an end and consequently
acts for no end beyond its existence: the good is no longer that
end of action toward which things are ordered as "desiring" their
perfection; the good becomes simply convertible with being and
law describes the "properties" of each nature. Aristotle had clearly

55. Cassirer, *The Philosophy of the Enlightenment*, 144–45.
56. Aristotle, *Physics*, III, 1, 200a22; *Nicomachean Ethics*, II, 1, 1103b3–6; V, 1,
1129b17.

distinguished this ontological "good" from the "good" to which law as an ordinance of practical reason ordains things to their ends in the actions that constitute their perfections.[57] In speaking of Hobbes, Maréchal has pertinently described the special character of modern natural law:

The good is defined in relation to the "ontological" perfection of each "nature"; *the moral problem is a problem of maximum being.* This "maximum being" must not be imagined to be an *end* pursued; it has nothing to do with ends pursued, but only with necessary effects. . . .
  In each "rational nature" the moral problem, the problem of the intensification of the power of existence, will be resolved without any liberty of choice. . . . [It will be resolved] by means of the correcting of inadequate ideas.[58]

Now in Plato's *Republic*—the "city according to nature," as Strauss calls it—there is no place for that law which depends on liberty of choice with respect to ends pursued; the "moral problem" is a problem of "maximum being," having nothing to do with ends pursued but only with necessary effects. It is a problem of the "ontological" perfection of each nature, the properties of which are adequately understood by the "wise rulers." As Sabine sagely remarks, in omitting the law that depends on the internal natural liberty of choice of the subject Plato failed "to perceive a striking *moral* aspect of the very society which he desired to perfect."[59]

Plato's philosophizing had, as Strauss indeed tells us, the character of direct ascent from the speculative consideration of the cosmos to the more adequate ideas of the best regime, constructed in speech:

This difference between Plato and Aristotle can be illustrated by the contrast between the relation of the *Republic* to the *Timaeus* on the one hand, and of the *Politics* to the *Physics* or *On the Heaven* on the other. Aristotle's cosmology, as distinguished from Plato's, is unqualifiedly separable from the quest for the best political order. Aristotelian philosophizing has no longer to the same degree and in the same way as Socratic philosophizing the character of ascent.[60]

For the eighteenth-century philosophers, the study of the cosmos was also not separable from the quest for the best political order:

57. Aristotle, *Metaphysics*, IV; *Nicomachean Ethics*, I, 1, 1094a1–18; V, 5 and 6, 1096a1–b36.
58. Joseph Maréchal, *Précis d'histoire de la philosophie moderne* (Brussels, 1931), I, 137, n. 77.
59. George H. Sabine, *A History of Political Theory* (New York, 1937), 65.
60. Strauss, *The City and Man*, 21.

composed of the same elements and combined according to the same laws, the cosmos presented to man the more modest task of increasingly adequate ideas on the ontological perfection of man's nature "which meets the cosmos half-way and finds its own essence there." It was this manner of reasoning that allowed Hobbes to declare that the State disintegrates not when the laws are "unjust" but when they do not "keep [the citizenry] in such motion as not to hurt themselves by their own impetuous desires."[61] The obligation to obedience lasts as long as the power lasts by which the parts of the State are held together. The right to revolt is a right not against tyranny but against weakness in the power of the body politic, in the ordering of material and efficient principles to the formation of the body politic.

The *mutatis mutandis* then of the eighteenth-century philosophers' appeal to nature as standard consisted, in effect, of overcoming the separation of reality from philosophy by transposing onto the real world what Plato had constructed in speech. All of them appeal to nature by moving toward that good which is simply convertible with being: not the "good," taken formally in the Aristotelian sense, but the good that is convertible with being. Self-preservation becomes the first principle of politics in the new "natural rights" philosophies of Hobbes, Locke, and Rousseau, and further, there is a tendency toward an identification in the real world of the individual with the species and the species with generic being, that "intensification of the power of existence" to which Maréchal refers. The movement culminates in Marx's celebrated doctrine of "the generic natural relation" according to which man is "a conscious generic being who relates himself to the species as to his own proper being and relates himself to himself as a generic being."[62] Marx resolves "religious essence" into "human essence" by the reduction of "the absolute metaphysical spirit to the real man standing on the foundation of nature."[63] Action not for an end, but the resolution of the antagonism between the region of thought and the region of reality, between man and nature, become the objective of modern political philosophy.

61. Thomas Hobbes, *Leviathan*, II, 30. See also McCoy, *The Structure of Political Thought, Chapter VII*.

62. Karl Marx, "Manuscript economico-philosophique, XXIV," cited in *De Marx au Marxisme*, Robert Aron (ed.) (Paris, 1948), 93.

63. Cited in Otto Rühle, *Karl Marx: His Life and Work* (London, 1929), 33.

Not until "all the pretended history of the world [is seen to be] nothing but the production of man by human work," Marx tells us, will man be restored, in the *real* world, on the human plane, to that generic life which defines him as universal producer, as "conscious generic being." Only then indeed will the principle "from each according to his ability, to each according to his needs" pass very rapidly, as Lenin put it, into a state of habitude.[64] But that this may come about, consciousness must cease, Marx tells us, "to flatter itself that it is conceiving something without conceiving something real."[65] This is that self-flattering consciousness of the seventeenth- and eighteenth-century revolutionary political philosophies that conceived "the fully developed political state"; for in that merely "political" form of the generic life, man continued in civil society to work as "a mere part" and to see in other men "simply means" and to become "himself swallowed up in the role of simple means . . . the plaything of forces extraneous to himself."[66] This is the same consciousness that is traceable back to the immoderation of thought that Strauss calls a virtue in Plato: the immoderation of thought that asserts that something is which in reality is not.

Pursuing the precise same principle of *mutatis mutandis* of nature as the standard and indissolubly joining—in the manner of Plato but at the opposite extreme—the quest for the best regime with the study of the cosmos, Marx fills the emptiness of the Platonic logical universals with real natural matter and makes matter (and its dialectical law of motion) the principle of all fecundity. By an obverse confusion of the logical and the real, Marx also refuses to treat of the various levels of beings on their own terms. The natural right is now defined by direct reference to the fact that the only life which is simply just is the life of the worker, of man as universal, material producer; the question as to what is by nature right or as to what is justice finds its complete answer only through the construction, not in speech, but in the "real community" of the generic man, of "socialized humanity." And this construction is carried out not by Plato's "wise rulers" but by "the armed workers." Instead of politics passing into philosophy (the radicalism of Plato) philosophy passes into practice (the radicalism of modern political philosophy).

64. V. I. Lenin, *The State and Revolution* (New York, 1932), 74.
65. Karl Marx and Friedrich Engels, *The German Ideology* (New York, 1939), 20.
66. Karl Marx, *Die Judenfrage*, in *Gesamtausgabe*, Sec. I, I, 1 (Berlin, 1927–32), 595.

Nature as standard in the Platonic sense, the universal cause in the orders of predication, could indeed only lead, when projected onto the real world, to that nature which Aristotle thought of as "substitute intelligence": substitute intelligence because it does not "know" with precision the individual it produces, nor does it "know" the species, either in themselves or in their diversity. The "generic natural relation," in which the individual life and the life of the species are not different, means in real life that the "intensification of the power of existence," to which we have alluded, will be accomplished without any liberty of choice; it means that, as Arthur Koestler has expressed it, individuals are without face and name, "having effaced their personality, their will and feeling, by orders of the Party."[67]

Strauss is confronted with the disastrous implications of the Platonic way of philosophizing: ignoring the various levels of beings and not treating them on their own terms. The implications are disastrous when made practical by "the modern secular movement which tries to guarantee the actualization of the ideal, or to prove the necessary coincidence of the rational and the real."[68] The Platonic forms, empty as logical universals, were filled by the "substitute intelligence" of the real world of nature.

Nonetheless Strauss appears to allow his fear of philosophy's transforming itself into theology to overcome his profound distaste for a philosophy that disappears into the political. He adheres persistently to the Platonic notion of the best regime as identical with the perfect moral order and has recourse, finally, to an acceptance *by contract* of Aristotle's essentially inferior polity. One may be forced to give it allegiance, but the allegiance will be de-

67. Arthur Koestler, *The Invisible Writing* (Boston, 1954), 41–42. "Death," Marx writes (*Die Judenfrage,* 583) "appears as a hard victory of the species over the individual, and seems to contradict the unity of the species; but the determinate individual is only a determinate generic being, and as such he is mortal. Each of his human relationships . . . is in its objective relationship . . . the appropriation of (the) object, the appropriation of human reality. This manifestation is as multiple as are *human determinations and activities,* human *activity* and human *suffering,* for suffering, taken in the human sense, is a pleasure proper to man." (*Oekonomische-Philosophische Manuskript,* 116). But the individual in his "essentiality" is "the product of industry and of the state of society, . . . the result of the activity of a whole succession of generations, each standing on the shoulders of the preceding one. . . ." (Marx and Engels, *The German Ideology,* 35). So that the individual's mortality is indeed not only quite indifferent to his real (species) life but rather contributes to it! The comrade agrees to be shot.

68. Strauss, *What is Political Philosophy?* 51.

rived from a "compromise of reason with unreason, of wisdom with folly"[69]:

In a passage of Plato's *Crito,* Socrates is presented as deriving his duty of obedience to the city of Athens and her laws from a tacit contract. To understand this passage, one has to compare it with its parallel in the *Republic.* In the *Republic* the philosopher's duty of obedience to the city is not derived from any contract. The reason is obvious. The city of the *Republic* is the best city, the city according to nature. But the city of Athens, that democracy, was from Plato's point of view a most imperfect city. Only the allegiance to an inferior community can be derivative from contract, for an honest man keeps his promises to everyone regardless of the worth of him to whom he made the promise.[70]

The contractual acceptance of Aristotle's inferior polity allows Strauss to retain the Platonic idea of the perfect moral order subjectified in the world but to retain it now through a mode of behavior: "the mating of courage and moderation" (just the right draught of wine) that allows one to *see past* the city with its obfuscations and dimnesses and while accepting the city, to embrace, hidden and shadowed by it, the city of the sun, the city according to nature. Strauss's solution to the problem of classic natural right is, after all, a quite personal one. "[Philosophy] is the highest form of the mating of courage and moderation. In spite of its highness or nobility, it could appear Sisyphean or ugly, when one contrasts its achievements with its goals. Yet it is necessarily accompanied, sustained and elevated by *Eros.* It is graced by nature's grace."[71] "Nature's grace" is evidently that spark of divine madness that allows the "wise rulers," against all odds, to aspire "to introduce order into the unlimited." This is a touching, even admirable faith; it is also, I believe, a quite desperate one: Strauss drinks wine with Plato and hemlock with Socrates.

69. Strauss, *Natural Right and History,* 152–53, 119.
70. *Ibid.,* 119.
71. Strauss, *What is Political Philosophy?* 40.

11. The Counter Culture: Its Sense of Life

[This previously unpublished essay (written between 1970 and 1975 and found among his papers) demonstrates the usefulness of McCoy's whole method in comprehending political and philosophical movements.[1] McCoy presents a general analysis of the Counter Culture in terms of its understanding of itself and its relation to the larger issues in political philosophy. The essay begins McCoy's endeavor to see how the Counter Culture had a definite philosophical origin, often unknown to itself, in its reaction to well-established views in modern political philosophy. McCoy finds in the methodology of modern political analysis a loss of contact with being which was somehow sensed in the Counter Culture movements. McCoy sees that this reaction to a politics based on pure scientific methodology sought the being which simply existed and was able to be encountered. In a brilliant Aristotelian discussion of the sense of touch (the normal way human beings encounter something outside of themselves) McCoy relates this movement to more fundamental ideas in classical political thought.]

In the course of examining the relation of Freud to literature Lionel Trilling distinguishes between a "limited reality, by which we get our living, win our loves, catch our trains and our colds," a "given reality," what is simply *there*, and a "taken" or "created reality" which the mind "helps create . . . by selection and eval-

1. This essay is a portion of a larger study of the Counter Culture. The first part of the study deals with the origin, nature, and development of the notion of "objective consciousness"—that consciousness which Roszak, Marcuse, Reich, *et al.* speak of as the chief characteristic of "one-dimensional man." The objective consciousness formed by what Roszak calls the "ideologically invisible." Technocracy supersedes, Marcuse maintains, the old ideological conflict between Marxism and Capitalism. It is this form of objective consciousness that is taken to be the prime enemy of the Counter Culture. In the portion of the study presented here, I am seeking to find in the Counter Culture's manifestations of opposition to the objective consciousness of the Technocracy some clue to the "way out" of one-dimensionality—where the road lies in the discovery of what Roszak calls "consciousness consciousness" and what Reich calls "consciousness III."

uation."[2] Trilling contends that "the reality to which (Freud) wishes to reconcile the neurotic patient is, after all, a 'taken' and not a 'given' reality. It is the reality of social life and value, conceived and maintained by the human mind and will. Love, morality, honor, esteem—these are the components of a created reality."[3] This, of course, had been the ancient understanding of what it was to be a freeman—one who moves himself to act by understanding the nature of things, by an idea that proceeds from the intellect itself "as a thing conceived and in a way contrived by it."[4]

Since the time of David Hume's critique of nature, order, and causality the sciences of society have allowed as scientifically acceptable knowledge only those matters that are embraced either by "given reality" or "limited reality." Hume's critique had cut the connection that former ages had believed existed between the "reason" that is nature, the "reason" that is the cause of nature, and human reason.[5] With the elimination of the "reason" that traditional philosophy had attributed to nature's operations, the conception of law as "an ordinance of reason" for the proper human good disappeared. Thus liberated, politics found its leading principle in the mere fact of regularity of behavior—measurable, indeed, but no longer recognized for what it had always been taken to be, namely, a *sign* of some determinate reason "why." Proceeding henceforth from a concept of nature that reduces it to a merely temporal sense of "that which happens always or for the most part," political actions, laws, and institutions came no longer to be subject to "understanding" but only to more or less elaborate descriptions and measurements. Sheldon Wolin very well expresses the general effect of Hume's critique in his observation that "[N]o longer able to communicate on the basis of a common interior of life [men] were reduced to knowing each other solely from the outside; that is, on the basis of socially acquired responses and values."[6] The "socialized conscience" begins to make its ap-

2. Lionel Trilling, *The Liberal Imagination* (Garden City, N.Y., 1957), 41–42.

3. *Ibid.*

4. St. Thomas Aquinas, *Summa Contra Gentiles*, II, 47. See Aristotle, *Metaphysics*, I, 2, 982b.26.

5. These various "reasons" are what Ernst Cassirer refers to when he speaks of Enlightenment thought having removed "the artificial barriers that had hitherto separated the human world from the rest of nature." *Essay on Man* (Garden City, N.Y., 1944), 30.

6. Sheldon Wolin, *Politics and Vision* (Boston, 1960), 340.

pearance, a conscience that develops by a whole series of "trop-isms" in response to outside stimuli. What Walter Lippmann observed, namely, the disappearance not of a ruling class but of "the functional [arrangement] of the relationship between the mass of people and the government"[7] (the substitution of veto-groups, Gallup-Pollsters, and inside-dopesters for genuine rule) had meant indeed that the state had begun to wither away.

Technology has served to bring this trend to completion. As Hans Morgenthau has pointed out:

It has become trivial to say . . . that the modern technologies of trans-portation, communication and warfare, have made the nation-state as principle of political organization, as obsolete as the first industrial revo-lution of the steam engine did feudalism. While the official governments of the nation-states go through the constitutional motions of governing, most of the decisions that affect the vital concerns of the citizens are rendered by those who control these technologies, their distribution, their operation, their price.[8]

Man is no longer "self-governing." As Marcuse puts it: "[I]deas, aspirations, and objectives that, by their content, transcend the established universe of discourse and action are either repelled or reduced to terms of this universe. They are redefined by the ratio-nality of the given system and of its quantitative extension."[9] It is in this way that there "emerges a pattern of *one-dimensional thought and behavior.* . . . The result is not adjustment but *Mimesis*: an im-mediate identification of the individual with *his* society and, through it, with society as a whole."[10] The person in his individ-uality *is* the "organization man," the "other-directed man," the "one-dimensional man."

In short, liberalism's primal act of imagination whereby it estab-lished its essence and existence in the enhanced sense of freedom consequent upon Hume's denial of a "reason" in nature which allows human reason to make distinctions perceptive of proper human values and consequences issued in anomie and other-direction and one-dimensionality. The growing awareness of this one-dimensionality of our culture marks the transition of the con-temporary form of "objective consciousness"[11] from "one-dimen-

7. Walter Lippmann, *The Public Philosophy* (Boston, 1955), 14.
8. Hans Morgenthau, "Decline of Democratic Government," *The New Republic*, 171 (November 9, 1974), 14.
9. Herbert Marcuse, *One-Dimensional Man* (Boston, 1969), 12.
10. *Ibid.*, 10.
11. "Objective consciousness" may be briefly defined here in the formulation

sionality" to "authenticity." It marks also its dilemma. For if the quantitative measurement of the "facts" observable in human behavior marks the phase of *anomie* and one-dimensionality of the contemporary form of objective consciousness, the movement toward authenticity calls for the conscious overthrow of all that is clothed with the stability of nature.[12] The only "creative act" open to the one-dimensional man *as one-dimensional* is indiscriminate destruction.

Hans Morgenthau, in the essay just cited, has called attention to this indiscriminate destruction. Pointing out the difference between traditional violence and its contemporary form, he states: "The violence that we witness in the form of hijacking, torture, indiscriminate killing, differs from traditional violence in the form of political assassinations and the destruction of political institutions in that it is in general politically aimless. Rather than being a rational means to a rational end, it is an end in itself, as such devoid of political rationality."[13] Marx himself put the point most succinctly: Objective consciousness is fully achieved when the philosophical activity of the individual is understood to be "sensuous practical activity" engaged in the overthrow of all "forms and products of a ['false'] consciousness [represented] by 'pure' theory, theology, philosophy, ethics, etc."[14] Technology has quietly made steady inroads on these forms and products of "false" consciousness—the State, the family, religion, private property. It remains only to carry authenticity to final expression by the conscious overthrow of everything clothed with the stability of nature.

The contention that indiscriminate destruction is the only "creative act" open to one-dimensional man receives confirmation from an observation made by Trilling in his last book, *Sincerity and Authenticity*. He writes: "A very considerable originative power had once been claimed for sincerity, but nothing to match the marvelous generative force that our modern judgment assigns to authenticity, *which implies the downward movement through all the cultural superstructures to some place where all movement ends, and*

---

of Ludwig Feuerbach: that consciousness by which the power of the object is seen to be the subject's own power objectified. *Essence of Christianity*, F. W. Strothmann, (ed.), (New York, 1957), 8. See also: Charles N. R. McCoy, *The Structure of Political Thought* (New York, 1963), Chapter IX.

12. See: Charles N. R. McCoy, "The Dilemma of Liberalism," in *The Structure of Political Thought*, 250–261. (See above, Chapter 6.)

13. Morgenthau, "Decline of Democratic Government," 16.

14. Karl Marx and Friedrich Engels, *The German Ideology* (New York, 1939), 20.

begins."[15] He concludes his essay by remarking that "not the organic, but the mechanical is to be the authenticating principle in modern life."[16] Not, of course, that aspect of the mechanical to which precisely the one-dimensionality of our technological society has been attributed. If the machine accounts for the political apathy of one-dimensional man, it accounts also for the political violence by which he seeks "authenticity." The marvelous generative force that our modern judgment assigns to authenticity and which is linked to the mechanical as "the authenticating principle in modern life" is revealed, Trilling suggests, by the "violent meanings which are explicit in the Greek ancestry of the word 'authentic.' *Authenteo*: to have full power over; also, to commit a murder. *Authentes*: not only a master and a doer, but also a perpetrator, a murderer, even a self-murderer, a suicide. These ancient and forgotten denotations bear upon the nature and intention of the culture of the period we call Modern."[17]

The ultimate irony of the machine culture lies before our eyes.[18] The "human" and authenticating principle is the machine in the capacity it gives man for taking apart the universe. We must look more deeply into this ultimate irony if we wish to see where man himself stands today in relation to what Ernst Cassirer called the "loss of intellectual center in the modern theory of man."[19] This loss of intellectual center bears directly on the ethos of the Counter Culture movement.

We may observe that the pure "exteriority" of the nature of the machine—i.e., the absence in it of what Marcuse calls "inner dimension," the inability of the machine to apprehend or state anything and to reflect on anything—is precisely what characterizes

15. Lionel Trilling, *Sincerity and Authenticity* (Cambridge, MA., 1971), 11–12.
16. *Ibid.*, 129.
17. *Ibid.*, 131. In "Demon in the Counterculture," a review of a book on the Charles Manson murders entitled *Helter Skelter* by Vincent Bugliosi and Curt Gentry, William Crawford Woods remarks, "It is hard to escape the conclusion that the counterculture of the 1960's—which offered us beautiful music, new ways to live our lives, and the will to end the war—gave birth as well to Charles Manson. . . . So, to an extent, one of the most hopeful movements in American life in this century created one of our darkest social chapters." *The New Republic,* 172 (January 4 & 11), 1975, 23, 25.
18. Roszak remarks that the ultimate irony of the machine consists not in the fact that man is replaced in all areas by the machine where the machine can do things better, "but rather [that] all things have been reduced to what the machine is capable of doing" (*The Making of a Counter Culture,* 231). I am suggesting, as the ultimate irony, something more disastrous.
19. Ernst Cassirer, *Essay on Man* (New Haven, CT., 1944), 29.

the nature of the primeval cosmos in its initial state—its pure exteriority, where things are separated one from another, wrapped in their obscurity. In the realm of the inorganic, things move only by being moved. The ultimate irony of the machine perfects the analogy between the origin of the world—as physics presents it to us—in the explosion of an immense atom and the human empathy in the one-dimensional society with the pure exteriority of the primeval cosmos wrapped in its own obscurity. Now the analogy is carried further in the authenticating principle of the machine—the capacity it gives man for destroying the universe by the bomb. We see what Roszak means by speaking at once of the "mere fact of the bomb" and the "total ethos of the bomb."[20] The bomb is the ultimate machine, the terrible external sign of defect at the heart of our modern culture and the sign of what Gabriel Marcel calls the process of "self-destruction that is taking place at every level of being."[21] We have, to be sure, as Trilling puts it, assigned a generative force to authenticity that "implies the downward movement through all the cultural superstructures to some place where all movement ends, and begins."

If indeed the Counter Culture gives much the appearance of pursuing authenticity by the downward movement through all the cultural superstructures, the evidence suggests that this movement is by way of rediscovering what Jacob Needleman calls, "the idea of *levels* of intelligence and consciousness in the universe."[22] The literature and behavior of the Counter Culture people show, more than anything else, "awe and solicitude for the whole of creation."[23] What is imperative for the Counter Culture is the redis-

20. Roszak, *The Making of a Counter Culture*, 47.
21. Gabriel Marcel, *The Philosophy of Existence* (New York, 1949), 32.
22. Jacob Needleman, "Winds from the East," *Commonweal*, 39 (April 30, 1971), 189.
23. In the *Notes and Comment* column for May 13, 1972, the editors of *The New Yorker* magazine remark that "the dominant note in any sane contemporary political philosophy should be a spirit of conservatism"; but they give an unexpected turn to this remark by immediately adding that this spirit of conservatism does not today, as it did in the past, embrace the preservation of the established political order. "It should be plain that a true conservatism today would have nothing to do with what now passes for conservatism in the United States. . . . Our most powerful institutions . . .—and the 'conservatives' who give them unquestioning support—are forces of extreme radicalism." If the established institutions are indeed forces of extreme radicalism, then, it would seem, the Counter Culture revolution may well be understood as a profoundly conservative movement. "A genuine conservatism," the editors of *The New Yorker* continue, "would ask the State and all other human institutions to approach the whole of creation with . . . awe and solicitude."

covery of *self*-consciousness, the need to ask "at what level of consciousness do I exist? and at what level of consciousness *may* I exist?"[24] Among the members of the Counter Culture there is a sense, made evident in a variety of ways, of the cosmos as a tendency toward life, and indeed, toward the life of intelligence in which all the parts of the universe are united and lived. We may well expect that the beginnings of such a movement will exhibit that peculiar paradox of empathy (of which I have spoken) with the pure exteriority of the primeval cosmos, existing, so to speak, entirely outside of itself, separated from itself—the experience of being "stoned." If indeed it is by drugs that the Counter Culture people are more often than not "turned on," the stoned pattern, as Jonathan Eisen tells us, "is more along the lines of instantaneous understanding, a kind of awareness that proceeds as though unencumbered by the kinds of defences that order thought in pre-ordained channels."[25] And Myron Bloy calls our attention to the "growth among today's young of what Eliade in *The Sacred and the Profane* calls the 'ontological obsession' of primitive man. Eliade argues that 'for the non-religious man of the modern age, the cosmos has become opaque, inert, mute; it transmits no message, it holds no cipher' but for religious man 'life is not possible without an opening toward the transcendent [because] the cosmos 'lives' and 'speaks.' "[26]

The primitive pieties move the mind in a profound way: We must not forget that if the great ideas of western culture are "formulated" in "systematic thought" this systematic thought is the means by which a highly developed culture keeps the primitive issues and concerns before it. Life and death, love, honor, the transcendent—that "created reality," in Trilling's phrase, that is specifically human and that embraces the awesomeness of creation—are thus kept.[27] It is by these concerns that the Counter Culture people are, body and soul, "turned on." It is important,

24. Needleman, "Winds from the East," 189.
25. Jonathan Eisen, *The National Catholic Reporter,* September 24, 1969.
26. Myron Bloy, "The Counter-Culture—It Just Won't Go Away," *Commonweal,* 95 (October 8, 1971), 29–34.
27. "The ultimate questions of conscious and rational thought about the nature of man and his destiny match easily in the literary mind with the dark *un*conscious and with the most primitive of human relationships." Lionel Trilling, *The Liberal Imagination,* 284. We may ponder Alfred North Whitehead's statement that "great ideas often enter reality in strange guises and with disgusting alliances." Cited in C. Vann Woodward, "What Became of the 1960's?" *The New Republic,* 171, (November 9, 1974), 18.

then, to note that it is a *kind* of concept of intellect that the Counter Culture—however unwittingly—is turned on by, the kind that the Technocracy is built upon. It is turned off by the quantifying and measuring intellect that expresses "objective consciousness" by confining itself to purely "operational concepts," concepts whose meaning is restricted to representing particular operations and actions. Protesting this concept of intellect and affirming the other, Mitchell Goodman says, "We are not against 'reason'; we are for *feeling intelligence.*"[28]

It is precisely the discovery that all existence is mysteriously infused with life that has precipitated the "ontological obsession" among the young. It is curious indeed that after the proclamation of "the death of God" and the inauguration of "the secular city" this concern for the sacred should have become so strong among the young. Although drugs contributed toward the sense of mystery by breaking "through the traditional culture's linear time and geometric space"[29] the drug culture is being replaced by a profoundly religious attitude toward the whole of nature. In this regard Myron Bloy asks us to

consider the recent works of Bob Dylan, George Harrison, Arlo Guthrie, and John Lennon and, of course the rock operas *Tommy* and *Jesus Christ Superstar.* Consider also the rhetoric of the Counter culture young in which a far more mysterious cosmos is consistently assumed than is true for the secular establishment: for example, 'vibrations' or 'vibes' emanate from persons, places and situations which betray their demonic or sacred character. . . . Furthermore, and this is the second, the negative cause, the failure in several major respects of the progressive, rationalistic culture to deliver on its claim to solve whatever ails man has given additional support to the possibility of seeing life as a mystery. The successful resistance of peasants to the organized terror of our military-industrial complex and of nature to our rapacious digging and delving have been prophetic voices from beyond, from a cosmos we had assumed was nothing but a bland backdrop for our struttings.[30]

This extraordinary element of the Counter Culture revolution is not overlooked in Professor Morgenthau's description of our "fractured democracy":

The decline of official government, both in general, and in its democratic form, has still another consequence, *transcending the confines of politics.* In

28. Mitchell Goodman, "The Nature and Dynamics of the Movement," *The Movement Toward a New America,* (Philadelphia, 1970), 1x.
29. Bloy, "The Counter-Culture—It Just Won't Go Away," 33.
30. *Ibid.*

a secular age men all over the world have expected and worked for salvation through the democratic republic or the classless society of socialism
rather than through the kingdom of God. Their expectations have been
disappointed. The charisma of democracy, with its faith in the rationality
and virtue of the masses, has no more survived the historic experience of
mass irrationality and the excesses of fascism and of the impotence and
corruption of the democratic governments, than the charisma of Marxism-
Leninism has survived the revelations of the true nature of Communist
government and the falsity of its eschatological expectations. *No new political faith has replaced the ones lost.* There exists then a broad and deep
vacuum where their was once a firm belief and expectation, presumably
derived from rational analysis.[31]

There is a broad and deep vacuum to be filled by a new faith,
or—to change the metaphor—there is a ladder to be built by which
to climb to a higher reality. And Bloy—to refer to him once again—
makes an observation strikingly similar to that made in 1958 by
William Barrett: that in our contemporary culture "the movement
of the spirit is *no longer vertical but horizontal.*" This is similar to the
statement made in 1971 by Trilling, that the movement is indeed
"downward . . . through all the cultural superstructures to some
place where all movement ends, and begins."[32] For Bloy concludes
his essay with the following remark:

When established spiritual assumptions and their cultural constructs collapse, *and when the flat surface of existence opens up to unimagined depths,* then
the self, frightened by the threat of chaos but, nevertheless exulting in
the discovery of an unexplored spiritual cosmos, must give absolute priority to establishing a secure spiritual identity.[33]

The "ontological obsession" of the Counter Culture is wholly at
odds with the Enlightenment teaching that the cosmos is unjus-
tifiably credited with a kind of "reason," that the nature of man,
meeting nature in the cosmos half-way finds its own essence to be
equally opaque, inert, mute, transmitting no message, holding no
cipher. On the contrary, the Counter Culture takes nature to be a
kind of "reason" put into it by the divine art—to use a phrase of
Aquinas which follows closely the argument of Aristotle in the
second book of the *Physics.* The cosmos is taken to be a function
of man, the beings below him considered to be open to one another, constituting in their ascension toward man a drive more

---

31. Morgenthau, "The Decline of Democratic Government," 18. Italics added.
32. See above, note 15. Cf. William Barrett, *Irrational Man* (Garden City, N.Y.,
1962), 49. Italics added.
33. Bloy, "The Counter-Culture—It Just Won't Go Away," 33–34.

and more determinate and powerful, culminating in the human consciousness.[34] The Counter Culture is engaged in an *upward thrust* from the point of almost non-being to which the Enlightenment principles had led us. The "movement" is described by Peter Marin as "a force coming up out of the unconscious, from the gods . . . divinities whose honor we have neglected."[35]

Given the history of modern culture, the task of recovering the fullness of life must indeed be so strenuous and radical that it should not surprise us to find it filled with ambivalences. For it moves from the "stoned pattern" of the drug culture in which the individual has empathy with the pure exteriority of the primeval cosmos—an inability to apprehend anything and to reflect on anything—to the "stoned pattern" that is along the lines of instantaneous understanding and is derived now from a sense of "interiority" that characterizes the highest kind of intellectual contemplation. The *upward thrust* is from the point where all movement ends, and begins (the lifeless Technocracy, the primeval cosmos) *in the direction of interiority*—of self-movement, of sensation, of life. If the stoned pattern is founded on drugs, behind the drugs "there is a new sexuality, and behind the new sexuality a new body and soul awareness that persists in flowing toward new . . . life styles."[36] It is, indeed, like a return from the dead: The phenomenon is reflected in the curious names of the rock music groups— "The Grateful Dead," "The Rolling Stones." Joseph Arntz has remarked that the Counter Culture's attitude toward sex is pre-conventional *"because [the] return to a direct experience of life means a return to the body as the point of entry into the world."*[37] "I see the Movement, then," says Mitchell Goodman, "as primitive culture. . . . It is primitive at least in the sense that it involves a return to sensation, to the living body and its senses, its capacity for feeling and imagining the life in others—that state in which a man knows again, 'at first hand,' through his own energies, the pos-

34. In by book, *The Structure of Political Thought,* I wrote, "[W]e must take careful note of the fact that the purely natural and the purely animal 'love' of the . . . good implies a profound participation of nature in intelligence: for it involves a movement toward a universal end, and universal forms cannot be received by non-rational natures." That is why nature was traditionally understood to be a "substitute intelligence"—a "reason" put into things by the Divine Art.

35. Goodman, "The Nature and Dynamics of the Movement," viii.

36. Eisen, *The National Catholic Reporter,* September 24, 1969.

37. Joseph Arntz, "Is There a New Openness to the Church's Charismatic Testimony?" *Perspectives of a Political Ecclesiology,* Johannes B. Metz, ed. (New York, 1971), 87.

sibilities of life."[38] Primitive, yes; but, Goodman continues: "[I]n what sense a 'culture'?"

I see the people of the Movement as New Americans, who recognize that the old America is destroying itself. They see the necessity, then to make a new culture: To *make it new*, because what we now have is not a culture at all but a mechanism for commerce and war, embellished with certain 'refinements' like museums and symphony orchestras, energized by money. A culture is a live organism: a body of thought, of things, of forms that sustain life, nurture it.[39]

These words of Goodman are reminiscent of the ancient and forgotten denotation of the word polity. In saying that "what we have now is not a culture at all but a mechanism for commerce and war," that "a culture is a live organism, a body of thought, of things, of forms that sustain life, nurture it," he suggests the distinction drawn by Aristotle between the aims that make a state and the aims that do not:

[I]f men met and associated out of regard for wealth only . . . the oligarchical doctrine would then be seen to carry the day. . . . But a state exists for the sake of a good life, and not for the sake of life only. . . . Nor does a state exist for the sake of alliance and security from injustice, nor yet for the sake of exchange and mutual intercourse; for, then . . . all those who have commercial treaties with one another would be citizens of one state. . . .

Again, if men dwelt at a distance from one another, but not so far off as to have no intercourse, and there were laws among them that they should not wrong each other in their exchanges, neither would this be a state. . . . Why is this? Surely not because they are at a distance from one another; for even supposing that such a community were to meet in one place, but that each man had a house of his own, which was in a manner his state, and that they made alliance with one another, but only against evildoers, still an accurate thinker would not deem this to be a state, if their intercourse with one another was of the same character after as before their union. It is clear then that a state is not a mere society, having a common place, established for the prevention of mutual crime and for the sake of exchange. These are conditions without which a state cannot exist; but all of them together do not constitute a state, which is a community of families and aggregations of families in well-being, for the sake of a perfect and self-sufficing life . . . Hence arise in the cities family connexions, brotherhoods, common sacrifices, amusements which draw men together. But these are created by friendship, for the will to live together is friendship. The end of the state is the good life, and these are the means toward it. And the state is the union of families and villages

---

38. Goodman, "What's Happening?" *The Movement Toward a New America*, viii.
39. *Ibid.*

in a perfect and self-sufficing life, by which we mean a happy and honorable life.[40]

The prominence of the body, of sensuality—of the sense of touch, of the things "which draw men together"—is the surest sign of the Counter Culture's search for the roots of intellect that have been neglected since the Enlightenment. It is important to recall the prominent place that Aristotle assigned to the sense of touch in all areas of culture. Suggesting an Aristotelian counterpart of the Cartesian "*Cogito, ergo sum*," ("I think, therefore I am"), Charles de Koninck unabashedly offers "*Sedeo, ergo sum*," ("I am sitting, therefore I am"). In his article on the subject of the sense of touch and the effects of its repudiation in our philosophy, our art, and our politics, de Koninck recalls for us the profound intellectual role assigned to it in Aristotle's teaching.[41] Touch is the most basic of our senses, and is *par excellence*, the sense of certitude. "*It is the sense of existence, of reality, of substance, of nature, of experience and of sympathy.*"[42] All these kinds of awareness have shrivelled away in the contemporary culture of the Technocracy. They have fallen away because of the neglect of this very sense of touch which is so prized by the people of the Counter Culture. We may note here, too, that in drawing the distinction between the "proper sensibles"—namely, objects that are proper to one sense and cannot be perceived by another (as color is perceived by the eye, not heard or touched, warmth and hardness are felt by the sense of touch, and neither seen nor heard—and the "common sensibles"—the objects which can be perceived by at least more than one sense—Aristotle draws attention to the fact that the common sensibles are movement, magnitude, number, figure or shape: all either quantity or quantitative modes. Now the knowledge recognized as valid and significant for the Establishment culture is, in contrast to the Counter Culture's inclination, confined to what can be expressed in quantitative modes.

If to be sure it is the sense of sight and not touch that is the sense *par excellence* of knowledge, it is nonetheless the case that the sense of touch has a quality in virtue of which it is the most important of man's external senses. For the sense of touch is the ultimate criterion of reality, of physical existence. Whenever we

40. Aristotle, *Politics*, Book III, 9, 1280a26–1281a.
41. Charles de Koninck, "Sedeo, ergo sum—Considerations of the Touchstone of Certitude," *Laval Théologique et Philosophique*, VI (#2, 1950), 343–348.
42. *Ibid.*, 343. Italics added.

wish to assure ourselves of the reality of something, of the existence of a sensible object, we want to verify it by touching it. It is for this reason especially that touch is called the sense of certitude, while sight is the sense of distinction, of clarity, and of representation. Where the fact of physical existence is involved, sight, notwithstanding its accuracy of discernment, yields less assurance than touch. "Phantoms" and "ghosts" are things visual indeed, and yet unreal, intangible, and we compare them to the kind of things that present themselves to us in dreams.

Although the sense of touch reveals little in the order of representation, it is, in Aristotle's psychology, considered to be *"the sense of intellect"*: it is, he tells us, by reason of the exactness of its discrimination in the human species that "man is the most intelligent of all animals."[43] The qualities we know by touch are, to us, the first principles of thought and action. This position is obviously very much down to earth. As Mitchell Goodman says, "We are for a *feeling intelligence*."[44] Philosophical thought from the time of the Enlightenment—of which Descartes is a prime example[45]—led quite logically to a "senseless liquidation of the human substance." As de Koninck points out:

[I]f there is a sense by which we feel ourselves within ourselves and distinct from other things about us, surely it is in the sense of touch. I begin down there and end up here. . . .
Touch, again, is the sense of experience. Experience involves passivity, and this sense is the most passive of all. Physical pain is associated with touch. This makes it at the same time the sense of sympathy. . . . If, to us, the other fellow merely has the existence of a purely visual object, we may be inclined to view him in a cold, detached, objective manner. . . . We might have no sympathy with *his* life. This kind of objectivity is surely a useful quality in the Commissar.[46]

43. Aristotle, *De Anima*, II, 9, 421a22–23.
44. Goodman, "The Nature and Dynamics of the Movement," ix.
45. "Confining himself to 'clear and distinct ideas,' [Descartes] reduces the external world to extension and modes of extension, to figure and movement. He expressly denies the reality of the proper sensibles; only what are called 'primary qualities'—which we term 'common sensibles'—are real. In his view, there are no such things as animals in the usual sense of the word. They are automatons, mechanisms; and even the human body is but a mechanical complex which our mind steers about like a buggy. Indeed the whole universe of what are called living bodies is no more than a machine, though comparatively involved. Quite logically, Descartes expels final causality from nature and consequently also the good—the idea of which is first conveyed to us by touch and taste." de Koninck, "Sedeo, ergo sum," 347.
46. *Ibid.*, 346.

This objectivity is also useful for the kind of behavioral scientist who views man as part of "homologous processes" that abstract from the real individuals making up political life; this kind of scientist wants to go back to the "particles" out of which, he tells us, "all social behavior is formed."[47] Where do we find here that "will to life together which is friendship" and which Aristotle had maintained is the internal creative force of society? The pernicious imbalance in our thoroughly bureaucratized political society has come about precisely from the loss of the sense of touch:

> [W]e now consider the community almost exclusively in terms of structure—something prevailingly visual. Formerly society was defined *in terms of the good* . . . *the idea of which is first conveyed to us by touch and taste.* . . . Now [society] is mainly correlations and functions. . . . Government becomes abstract and remote; it becomes a system.[48]

In contemporary social science Hobbes's ambition "to insinuate and impose upon men . . . a vocabulary of ethics, law, and politics entirely neutral in tone" has been fully achieved.[49] Conduct has become "the plotted curve of behavior." We have been told that the aim of social science is "to bring into being a democratic equilibrium in societal relations in which deviations are promptly rectified."[50] This can be accomplished in the way in which, by constructing a machine, we might "build in a set of servo-mechanisms which perform [the] re-stabilizing operation."[51] This Lasswellian political prescription is the apotheosis of Hobbes's prescription for insinuating and imposing upon men a vocabulary of politics entirely neutral in tone "which will serve as an anaesthetic to quiet the mutinous passions."[52]

47. David Easton, "The Current Meaning of Behavioralism," in James C. Charlesworth (ed.) *Contemporary Political Analysis* (New York, 1967), 24.

48. De Koninck, "Sedeo, ergo sum," 348. It is one merit of Marcuse's diagnosis of our social illness that he perceives the importance of our disregard for what he calls "radical sensibility." He explains "radical sensibility" in terms that suggest the Aristotelian principles we have been reviewing: ' "Radical sensibility': the concept stresses the active, constitutive role of the senses in shaping reason. . . . Our world emerges not only in the pure forms of time and space, but also, and *simultaneously,* as a totality of sensuous qualities—object not only of the eye . . . but *all* human senses (hearing, smelling, touching, tasting). It is this . . . pre-conscious constitution of the world of experience . . . which must change radically if social change is to be radical, qualitative change." *Counter Revolution and Revolt* (Boston, 1972), 63.

49. Norman Jacobson, *Hobbes as Creator* (New York, 1971), 3.

50. Harold D. Lasswell, *The Political Writings of Harold D. Lasswell* (New York, 1951), 513–514.

51. *Ibid.*

52. Jacobson, *Hobbes as Creator.*

Wholly in revolt against this kind of objectivity is the view of the Counter Culture. In "The Nature and Dynamics of the Movement," Mitchell Goodman writes:

Immediacy of feeling. Immediacy of experience. Impelled by conscience, by conviction, by a vision of what life might be. *Love* the young have called it. And have heard the sneers of those who 'have no options, no sense of alternative or growth' (Marin). What do they mean by *love*? I think they mean a quality of attention to each other, to all that is around them. Through the senses—an appetite, a reverence, love of life, of living things, of what's held in common. A sharing, a communion, a community. . . . Members one of another.[53]

Is it to be wondered at that the Counter Culture insists that "a revolutionary is not merely one who tries to make political changes; *he is out to change the meaning of the word politics.*"[54] He is out to change a vocabulary of politics entirely neutral in tone.

"[T]o change the meaning of the word politics," says Goodman. But how can this change come about? We have spoken of Aristotle's idea of the state as a *communication*—a community of friends for the sake of a good and noble life, and we have taken note of the closeness of the Counter Culture's idea of community to this classical conception. Now we may also note that the "ontological obsession" of the Counter Culture young people—their concern for the sacred, for "divinities whose honor we have neglected"— is not unrelated to the new feeling for community. Kenneth Keniston, alluding to the appearance among the young of more communal forms of human existence, relates this development to the concern for the sacred. As Myron Bloy presents it: "[Keniston] sees a 'universalization of identity' in which primary self-identity is communal rather than isolate—in which, for example, personal salvation is understood to be inextricably bound up with that of Vietnamese peasants and ghetto children rather than with career success."[55] And here, again, a remark of Aristotle profoundly joins regard for the sacred with community life. For Aristotle says that if the good is the same for a single man and for a whole community, the good for a whole community of men is *"more godlike."*[56] He calls it "more godlike" because it is a more perfect likeness of the good of the entire universe and of the ultimate essential good-

---

53. Goodman, *The Movement Toward a New America*, viii.
54. *Ibid.*, ix.
55. Bloy, "The Counter Culture—It Just Won't Go Away," 30.
56. Aristotle, *Ethics*, I, 2, 1094b8–10.

ness which draws all things to itself. Aristotle thinks of man as sharing proportionately in the activity of God by being the cause of goodness in all that exists. There is, then, in the thought of Aristotle an element that transcends the confines of politics and serves to sustain and perfect the whole of political life.[57]

Finally we must return to the suggestion made by a number of students of the Counter Culture that the "stoned pattern" of the drug culture and its sexuality betoken a "new body and soul awareness that persists in flowing toward new . . . life styles"[58]— that upward thrust from the point where all movement ends, and begins, in the direction of *interiority*, of self-movement, of sensation, of life. All these considerations seem to point not only toward a new meaning of the word politics, but toward, indeed, a consequence which transcends the confines of politics by carrying us toward a form of contemplation that passes into practice. A new religious consciousness appears to be taking the place of the dead faith in secular democracy and the dead faith in Marxism—the need for which, as we have seen, Hans Morgenthau takes account of. But this demands a further exploration of the notion of *interiority* which is at the root of the Counter Culture's "life style," and which more than anything else distinguishes the Movement from the surface existence in the lifeless Technocratic culture. It is this further exploration into the notion of *interiority* that will lead us to the new consciousness and its significance for political renewal.

57. These considerations transcend the confines of politics because none of them are required for citizenship. See: Charles N. R. McCoy, "The Value-Free Aristotle and the Behavioral Sciences," *The Western Political Quarterly*, XXIII (March 1970), 57–73 (above, Chapter 8).

58. Eisen, *National Catholic Reporter*, September 24, 1969.

12. The Counter Culture: Its Place in the History of Political Thought

[This second essay on the Counter Culture (also written between 1970 and 1975) takes up and deepens the general theme of the previous chapter. Probably no single essay of Charles N. R. McCoy deals with as many of his basic themes as this one. He was concerned to trace the lineage of ideas in political philosophy. Central is the place of post-Aristotelian political philosophy. The "a-political" nature of this philosophy has two forms, one which had become the established liberal view and the second, represented by the Counter Culture, which sought to return to some of the more anti-political notions of the post-Aristotelian systems. McCoy was intellectually convinced that Marx understood the direction and nature of this post-Aristotelian system and indeed sought to bring it to perfection in his own peculiar manner. Contained within this discussion is the subtle relation of thought to being which McCoy always argued must be clarified, since the development of modern political philosophy had almost succeeded in replacing given being with its own intelligible structure, with the being found in an intellect presupposed to no order. McCoy sees in the Counter Culture a confused effort to restore the actual relationships of given beings. The place of classical metaphysics in re-establishing the meaning of the practical sciences and the order of actual being is McCoy's contribution to understanding the meaning of the Counter Culture.]

The meaning of the Counter Culture is, of course, ambiguous. I shall attempt to move toward a resolution of the ambiguity by considering two related alternative interpretations: (1) the Counter Culture is a coming full circle, through the centuries, of the early philosophies of withdrawal and protest of the Hellenistic-Roman world; (2) the Counter Culture—despite surface resemblances with the ancient philosophies of withdrawal and protest—points the way to principles other than those that characterized the early movements.

166

With regard to the first alternative: the present-day "Establishment" is the heir of the eighteenth-century political philosophies and is the *political* expression (as the Carlyles and other historians of political thought have shown) of the *a-political* principles of the post-Aristotelian philosophies of withdrawal and protest; hence, the dissolution of the Establishment, implicit in the Counter-Cultural revolution, may be read directly as a return to the radical origins of the Establishment. On this reading the Counter Culture is indeed a paradigm of the Establishment against which it protests.

Regarding the second alternative (which is not altogether incompatible with the first) we may note that it is supported by the fact that the Counter Culture, as a repudiation of the *political* outcome (embodied in the Establishment) of its radical a-political origins, points toward other principles of life in society. The "life style" of the Counter Culture, which at first glance appears to express Rousseau's "sweetest natural sentiments"—that "sentiment of being" at whose expense the morality of the State is said by Rousseau to have been purchased[1]—may possibly rather be interpreted in the light of that "poverty of existence" evocative of both Heidegger and Marx, and may signal the Heideggerian "call" which, he tells us, opens up the lifeless world of our Technocratic culture to the "world-creating impulse of the spirit."[2] On this reading, the Counter Culture, unlike the early philosophies of withdrawal and pro-

---

1. Compare Professor Allan Bloom's remarks: "Rousseau resisted the temptations to which his successors succumbed. Because he was aware that man's morality was purchased at the sacrifice of his sweetest natural sentiments and is partly only a means to the preservation of the state, he did not try to absolutize that mortality to the exclusion of all else that is human." In *A History of Political Philosophy*, eds. Leo Srauss and Joseph Cropsey (Chicago, 1963), 533. In the "withering away of the State," Marx may be said to have tried to "absolutize" man's sweetest natural sentiments; and the "one-dimensional society" of mature industrialism—both Marxist and Capitalist—accomplishes the "withering away of the State" in behalf, too, it may be said, of "man's sweetest natural sentiments."

2. The "crux of the matter" of authenticity, Heidegger tells us, is the masquerading of spirit as intelligence: "The spirit falsified into intelligence falls to the level of a tool in the service of others." *An Introduction to Metaphysics* (Garden City, N.Y., 1961), 38. Spirit is to be found neither in "the regulation and domination of the material conditions of production" nor in "the intelligent ordering and explanation of everything that is present and already posited at any time" (*ibid.*, 38–39). Werner Brock in his commentary on Heidegger's essay "What Is Metaphysics?" remarks that Heidegger's vision and outlook in delineating man's experience of 'nothingness' has in its favor its evocation of the beginning of *Genesis*. Martin Heidegger, *Existence and Being*, with an Introduction by Werner Brock (Chicago, 1949), 215.

test, is calling for a new society, qualitatively different from that of the Establishment and its principles.

I have said that these two quite different interpretations are not entirely incompatible. In the *Notes and Comment* column for May 13, 1972, the editors of *The New Yorker* magazine make a remark whose elucidation gives the remark itself a quite unexpected turn. The editors observe that "the dominant note in any sane contemporary political philosophy should be a spirit of conservatism," but they immediately go on to say that this spirit of conservatism does not today, as it did in the past, embrace the preservation of the established political order. "It should be plain that a true conservatism today would have nothing to do with what now passes for conservatism in the United States. . . . Our most powerful institutions . . .—and the 'conservatives' who give them unquestioning support—are the forces of extreme radicalism." These institutions are said by the editors to be forces of extreme radicalism because they subvert a political order that—quoting Burke— the editors say "works after the pattern of nature" and "a political system [that] is placed in a just correspondence and symmetry with the order of the world. . . ." A genuine conservatism "would ask the State and all other human institutions to approach the whole of creation with . . . awe and solicitude." Contrary to this philosophy, our American "conservatism" defies any just correspondence with the order of the world and approaches nothing in nature with "awe and solicitude." It threatens us with "radiation which can corrupt the gene pool and destroy the very frame of man; . . . with the sheer explosive force of nuclear weapons which . . . would be great enough to kill every human being; . . . with pollution which destroys the land, the sea, the air, our plants and animals."

If the established institutions are indeed forces of extreme radicalism, then, it would seem, the Counter-Cultural revolution may be understood to be a conservative movement. And just as the extreme radicalism of the Establishment refers only reductively to political and economic structures while it refers primarily and at root to an attitude toward the whole of nature, so the Counter-Cultural revolution may be taken to be aiming at the resuscitation of a conservative view of nature, at approaching the whole of creation "with awe and solicitude." To understand how profound is the conservatism which the Counter Culture may be nurturing we must first inquire into the genesis of the extreme radicalism which it opposes.

The core principle of the post-Aristotelian philosophies of conduct to which the Establishment traces its ultimate philosophical origins was an active rejection of the mundane reality which was felt to stand between man and his liberty. There is no change in political theory so startling in its completeness, Carlyle tells us, as the change from the classical Greek philosophies to the later philosophical views of the Hellenistic-Roman world. It is here that "we are indeed at the beginnings of a theory of human nature and society of which the 'Liberty, Equality, and Fraternity' of the French Revolution is only the present-day expression."[3] The character of all the post-Aristotelian philosophies of conduct is suitably suggested in Professor Catlin's description of early Stoicism:

Stoicism . . . asserted as central in its philosophy that Man, autonomous in his Will, was master of his soul and hence captain of his fate. The right to suicide—in the final need, the right to turn the keys of the portals of death—was at once a theoretical concession and a practical corollary. . . . The resolve to do nothing save on one's own moral choice and at one's own will, was the core of the philosophy.[4]

The Stoic principle of the autonomy of the human reason was curiously unlike everything that the Greek classical philosophers had to say about man, whom they regarded as the most dependent and uncertain of intelligent creatures. The "rights" asserted for man in the philosophies of conduct strangely free the *form* of human life from all determinations. In Aristotle's view the form of human life is made determinate and complete through (good) acts, habits, laws and institutions—all manifestations of self-government; for Plato the "natural justice" reveals itself to man in his study of the order of the cosmos.[5] The early Stoic concept of self-

---

3. R. W. and A. J. Carlyle, *A History of Mediaeval Political Theory in the West* (Edinburgh and London, 1930), I, 9.

4. George Catlin, *The Story of the Political Philosophers* (New York, 1939), 105.

5. There is indeed an affinity between the early Stoic and the Platonic ideas of natural right as well as between the revised Stoicism of Cicero and Seneca and the Platonic idea of natural right. "As regards the Stoics, it seems to me that their natural right teaching belongs to the Socratic-Platonic type." Leo Strauss, *Natural Right and History* (Chicago, 1953), 146. I shall treat of this matter later, but for the moment it is enough to stress the difference between the early Stoic assertion of the autonomy and self-sufficiency of man and the Platonic assertion that man must conform to the moral order and pattern of justice in the cosmos in order to fulfill his nature.

sufficiency demanded a "natural right" and a "higher law" that were the expression of a nature that is universal in the sense of being tied to no determinate form: This "higher law" binds only in ensuring the free act of man which creates a world of his own total making. Thus the Stoic teachings on equality and freedom and self-sufficiency define precisely a self-dependent reason which makes one's moral worth depend exclusively on one's own judgment, in merging moral, domestic, and political distinctions "in a far-off dream of the fellowship of cosmopolitan philosophers."

If these ideas strike the reader as the familiar fare of the Counter Culture one must consider the fact—attested to by the great historians of political thought—that they are the inarticulated beginnings, as the Carlyles put it, of the present-day theory of human nature and society of which the "Liberty, Equality, and Fraternity" of the French Revolution is the paradigmatic expression. They were given *political*—and *scientific* political meaning—by the seventeenth- and eighteenth-century theory of the social contract— the theory from which the Establishment ideas of government derive. The special character of seventeenth- and eighteenth-century political philosophy becomes clear, says Cassirer, "if, instead of analyzing its first principles, we look at its general method."[6] And what was this method?

The doctrine of the state-contract becomes in the seventeenth century a self-evident axiom of political thought. . . . This fact marks a great and decisive step. For if we adopt this view, if we reduce the legal and social order to *free individual acts, to a voluntary contractual submission of the governed, all mystery is gone.* . . . If we can trace the state to such an origin, it becomes a perfectly clear and understandable fact.[7]

Professor Sabine agrees that the surpassing importance of the theory of human nature and society in the seventeenth and eighteenth centuries was due not to its content but to its methodology. "The importance [of it] was methodological. . . . It was essentially an appeal to the reason, as the ancient versions had always been, but it gave a precision to the meaning of reason such as it had not had in an equal degree in antiquity."[8] This precision derives from the ascendancy accorded by the social contract theorists to the practical reason over the speculative reason: ". . . if we reduce the legal and social order to free individual acts . . . all mystery is

6. Ernst Cassirer, *The Myth of the State* (New Haven, CT., 1946), 172.
7. *Ibid.*
8. George H. Sabine, *A History of Political Theory* (New York, 1937), 425.

gone. . . . [The state] becomes a perfectly clear and understandable fact."⁹ There is no need to approach "the whole of creation
with awe and solicitude"; rather, we will begin with protest against
the imposition of nature's "authority" and create a world of our
own.

Aristotle had called attention to the speculative reason—that
part of man's reason that considers the natures of things but does
not make them—as "too high for man"; and because of this there
is in man a tendency to accord primacy to what he called the
"practical reason"—the reason concerned with human things,
with morals and art. Now in practical knowledge—insofar as it is
practical and prescinding from its dependence on the speculative
reason—*the intelligence is the measure of its object*. Man *knows* the
nature of the foot; he doesn't *make* it. The "precision" which is
given to reason by the seventeenth- and eighteenth-century theoreticians (to which Sabine alludes) is the independence that is
granted it from the "givenness" of things: Reason will no longer
need to "find" the nature of man and of society; it will make a
world of its own.¹⁰ The idea of contract is well suited to express a
naturalness which demands an innate social propensity which is
raised to the level of a sufficient explanation of social groupings
in such a way as to leave no law to be observed which in any sense
is imposed from without, but to leave only a "natural law" which
the moral subject gives to himself. And in the political theories of
the seventeenth and eighteenth centuries the State, far from having its origin even remotely in the "givenness" of man's nature,
is on the contrary something wholly produced by man who, in the
fashion of the early philosophies of withdrawal, is conceived as
being originally quite independent and "withdrawn." The ethics
of withdrawal and protest assume in this late revival a specifically

9. Cassirer, *The Myth of the State*, 172.
10. The physical universe is at the same time having all mystery removed from
it through the mathematization of physics: "Both [nature and knowledge] must be
understood in terms of their own essence, and this is no dark, mysterious 'something,' impenetrable to intellect; this essence consists rather in principles which are
perfectly accessible to the mind since the mind is able to educe them from itself
and to enunciate them systematically." Ernst Cassirer, *The Philosophy of the Enlightenment* (Boston, 1955), 45. Aristotle had pointed out that the mathematical object
is the object most proportionate to the human intellect; he understood, indeed, the
use of mathematics in physical investigations, but he agreed with Heraclitus (and
as contemporary physicists acknowledge) that "nature loves to hide." He realized
that mathematics cannot lead us directly to the natural object itself any more than
the curved line can express the reality of the snub nose.

political character in the notion of the State arising out of an original "equality of nihilism" and coming into existence by "free individual acts." These are the decidedly novel meanings of "equality," "freedom," "Fraternity," "self-sufficiency" that make the post-Aristotelian period rightly thought of as a turning point in the history of political thought.

The acceptance of these ideas by Marx is equally as hearty as is their acceptance by scholars writing in the tradition of the social contract theorists; but his appreciation of them is more astute. The post-Aristotelian philosophers were, according to Marx, a natural outcome of classical Greek philosophy which "closes itself into a complete, total world" and which thereby forces its heirs to turn against their age. Marx observes that "it is a psychological law that the theoretical mind, when it becomes free in itself, is transformed into practical energy, and as *will* turns against the mundane reality which exists independently of it."[11] This is an important step, but Marx describes it as resulting—in the philosophies of withdrawal and protest—in an intolerable attitude of half-contemplation and half action.[12] Nor, in Marx's estimate, did the bourgeois revolutions and their rights of man, inspired as they were by the revival of post-Aristotelian philosophy, particularly the Stoic conception of the *autarky* of human reason, move effectively beyond the spirit of individual revolt against mundane reality. We are not accustomed to thinking of the Establishment having its origin in this spirit of individual revolt against the mundane reality that exists independently of man's practical will; we are apt, on the contrary, to attribute this spirit of revolt against "reality" to the Counter Culture. But indeed, as the editors of *The New Yorker* point out in the observation to which we have made reference, it is the powerful institutions of the Establishment that subvert a political order that works or ought to work "after the pattern of nature."

The achievement of man's political emancipation in the eighteenth century "constitutes a great progress," Marx says, but it is not "the final form of human emancipation but [only] the last form within the actual social order."[13] He points out that "none of the pretended rights of man goes beyond the egoistic man, man such

---

11. Karl Marx, *Über die Differenzen der demokritischen und epikureischen Naturphilosophie* (Marx-Engels, *Gesamtausgabe*) Sec. I, Vol. I, Pt. I, 1.

12. *Ibid.*, 131.

13. Karl Marx, *Die Judenfrage* (Marx-Engels, *Gesamtausgabe*) Sec. I. Vol. I, Pt. I, 585–86.

as he is, a member of bourgeois society, that is to say, an individual separated from the community, folded back on himself, uniquely preoccupied with his own private interests."[14] The final emancipation of man (which Marx calls "human" as distinguished from "political") can be achieved only with the full resolution of the conflict between the theoretical mind (which, though it has assuredly won its independence from the "givenness" of things, remains frustrated on the practical level) and the mundane reality which exists independently of it. If philosophy is to be made capable of advancing beyond the declarations of the seventeenth- and eighteenth-century philosophers, the division between speculative and practical reason needs to be corrected by transposing into practice an attitude toward the whole of nature implicit in those declarations but not realized by them on "the human plane" and in "real life." This means that far from approaching the whole of creation with awe and solicitude, man must come to see that he *is* all that he knows, that as universal producer he is the act whereby all things are what they are, that, in Marx's famous phrase, man is a "generic being." The seventeenth- and eighteenth-century declarations of independence continue to alienate properly human forces; they leave man separated from the community, from the political community which is allowed to substitute for the generic life of man. Indeed, had not Rousseau purchased the morality of the State at the expense of man's sweetest natural sentiments?[15] For Marx the "real life" of man is that of "universal producer," and it is at the expense of this generic activity that the morality of the State is purchased. The radical independence of man is to be found only on condition that philosophy pass into the world itself as a radical critique, that it be transposed into practice. The conception basic to this final step, and its achievement, is the conception of "objective consciousness."

The notion of "objective consciousness,"[16] implicit in the a-

14. *Ibid.*, 595.

15. See above, note 1. Professor Joseph Cropsey speaks of "Marx's radicalization of Rousseau," and remarks that "Rousseau may be said to have suggested . . . that government may be more and more replaced by society. . . . What in Rousseau was a limited suggestion, although an emphatic one, came to be the dogmatic core of a confident prognosis, a strident propaganda, and a revolutionary incitation in Marx." *A History of Political Philosophy*, 719–20.

16. Theodore Roszak in *The Making of a Counter Culture* speaks of "objective consciousness" as the psychic style cultivated by the Technocratic society and declares it to be the chief enemy of the Counter Culture. This shall be treated below.

political philosophies of the Hellenistic-Roman world, was given explicit and "scientific" formulation by Marx and applied by him to man's role in nature. It derived its psychological basis from Ludwig Feuerbach, to whom Marx expressed his indebtedness. Reducing Hegel's "absolute metaphysical spirit" to the "real man standing on the foundation of nature," Feuerbach had said that

[m]an is nothing without an object. . . . But the object to which a subject essentially, necessarily relates, is nothing else than this subject's own but objective nature. The *absolute* to man is his own nature. The power of the object over him is the power of his own nature. Thus the power of the object of feeling is the power of feeling itself; the power of the object of the intellect is the power of the intellect itself.[17]

One's material individuality, Feuerbach tells us, must not be considered to contract thought to a mode of knowing that is not identical with the plentitude of being: Feuerbach immediately adds, "[D]oes not the subject precede the predicate? The predicate is nothing without a subject; the subject is a human being, a sensate nature."[18] This position implies a consciousness in the material individual man that is "generic" or universal by reason of embracing all objects in and through the knowledge of the self; in Marx's language, all objects henceforth must be seen as the "objectification of man." This is the apotheosis of all past efforts to overcome the mundane reality existing independently of the mind of man, to assert the absolute primacy of man's practical reason over the reason that *knows* but does not *make*.

Consciousness in the strictest sense is present only in a being to whom his species, his essential nature, is an object of thought. . . . But only a being to whom his own species, his own nature, is an object of thought, can make the essential nature of other things or beings an object of thought.
    Consciousness in the strict or proper sense, is identical with consciousness of the infinite; . . . *in the consciousness of the infinite, the infinity of one's own nature is the object of consciousness.*[19]

Feuerbach, as Marx indeed points out, represents an advance over the Enlightenment political philosophies, for these philosophies retained an "idealistic" character: they had achieved an "ideal" generic being—one that existed in the mere order of ideas—through the intermediary of the State:

17. Ludwig Feuerbach, *Das Wesen des Christentums*, in *Sämmtliche Werke* (Stuttgart, 1903), VI, 4.
    18. *Ibid.*, 15.   19. *Ibid.*, 1–3.

The state is the intermediary between man and the liberty of man. Just as Christ is the intermediary whom man charges with all his [own] divinity, with all of his religious limitation, so the State is the intermediary which man charges with all of his humanity, with all of his human limitation. . . .

Consequently, it is by the mediation of the state, it is politically, that man frees himself from a barrier by raising himself above this barrier, in contradiction with himself. . . . *The perfect political state, according to its essence, is the generic life of man by opposition to his material life.* All the suppositions of the egoistic life continue to subsist outside of the political sphere, but as properties of bourgeois society. There, where the state has reached its full development, man leads, not only in his thought, in conscience, but in reality, in life, a double existence, heavenly and earthly, the existence in the political community, where he considers himself a generic being, and the existence in civil society, where he works as a mere part, sees in other men simply means, and becomes the plaything of forces extraneous to himself.[20]

Feuerbach is able to advance beyond these "idealistic" revolutionary political philosophies because he is "not satisfied with abstract thinking": man's generic being is fulfilled in "the real life," in the life of the sensuous, material world.[21] But there remains an inadequacy in Feuerbach's capturing of the material world for man. The criticism that Marx makes of Feuerbach is that his notion of "objective consciousness" abstracts from the historical process and fixes the power of the subject over the object as "passive practise." Feuerbach sees the total philosophical activity of the individual to be nothing but the theoretical form of the sensuous world: "Feuerbach, not satisfied with *abstract thinking,* appeals to *sensuous contemplation,* but he does not conceive sensuousness as a practical human-sensuous activity."[22] Feuerbach did not understand that man's absolute mastery of nature is "not a thing given from all eternity . . . but [rather] the product of industry and of the state of society; and indeed, in the sense that it is an historical product, the result of the activity of a whole succession of generations, each standing on the shoulders of the preceding one, developing its industry and its intercourse . . . modifying its social organization according to the changed needs."[23] When in this way all objects are converted into human objects *they* may be *said*

20. Marx, *Die Judenfrage,* 583 and 595.
21. Marx, "Theses on Feuerbach," No. V. in Engels, *Ludwig Feuerbach and the Outcome of Classical German Philosophy* (New York, 1941), 83.
22. *Ibid.*
23. Marx and Engels, *The German Ideology,* (New York, 1939), 35.

to be the *"objectification"* of man in *real* life, the life of "human-sensuous activity." Contemplation will have passed into practice. The "sense of having," of using and possessing objects, retains a *contemplative* attitude toward objects; this is overcome by its replacement by the "sense of being" (Rousseau's "sweetest natural sentiments" translated, now, to the real world):

The need of the spirit has lost its egoistic nature, and nature has lost its simple utility from the fact that the utility has become a *human utility*.
   From the fact that everywhere in Society the objective reality becomes for man the reality of human forces, human reality, and consequently the reality of his own forces, all *objects* becomes for him the objectification of himself, objects which manifest and realize his individuality, *his* objects, that is to say, the object of himself.[24]

But we must now notice that if the "sense of having" is acquired at the expense of the "sense of being," the recovered "sense of being" is acquired at the expense of every natural object as object. Marcuse has recently pointed out that "in marxism too, nature is predominantly . . . the adversary in man's 'struggle with nature', the field for the ever more rational development of the productive forces."[25] In Marxist society as well as in the "Establishment" society Marcuse observes,

"[C]ommercialized nature . . . deprives man from finding himself in nature, beyond and this side of alienation; it . . . prevents him from recognizing nature as a *subject* in its own right—a subject with which to live in a common human universe. . . . Marx's notion of human appropriation of nature retains something of the *hubris* of domination. 'Appropriation', no matter how human, remains appropriation of a [living] object by a subject. It offends that which is essentially other than the appropriating subject, and which exists precisely as object in its own right—that is, as subject!"[26] The consequence of this attitude for the development of political consciousness is that no concern is felt for "the roots of liberation in individuals, i.e. with the roots of social relationships there where individuals most directly and profoundly experience their world and themselves: in their *sensibility*, in their instinctual needs."[27]

   24. Marx, *Oekonomische-philosophische Manuskript*, 117.
   25. Herbert Marcuse, *Counter Revolution and Revolt* (Boston, 1972), 61–62.
   26. *Ibid.*, 68–69.
   27. *Ibid.*, 62. Here Marcuse appears to return to a Feuerbachian deification of love. Engels tells us that it was Feuerbach's "extravagant deification of love to

We are confronted with an arresting paradox: Marx had criticized Feuerbach's "passive practise" ("sensuous contemplation") for its inability to develop a political consciousness. We now find Marcuse pointing out that the development of political consciousness by the active appropriation of objects neglects "the roots of liberation in individuals" and these are to be found, one may say, by approaching the whole of nature "with awe and solicitude." There is alienation of man both from himself and from nature as well as alienation of nature from herself and in the *hubris* of Marx's "human appropriation" of the object. As Marcuse observes, the "object"—nature—is deprived of its own independent ontological status, and men themselves, treated exclusively in terms of their capacity to "operate" upon and dominate the object are deprived of that in them by which "they most directly and profoundly experience their world and themselves: . . . [their] sensibility." The "precision"—to which I earlier alluded—given to the meaning of reason by the revolutionary political philosophies of the seventeenth and eighteenth centuries has issued in a truncating of human nature.

Apparenatly the *sense of being*, whether taken in the manner of Feuerbach's generic sensuous-contemplative consciousness, issues in a deformed political consciousness. How has it happened that "objective consciousness," finding its new definition of man in "the generic natural relation"—in which, Marx tells us, "[T]he relation of man to nature is directly his relation to man, and the relation of nature to man is his own relation to the origin of his natural determination"[28]—has brought about the contraction of both man and nature?

This consequence appears to come from the loss of intellectual center in the modern theory of man, a loss that was entailed in the effort to free the human mind from a mundane reality existing independently of it. In his *Essay on Man*, while giving general approval to this "liberating" movement—he speaks of it in terms of the "removal of the 'artificial barriers' that had . . . separated the human world from the rest of nature."[29]—Cassirer enters a

---

which 'true socialism' . . . in Germany after 1844 became linked, putting . . . the liberation of mankind by means of 'love' in place of the emancipation of the proletariat through the economic transformation of production." *Ludwig Feuerbach and the Outcome of Classical German Philosophy*, 19.

28. Marx, *Oekonomische-philosophische Manuskript*, 1844 (Marx-Engels *Gesamtausgabe*), Sec. I, Vol. III, 113.

29. Ernst Cassirer, *Essay on Man* (New Haven, 1944), 30.

caveat to his approval by remarking that a consequence of this emancipation has been the "loss of intellectual center" in our theory of man. And the loss of intellectual center left man without any inner resources for directing his life; he lost what David Riesman has called "inner direction" and became henceforth "other directed" by abstract social controls. It has been the intellectual center occupied by man in the variety and multiplicity of natural things that had in the past been relied upon to conquer the centrifugal forces of society. I shall treat of this matter at a later point, for it appears to be at the heart of the Counter-Cultural revolution whose principal enemy, as I have said, is the myth of "objective consciousness."

The loss of intellectual center in the modern theory of man was inevitable because the overcoming of nature as "object" standing over against man and his liberty proscribed treating the various levels of beings on their own terms. It required indeed that man affirm the unity and homogeneity of nature. If the cosmos were to become perfectly accessible to him, and thus perfectly "operable" by him, man had to be considered to be "composed of the same elements and combined according to the same laws" as the rest of nature. As Cassirer puts it, "[N]ature in man, as it were, meets nature in the cosmos half-way and finds its own essence there."[30] Only in this way could nature be treated as the field for the ever more rational development of human productive forces: Nature as object must be pared down to whatever in it is perfectly accessible to the human mind, that is to say, to nature as fundamentally "operable."[31] Making all objects the "objectification" of man means introducing order into the unlimited by transcending the variousness, the heterogeneity of nature's manifestations. In lieu of occupying a central position in the hierarchy of natural things—for man had been thought to be "a little world," to comprise within himself all the degrees of natural being—man and his world were contracted to such operational "natures" as "magnitudes," "numbers," "structures," "systems," "functions."

This "freeing" of man, both theoretically and practically, from a mundane reality existing independently of him, has meant indeed that man has been *disjoined* from reality. Nature has been forced on to a Procrustean bed whereon the distinction between

30. Cassirer, *The Philosophy of the Enlightenment*, 45.
31. See above, note 10.

beings is obliterated.[32] The "humanizing" of nature (a goal altogether worthy of pursuit) has evidently been pursued in the wrong way; it has issued in the dehumanizing of both nature and man. The illusion of overcoming the object so that the power of the object is seen to be the subject's own power (Feuerbach and Marx) is created by the unique character of generic thought, a mode of thought peculiar to the intelligence of man.[33] We may advert to the fact that the very first object of the human mind is some material thing under a concept most indeterminate and confused— the concept of *being* that is common or universal in the sense that it is predicable of whatever has real existence, of whatever *is*. The "object," the material thing of nature, is "overcome"—is seen to be the power of the subject—in the measure that its difference from other objects is surmounted in the vague generality of a common genus which fails to express the nature of anything that *is*. Thus indeed there is a certain adequation between the most indeterminate and confused universal concept and the human intellect: It is the most purely potential concept which best reflects the pure potentiality of the most imperfect of intelligences. This is the ground, we may observe, for Feuerbach saying that in the object man has his own nature—his "objective," "infinite" na-

32. An impressive early modern example of reducing the various levels of beings to a homogeneity and unity of explanation is to be found in Hippolyte Taine's *History of English Literature*. Taine writes: "Here as elsewhere we have but a mechanical problem; the total effect is a result, depending entirely on magnitude and direction of the producing causes. . . . Though the means of notation are not the same in the moral and physical sciences, yet as in both the matter is the same, equally made up of forces, magnitudes, and directions, we may say that in both the final result is produced after the same method." *Histoire de la litterature anglaise*, Intro. English trans. by H. van Laun (New York, 1872), I, 12ff.

33. Speaking of this purely logical universal which has no real existence as a universal, Aristotle remarks: "It is now evident that a general notion can be given of soul only in the same sense as one can be given of figure. For, as in that case there is no figure distinguishable and apart from triangle, etc., so here there is no soul apart from the forms of soul just enumerated. It is true that a highly general definition can be given for figure which will fit all figures without expressing the peculiar nature of any figure. So here in the case of soul and its specific forms. Hence it is absurd in this and similar cases to see a common definition which will fail to express the peculiar nature of anything that *is*. . . . The cases of figure and soul are exactly parallel; for the particulars subsumed under the common name in both cases—figures and living beings—constitute a series, each successive term of which potentially contains its predecessor, e.g., the square the triangle, and the sensory power the self-nutritive. Hence we must ask in the case of each class of living things, What is its soul, i.e., What is the soul of plant, animal, man?" (*De Anima* II, 414b–415a). It is clear then that what we first apprehend is not anything according to the order of nature, i.e., as it actually is in nature.

ture—for object. The infinite object (which is the subject's own power, Feuerbach tells us) is finite only by reason of its pure potentiality; it has no formal termination apart from the specific and individual natures to which being is attached in the real world.

The deformed political consciousness that is a consequence of Feuerbach's doctrine of species-being (or generic being) is brought sharply before us by Marx's overhauling of the doctrine in terms of "sensuous practical activity." For it is clear that Marx's statement that society is "not an abstraction" confronting the individual—the individual life and the species-life are not different[34]—must be understood to mean that man's life in its individuality is not his real life; his real life is his *species-being* and this is the life of social humanity. Just as in Feuerbach's doctrine the individual himself *is* his species, so that there are in him no parts that are not parts of humanity, so, similarly, in Marx's doctrine the individual is himself "socialized humanity" and there is in him nothing not "the result of the activity of a whole succession of generations, each standing on the shoulders of the preceding one, developing its industry and its intercourse, modifying its social organization according to the changed needs."[35] It is in this curious way that Marx conceives the deliverance of the individual from the role of "a mere part . . . swallowed up in the role of a simple means . . . the plaything of forces extraneous to himself."[36] This is the apotheosis and transfiguration of the "withdrawal" and "protest" of the early post-Aristotelian philosophies of conduct which Marx accused of having issued in a frustrated condition of half-contemplation and half-action. It is said to issue here in the "consubstantiality" of the individual's existence and his social existence—contemplation having passed into practice.

It is with vengeance that this teaching overcomes man's need for "having"; the *sense of being*, which replaces the sense of "having," is achieved through the absolute aseity of socialized humanity—the radicalization, alluded to above, of Rousseau's "sweetest natural sentiments." The individual's liquidation itself is carried out by his own "substantial forces," his "essentiality." In describing a play by the German poet Bertolt Brecht, Arthur Koestler shows us the dread facelessness of the new generic man. It deserves quotation at some length:

34. Marx, *Oekonomische-philosophische Manuskript*, 117.
35. Marx and Engels, *The German Ideology*, 35.
36. Marx, *Die Judenfrage*, 583.

The play takes the form of a trial. Three Comintern agents return from a secret mission to China, and explain before a Party tribunal, in the form of flashbacks, why they had been obliged to kill their fourth, young comrade and to throw his body into a lime pit. The tribunal is represented by an anonymous, Greek 'Controlchorus'. The three agents are equally anonymous—they wear masks on their mission, having effaced their personality, their will and feeling, by order of the Party:

'You are no longer yourselves. No longer are you Karl Schmitt of Berlin. You are no longer Anna Kyersh of Kazan, and you are no longer Peter Savich of Moscow. You are without a name, without a mother, blank sheets on which the Revolution will write its orders.

'He who fights for Communism must be able to fight and to renounce fighting, to say the truth and not to say the truth, to be helpful and unhelpful, to keep a promise and to break a promise, to go into danger and to avoid danger, to be known and to be unknown.'

The 'young comrade', however, was unable to live up to this ethical code. He was guilty of four crimes, having successfully fallen into the traps of pity, of loyalty, of dignity and of religious indignation. In the first episode he is described as one of a gang of coolies pulling a boat up the river. He tries to help some exhausted comrades, thereby attracts attention, and the agents have to decamp. In the second episode he comes to the defense of a workman beaten up by the police, with the same result.

In the third, he is sent to negotiate with a representative of the Chinese bourgeoisie, who is willing to arm the revolutionary coolies to get rid of his British competitors. All goes well until the fat bourgeois sings a song in praise of business profits; the young comrade is so disgusted that he refuses to accept food from the bourgeois, and the deal falls through. The moral is driven home by the Controlchorus, who asks the rhetorical question:

Controlchorus: But is it not right to place honor above all?

The Three Agents: No.

Controlchorus: What vileness would you not commit to exterminate vileness? . . . Sink into the mud, embrace the butcher, but change the world: it needs it.

The climax of the play is the fourth episode, in which the young comrade deviates from the Party Line. The line, it should be remembered, was the Stalin-Chiang pact of 1927, one of the most terrible episodes of Comintern history, which led to the wholesale massacre of Chinese Communists by Chiang, and with Stalin's passive complicity. . . . The young comrade in the play refuses to implement that line. He tears up 'the scriptures of the Party classics', and cries out:

'All this no longer has any bearing. At the moment when the fight is on, I reject all that was valid yesterday and do my human duty. My heart bleeds for the Revolution.'

He tears his mask off and shouts to the coolies:

"We have come to help you. We come from Moscow."

So the agents, who 'in the dusk saw his naked face, open, human, guileless,' have to shoot him. But before they do that, they ask the young comrade whether he agrees to be shot. He answers:

'Yes. I see that I have always acted incorrectly. Now it would be better if I were not.'
The three agents: 'Then we shot him and threw him into the lime pit and when the lime had absorbed him we returned to our work.'
Controlchorus: 'Your work has been blest. You have propagated the Principles of the Classics, the ABC of Communism. . . .'[37]

Marx, as we know, had envisioned the achievement of "objective consciousness"—the "achieved consubstantiality of man with nature, the veritable resurrection of nature, the realization of the naturalism of man and the humanism of nature."[38]—as possible only by means of the revolutionary overthrow of all those manifestations of an independent "nature" that the political philosophies of the seventeenth and eighteenth centuries had allowed to stand in civil society and which had stood in the way of man's attaining his generic being in the "real life," (*viz.* the family, religion, law, private property, and the State itself). It is today the common view of social critics that maturing industrialism has become the "ideologically invisible" force that has obliterated the theoretical differences between the bourgeois state and Marx's society. Marx's vision of species-being or generic being of man which resolves the "contradictions" of every hitherto existing society by the overthrow of the capitalist class has been superseded by the ideologically invisible "one-dimensional" view of man which Technological society imposes. As Herbert Marcuse puts it:

Our society distinguishes itself by conquering the centrifugal social forces with Technology [rather] than Terror, on the dual basis of an overwhelming efficiency and an increasing standard of living. . . .
Technical progress, extended to a whole system of domination and coordination, creates forms of life (and of power) which appear to reconcile the forces opposing the system and to defeat or refute all protest

37. Arthur Koestler, *The Invisible Writing* (Boston, 1954), 41–42. "Death," Marx writes (*Die Judenfrage*, 583), "appears as a hard victory of the species over the individual, and seems to contradict the unity of the species; but the determinate individual is only a determinate generic being, and as such he is mortal. Each of his human relationships . . . is in its objective relationship . . . the appropriation of [the] object, the appropriation of human reality. This manifestation is as multiple as are *human determinations and activities*, human *activity* and human *suffering*, for suffering, taken in the human sense, is a pleasure proper to man."
38. Marx, *Oekonomische-philosophische Manuskript*, 116. But the individual is his "essentiality" is "the product of industry and of the state of society . . . the result of the activity of a whole succession of generations, each standing on the shoulders of the preceding one." (Marx and Engels, *The German Ideology*, 35.) So that the individual's mortality is indeed not only quite indifferent to his real (species) life but rather contributes to it! The comrade agrees to be shot.

in the name of the historical prospects of freedom from toil and domination. . . . This containment of social change is perhaps the most singular achievement of advanced industrial society. . . .[39]

We have seen how in Marx's version of "generic being" Terror surmounts the contrarieties of existence: as we find them in the passions and actions of individual men they are "overcome" by one's generic self's agreement that one's individual self be shot! The science of the Technocracy overcomes these contrarieties without shooting. The ideological point of connection between Technology and Terror is that both are efforts to find a "system" or "method" that will quell the passions and appetites of men, that will substitute itself for the substantive problems of political life by imposing itself as the sufficient reason for all that goes on in the world.

We have taken notice of Marx's criticism of the seventeenth- and eighteenth-century political philosophies: that they had failed to achieve the individual's generic being in the "real" life; that, on the contrary, they had separated the individual from the community. These political philosophies had achieved an "ideal" generic being for man through the "intermediary" of the State: "The perfect political state, according to its essence, is the generic life of man by opposition to his material life."[40] Marx points out that "none of the pretended rights of man goes beyond the egoistic man, man such as he is, a member of bourgeois society, that is to say an individual separated from the community, folded back on himself, uniquely preoccupied with his own private interests."[41] The overcoming of nature as "object" standing between man and his liberty—"objective consciousness"—was not achieved in the real world by these philosophies. The "natural rights" philosophies had, to be sure, proceeded from the principle of the unity and homogeneity of nature, and had affirmed that man and the rest of nature are "composed of the same elements and combined according to the same laws." These philosophies had, then, established the foundation upon which the whole of nature could become "operable" by man. But whereas for Marx, human nature, meeting nature in the cosmos half-way and finding its own essence there, had meant that "my *theoretical* existence as a social being [is] the theoretical form of that of which the living form is *real*

---

39. Marcuse, *One-Dimensional Man* (Boston, 1969), x, xii.
40. Marx, *Die Judenfrage*, 595.
41. Cited above, note 13.

common matter,"[42] for the British philosophical tradition it came to mean cutting the connection that former ages had believed existed between the "reason" that is nature, the "reason" that is the cause of nature, and human reason.[43] This is a process that is the reverse of Marx's. Here man's knowing powers will be reduced—traced back, as it were—from the knowledge of universal or generic being to experience, memory, and mere sensation. The way to "objective consciousness" will have to lie, for this tradition, in some device other than that of generic thought.

While objective consciousness for Marx is something sought in terms of the real identity of individual and social life (the generic life of man and his individual life are not different)[44] the tradition of British philosophy is different. It begins with the achievement of objective consciousness through some intermediary—either that of the State, or later, after Locke, that of the more skillful accumulators of wealth—but, it will end by closing the gap between the intermediary and the individual. An adumbration—more than an adumbration—of this technique is to be found in the political theory of Hobbes, as Norman Jacobson has shown:

[T]here is . . . a feature of [Hobbes'] thought that has scarcely received attention at all. I refer to Hobbes' scheme not only for suppressing the outward expression of anti-social passions, but for stilling those very passions. . . . If we could but know 'the nature of human actions' as distinctly as we know 'the nature of quantity in geometrical figures,' the strength of avarice and ambition . . . would presently faint and languish; and mankind would enjoy immortal peace. . . .

If a vocabulary of ethics, law, and politics entirely neutral in tone may be insinuated and imposed upon men—insinuated into their thoughts and imposed upon their speech—it might serve as an anesthetic to quiet the mutinous passions. . . .

A further point. Unlike the rhetoric of theology or of classical political philosophy or heroic poetry, the rhetoric of Hobbes is itself ideally suited to the task. It is, above all, neutral. Men presumably do not come to blows over geometrical theorems. . . . Henceforth, to discuss politics would be to discuss geometry. 'The skill of making and maintaining Commonwealths consisteth in certain rules, as doth arithmetic and geometry. . . .'

---

42. Italics in original. "Real common matter," through the operation of the dialectic comes to mean, in its social expression, "the real community," or "socialized humanity." The quotation is from *Oekonomische-philosophische Manuskript*, 116.

43. These various "reasons" are what Ernst Cassirer refers to when he speaks of Enlightenment thought having removed "the artificial barriers which had hitherto separated the human world from the rest of nature." *Essay on Man*, 30.

44. Cited above, note 34.

To discuss politics is to become objective and remote, a neutral rather than a heated disputant.[45]

There is no need for shooting here. The mathematical way will supersede the generic way of thought, and the mathematical way of thought will close the gap between the "ideal" generic life led through the intermediary of State or economic class and the real individual. Thanks to David Hume's critique of nature, order, and causality, science is reduced to the service of tool, and the tool is mathematics.

David Hume pretended to prove what was already implicit in Locke: that there are no universal and necessary reasons in nature, that the universal ideas that Locke had admitted as being "nothing but the capacity they are put to, by the understanding, of signifying or representing many particulars" have no root in reality. The test of utility for any political and moral action, for every law and institution henceforth came to lie in no relation whatsoever to any "natural law" such as Hobbes and Locke had assumed. With the elimination of the "reason" that traditional philosophy had attributed to nature's operations, law as "an ordinance of reason" for the proper human good disappears entirely. Thus liberated, politics will find its leading principle in the mere fact of regularity of behavior—measurable, indeed, but no longer recognized for what it had always been taken to be, namely a *sign* of some determinate reason. Proceeding henceforth from a concept of nature that reduces it to a merely temporary sense of "that which happens always or for the most part," political actions, laws, and institutions will no longer be subject to "understanding" but only to more or less elaborate descriptions and measurements. It is not to be

45. Norman Jacobson, *Hobbes as Creator* (New York, 1971), 3, 13. In the editorial in *The New Yorker* earlier alluded to, the editors call attention to the decay of language in Establishment discourse. What they call "the arrogance" of Establishment radicalism "dominates our handling of another legacy from the past—our language. Conservatives today should be worried about what is happening to language. Common speech and writing are being drowned out, and the air is choked with voices that hardly seem to come from a human source, speaking words that seem to have been composed by the computers and mimeograph machines they issue from. . . . We are doing to language what we are doing to our natural inheritance. . . . Languages and societies both have [a nature], and we disrupt this with our impatient, self-centered procedures."

In the same vein, Mary McCarthy has observed that "modern science, which is able to do things that can be made intelligible not in words, but only in formulae, has, in a sense, abolished speech as vital communication between men, and this implies that the life of action, the matching of great words with great deeds, is finished." Mary McCarthy, *On the Contrary* (New York, 1961), 163.

wondered at that, as Professor Sabine says, after Hume's critique of natural causality, values came to be nothing but "the reaction of human preference to some state of social and physical fact; in the concrete they [were] too complicated to be generally described even with so loose a word as utility."[46] The first effect in the order of morals and politics was the abandonment of the meaning of "government" even in the caricature that Hobbes and Locke had made of it. The place of the State was taken by "society" which was conceived as having principles of operation presupposed to no intelligible form. Sheldon Wolin expresses very well the general effect of Hume's critique:

The offspring of this kind of theorizing was a non-political model of a society which, by virtue of being a closed system of interacting forces, seemed able to sustain its own existence without the aid of an 'outside' political agency. . . . The effect . . . was to accept existing society as a datum, susceptible to minor modifications but always with the frame of reference supplied by the *status quo*. . . . Hence what was truly radical in liberalism was its conception of a society as a network of activities carried on by actors who know no principle of authority. Society represented not only a spontaneous and self-adjusting order, but a condition untroubled by the presence of authority.[47]

The reduction of nature to the mere fact of regularity in the operation of its material and efficient principles left man not only without proper first principles for a science of politics—these had been already lost by Hobbes and Locke. Hume's critique left man without any clear and consistent idea of human nature itself. As Professor Wolin observes, "[N]o longer able to communicate on the basis of a common interior life [men] were reduced to knowing each other solely from the outside; that is, on the basis of socially acquired responses and values."[48] The "socialized conscience" begins to make its appearance: A conscience that develops by a whole series of "tropisms" in response to outside stimuli. Thus it was that Hume reduced the science of politics as the substantive sense of a science dealing with concept formation and demonstration to science as mere tool—the mathematical measurement of responses to stimuli. What Walter Lippmann observed, namely, the disappearance, not of a ruling class but of "the functional [arrangement] of the relationship between the mass of people and the government"[49]

46. Sabine, *A History of Political Theory*, vi.
47. Sheldon Wolin, *Politics and Vision* (Boston, 1960), 292, 298, 301.
48. *Ibid.*, 340.
49. Walter Lippmann, *The Public Philosophy* (Boston, 1955).

(the substitution of veto-groups, Gallup-Pollsters, and inside-dopesters for genuine rule) means indeed that the State "withers away." It means that man's generic (social) life and his individual life are not different, that the State has ceased being the intermediary between man and his liberty. The person *is* in his individuality the "organization man," the "other-directed man," the "one-dimensional man." As Marcuse puts it, "[I]deas, aspirations, and objectives are redefined by the rationality of the . . . system and of its quantitative extension. . . . Thus [emerges] a pattern of *one-dimensional thought and behavior*. . . . The result is not adjustment but *mimesis*: an immediate identification of the individual with *his* society and, through it, with society as a whole."[50] Thus the Western tradition of thought closes the gap between state or economic class as intermediary between man and his generic (social) life and the individual's life.[51] This phenomenon is described in the following passages from Marcuse:

To the degree to which freedom from want, the concrete substance of all freedom, is becoming a real possibility, the liberties which pertain to a state of lower productivity are losing their former content. Independence of thought, autonomy, and the right to political opposition are being deprived of their basic critical function in a society which seems increasingly capable of satisfying the needs of individuals through the way in which it is organized. . . . In the contemporary period, the technological controls appear to be the very embodiment of Reason for the benefit of all social groups and interest—to such an extent that all contradiction seems irrational and all counteraction impossible. . . . It is a good way of life—much better than before—and as a good way of life, it militates against qualitative change. Thus emerges a pattern of *one-dimensional* thought and behavior in which ideas, aspirations, and objectives that, by their content, transcend the established universe of discourse and action are either repelled or reduced to terms of this universe. They are redefined by the rationality of the given system and of its quantitative extension.[52]

---

50. Marcuse, *One-Dimensional Man* (Boston, 1969), 10.

51. Erich Fromm observes that "the change from the overt authority of the nineteenth century to the *anonymous authority* of the twentieth was determined by the organizational needs of our modern industrial society. . . . Modern man is obliged to nourish the illusion that everything is done with his consent, even though such consent be extracted from him by subtle manipulation. His consent is obtained, as it were, behind his back, or *behind his consciousness*." Erich Fromm, Introduction to A. S. Neill, *Summerhill: A Radical Approach to Child-Rearing* (2nd edition; New York, 1964), x–xi. Italics added. See also: Staughton Lynd, "The New Left," in *The Annals of the American Academy of Political and Social Science*, 382 (March 1969), 64–72.

52. Marcuse, *One-Dimensional Man*, 9, 1–2, 12.

Marcuse relates this trend toward one-dimensional thought and behavior to the current view of science: "operationalism in the physical, behaviorism in the social sciences." The intellectual auxiliary of the Establishment retains science as tool by restricting the meaning of concepts to their operation value. "Many of the most seriously troublesome concepts are being 'eliminated' by showing that no adequate account of them in terms of operations or behavior can be given."[53]

Indeed the prevailing trend among the extreme Behavioralists is to take their world of measured activity for the substance of the political world. "If we can get our social life seated in terms of activity, and of nothing else," Arthur Bentley advised,

we have not indeed succeeded in measuring it, but we have at least reached a foundation upon which a coherent system of measurement can be built up. . . . [W]e shall cease to be blocked by the intrusion of immeasurable elements, which claim to be themselves the real causes of all that is happening and which by their spool-like arbitrariness make impossible any progress towards dependable knowledge.[54]

The extrusion from the world of politics of what Bertrand Russell called "the metaphysical . . . about which we can never feel sure that it exists or that we have tracked it down" means that observable behavior patterns and actions alone remain, and from these a measure-number results. "Conduct," T. V. Smith wrote, "is, in a word, the plotted curve of behavior."[55] As Bentley says, measure conquers chaos: "It is of the very definition of activity that it is systematized. . . . All the actions that enter into the behavior of an idiot are correlated."[56] Applying this methodology to politics Berelson in the study of *Voting*[57] found that the combination of the *political* idiot and the politically competent "makes for enough consensus to hold the system together and enough cleavage to make it move." We all become "X's" on the plotted curve of behavior that indicates the degree of "equilibrium" of the "system." The ambition of Hobbes is fulfilled: to discuss politics is to discuss arithmetic.

It is this aspect of science as tool that, Jeremy Shapiro suggests,

53. *Ibid.*, 12, 10.
54. Arthur Bentley, *The Process of Government* (San Antonio, 1949), 215.
55. "Conduct," in the *Encyclopedia of the Social Sciences* (New York, 1937), IV, 177.
56. Bentley, *The Process of Government*, 285.
57. Bernard Berlson *et al.*, *Voting* (Chicago, 1954), 322, 316, 318.

"broke down two-dimensional into one-dimensional civilization (where-in) the world is transformed operationally so that subject and object . . . are mediated through action, operation, and function."[58] Speaking of the machine—most especially in the form of the computerized process—Shapiro observes that one "cannot speak of the work of a machine but only of its function, which is an ordered totality of operations. Form and content, if they still exist, are on the same level, are part of the same system; there is continuity between technology and nature."[59] At the same time, Shapiro adds, "The machine as mediator between man and nature, creates continuity not only between technology and nature but also between technology and man, whose structure is assimilated to that of the machine and technologically shaped natural objects. . . . The genesis of this new form of functional, structural unity, eliminates the hierarchical, vertical relations of the two-dimensional world, transposing them into a single, horizontal level."[60]

This aspect of the machine—especially in the form of the computerized process—may be grasped from a remark of Hermann Weyle concerning the new mathematics: "For the mathematician it is irrelevant what circles are. It is of importance only in what manner a circle may be given."[61] Or again, it is irrelevant for us what length is, it is important only to know how its measurement is actually made. And this is the case because as tool science is almost entirely concerned with a process of measurement which results in a measure-number. It is precisely this that accounts for the rigor of the technique. It is clear, for example, that while computing, say, with 2, we need not trouble ourselves as to whether 2 is in fact one two having a *per se* unity, or whether 2 is simply two ones, a class or a collection—so that $1 + 1 = 2$ is nothing other than $1 + 1 = 1 + 1$. Bertrand Russell's appreciation of this distinction is clearly put:

There is no doubt about the class of couples; it is indubitable and not difficult to define, whereas the number 2, in any other sense, is a metaphysical entity about which we can never feel sure that it exists or that we have tracked it down. . . . Accordingly, we set up the following definition:

58. Jeremy Shapiro, "One-Dimensionality: The Universal Semiotic of Technological Experience," in *Critical Irruptions—New Left Perspectives on Herbert Marcuse,* ed. Paul Breines (New York, 1970), 153.

59. *Ibid.,* 154.   60. *Ibid.,* 155.

61. Cited in Charles de Koninck, *The Hollow Universe* (Quebec, 1945), 13.

The number of a class is the class of all those classes that are similar to it. . . .

[I]n fact, the class of all couples will be the number 2, according to our definition.[62]

This is what Jeremy Shapiro is saying when he writes that in the function of a machine "form and content, if they still exist, are on the same level, are part of the same system; . . . The Genesis of this new form of functional . . . unity, eliminates the hierarchical, vertical relations of the two-dimensional world, transposing them into a single, horizontal level."[63]

It should be noted that if 2 were taken as something other than 1 + 1—if 2 were taken to enjoy its own irreducible unity so that by taking one of its units away the new thing which is 2 would be destroyed (if "animal" were taken out of the definition of man as "rational animal," Socrates would cease to be what he is—a man)—this number would not be just 1 + 1. Now this aspect of number—the two that is once two and not twice one—will have to be ignored by any computer, machine or man; for the computer must be indifferent to *what* things are, apart from their being collections, "as a highway policeman who checks the weight of trucks is indifferent as to whether the loads are potatoes, cement, horses, or men. From the computer's point of view, the only thing found in 2 which is not found in 1 + 1 is the symbol, and who is responsible for that?"[64] We notice, then, that the art of calculation enjoys a peculiar freedom which is not that of science as such: it is manifest in the simple fact that when carried on there is no interest involved with what those things are which we calculate about, but only with how we can operate upon them.

And so we come, as Theodore Roszak says, to "the ultimate irony: the machine which is a creature of the human being becomes—most fully in the form of the computerized process—its maker's ideal. The machine achieves the perfect state of objective consciousness, and becomes the standard by which all things are to be gauged. . . . Man is replaced in all areas by the machine, not because the machine can do things 'better' but rather because all things have been reduced to what the machine is capable of doing."[65] This is what Marcuse appears to be speaking of when

62. Cited in *Ibid.*, 13–14.
63. Shapiro, "One-Dimensionality," 155.
64. De Koninck, *The Hollow Universe*, 230–31.
65. Theodore Roszak, *The Making of a Counter Culture* (New York, 1969), 230–31.

he says that "the 'inner' dimension of the mind . . . is whittled down."[66] It must be agreed by those who confine themselves to what machines can do that problems touching on the question of *what* things are, are properly ignored. As we have seen, Shapiro remarks, "The world is transformed operationally so that subject and object are mediated through action, operation, and function. . . . Form and content, if they still exist, are on the same level, are part of the same system." The vertical, hierarchical relations of the two-dimensional world are "transposed into a single horizontal level."[67] Similarly with symbolic constructs, as de Koninck points out,

To pass judgment on $1 + 1 = 1 + 1$ is not part of their business after all; they do not even have to *know* these elements. The symbols and functions are ultimate data and will eventually appear 'out there' as actual mechanical entities. Whether their meaning be grasped or not does not invalidate their computation which may be ground out by a machine. Computation, let it be repeated, does not require understanding of what is being computed. Even when performed by man, a computation can be purely mechanical and, in fact, ought to be.[68]

But indeed, as de Koninck goes on to observe, "[A] curious compliment is being paid to the human mind by the assertion that its supreme degree of precision is achieved when nothing is either apprehended or stated, and when reflection is more of a hindrance than a help."[69] This is the only kind of "thinking" of which the machine is capable. This is that "ultimate irony" of which Roszak speaks: This form of "objective consciousness" which "overcomes" the object by restricting the meaning of concepts to what is operational is achieved at the expense of all distinctions between beings—distinctions which can be made only by the "inner dimension" of the mind.

We must look more deeply into this "ultimate irony" if we wish to see where man himself stands today in relation to his loss of intellectual center. First we may observe that the pure "exteriority" of the nature of the machine,—i.e., the absence in it of what Marcuse calls "inner dimension," the inability of the machine to apprehend or state anything and to reflect on anything—is precisely what characterizes the nature of the primeval cosmos in its initial

66. Marcuse, 10.
67. Shapiro, *One-Dimensional Man*, 155.
68. De Koninck, *The Hollow Universe*, 28.
69. *Ibid.*

state—its pure exteriority, where things are separated one from another, wrapped in their own obscurity. In the realm of the inorganic, motion is wholly transeunt, i.e., there being no self-motion, no life, inorganic things move only by being moved. The kind of thinking of which the machine is capable and to which human thinking today is increasingly confined, opens to man an experience where in the transeuncy and pure exteriority of the cosmos in its initial state is interiorized in such a way that it is as if the cosmos itself were imaginatively projecting a "consciousness" of pure exteriority, of one-dimensionality to *man*: a paradox of empathy, to be sure, whereby the "inner dimension" of the mind is "whittled away" by the mind itself.[70] In speaking of the different durations of natural things, de Koninck has these enlightening remarks on the matter we are considering:

[Life] is a kind of triumph over the diffusion of time. . . . [W]e find the most manifest sign of this in the knowledge of animals and men, and especially in the memory. In the measure that a being lives, it rises above the conditions of space and time. . . . A knowing being is present to itself and assimilates to itself its surroundings, while there where space dominates, things are separated one from another and lost in the night. . . . A living being . . . [has] a duration infinitely more rich, if infinitely shorter, than that of the stars; it is infinitely closer to eternity than anything of the oldest inorganic world. . . . It is the notion of physical time, first in the experimental order, that leads us to suppose that quantity is an essential property of duration. . . .

It is understood, of course, that the different durations of natural beings are all of them truly temporal, that is to say, successive and continuous. But some are less so than others. And when we consider the hierarchy of durations in the sense of their lower limit where they become experimentally measurable, we notice that they tend to lose their identity and to disappear in physical time to the point of the obliteration of all distinctions between *beings*. If the principle of the conservation of energy is true, and if the mass of the universe is constant, physical time is, under this aspect, absolutely one; in this perspective, which abstracts from the real breaks or incisions dividing the world in individuals, the different

---

70. An interesting example of this paradox at work is provided by William Barrett's exposition of the testimony of modern art to the "horizontal" rather than the "vertical movement of the spirit":: "What happens if we try to apply [the] classical Aristotelian canon to a modern work like Joyce's *Ulysses*, . . . where the movement is always horizontal . . . and where we detect not the shadow of anything like a climax, in the traditional sense of the term? *If Joyce's had been a disordered mind, we could dismiss all this as a sprawling chaos*; but he was in fact an artist in superb control of his material, so that the disorder has to be attributed . . . to life itself. It is in fact the banal, gritty thing that we live that Joyce gives us. . . . *This world is dense, opaque, unintelligible.*" *Irrational Man* (Garden City, N.Y., 1962), 51.

physical times proper to beings, the life of a cat, for example, are only local condensations of an identical time which goes back to the origin of things.[71]

In the reduction of conduct to "the plotted curve of behavior," to the activity that is of its very definition systematized, to—indeed—the "homologous processes" that abstract from the real, heterogeneous order of social-political life and go back to those "particles" out of which David Easton says "all social behavior is formed,"[72] behavioral science—the intellect auxiliary of the Establishment—would appear to be seeking to reduce the heterogeneous whole of society in the way in which durations can be reduced to their lower limit where they become experimentally measurable. The "stable units of analysis" that behavioral science strives to locate are, it is said, "ubiquitous, uniform, and repetitious." Has not Arthur Bentley told us that all actions—those that enter into the behavior of an idiot as well as those that enter into the behavior of the mentally competent—"are equally correlated"?[73] Despite the claim of behavioral science to take its departure from the individual actor, it brings us to a sense of unity of man with man that abstracts from the real breaks and incisions dividing the world in individuals; they become only local condensations of an identical "stuff" that goes back to the origin of things. The heterogeneous whole of society is reduced to the point of obliteration of the distinctions between *beings*—to "one-dimensionality." The "psychic style" cultivated by the Technocratic machine culture has painlessly achieved the "essentiality" of man proclaimed by Marx's "generic being": "You are no longer yourselves. . . . You are without a name, without a mother, blank sheets on which the Revolution will write its orders."[74] We will recall Norman Jacobson's observations on Hobbes:

> If a vocabulary of ethics, law, and politics entirely neutral in tone may be insinuated and imposed upon men—insinuated into their thoughts and imposed upon their speech—it might serve as an anaesthetic to quiet the mutinous passions. . . .
> To discuss politics is to become objective and remote, a neutral rather than a heated disputant.[75]

71. Translated by Charles N. R. McCoy from Charles de Koninck, "Le Cosmos comme tendance vers la pensée," *Itinéraires*, N. 66 (Sept.–Oct. 1962), 174, 176, 178.

72. In "The Current Meaning of Behavioralism," in James C. Charlesworth (ed.) *Contemporary Political Analysis* (New York, 1967), 24.

73. Bentley, *The Process of Government*, 285.

74. Koestler, *The Invisible Writing*, 141.

75. Jacobson, *Hobbes as Creator*, 13.

Jacobson very significantly concludes this passage with the following remark: "We witness in the disciplined austerity of academic political, social, and historical studies today similar tendencies, but with this significant difference: the academic scientist is not always aware of what exactly has been sacrificed. But Hobbes knew."[76]

What has been sacrificed is life—human life in its fullness. If we recall what was just said about the contemporary form of "objective consciousness" bringing us to an empathy with the original "stuff" of the primeval cosmos, the words of Gabriel Marcel take on profound meaning: "[I]n whatever direction we may look today, it is hard to escape the conclusion that we have entered upon what . . . might [be described] as an eschatological age. This does not necessarily mean that the end of the world is chronologically imminent. . . . But what is clear is that men today . . . know that they have it in their power to destroy the universe. Moreover, one would have to be blind not to see that, at every level of being, a clearly traceable process of self-destruction is taking place."[77] In these sentences Gabriel Marcel speaks of self-destruction at every level of being, and he joins this observation with the demurrer concerning the chronological imminence of the end of the world. The suggestion seems to be that the bomb is only the terrible external sign of that "darkening of the world, the flight of the gods, the destruction of the earth"[78] whose prototype is an intensity of defect in the very heart of man's being. Marcel's phrasing suggests a link with the Heideggerian proposal of the destruction of the history of ontology. Heidegger's proposal opens to man the curious experience alluded to earlier. That experience is the one wherein the transeuncy and pure exteriority of the cosmos in its initial state—separated from itself, wrapped in its own obscurity— is interiorized in such a way that it is as if the cosmos itself were imaginatively projecting a "consciousness" of pure exteriority and "irrelationality" to *man*. The Heideggerian proposal for the destruction of the history of ontology induces in the region of intellect a consciousness of primeval being such as the primeval atom— from the explosion of which, physics tells us, the world first arose—and the atom bomb alike establish in the region of reality.

76. *Ibid*.
77. Gabriel Marcel, *The Philosophy of Existence* (New York, 1949), 32.
78. Martin Heidegger, *An Introduction to Metaphysics* (Garden City, N.Y., 1961), 31.

Nature in man meets nature in the cosmos half-way indeed, and finds its own essence there.

Now then, as Theodore Roszak remarks, "The counter culture takes its stand against the background of this absolute evil, an evil which is not defined by the sheer *fact* of the bomb, but by the total *ethos* of the bomb, in which our politics, our public morality, our economic life, our intellectual endeavor are now embedded with a wealth of ingenious rationalizations."[79] We see then that the Counter Culture takes its stand against that process of self-destruction that Marcel says is taking place "at every level of being," and which Heidegger describes in terms of the "destruction of the history of ontology."

In Heidegger's philosophy, existence is peculiarly human existence (*Dasein*) and it is experienced in the feeling of the exteriority of the primeval cosmos (being in "the throw"). In the movement of *Dasein* toward its innermost potentiality, toward "authenticity," there is a sacrifice of time from the point of view of quantity—the everydayness of the one-among-many. Quantity of time is, to be sure, a sign of slackened existence.[80] In the perspective of Heidegger's temporality as the ontological meaning of *Dasein*, "The dimension of extension and number" which prevails in the mode of "fallenness" (in the everydayness of the one-among-many) is overcome by the emergence of "the self-alone" through a reduction of the quantitative measurability of beings: The projection of *Dasein* toward its innermost potentialities, to "the origins," to "the poverty of existence," is accomplished not by intensifying the duration but by shortening it.[81] Death, because it discloses all the potentialities that precede it, is said to be the "whole" of *Dasein*.

It is here that an unexpected turn brings us in view of the historical position of man himself today. How is it that the "existential solipsism" of the Being-toward-Death as the "whole" of the being of *Dasein*" is so little an isolated subject-thing, that, on the con-

79. Roszak, *The Making of a Counter Culture*, 47.
80. In speaking of the idea of evolution, Charles de Koninck writes: "The natural species below man ought to be considered as attempts, more and more audacious, to detach themselves from the dispersion of time, and to dominate it. This ascension accomplishes itself in sacrificing time from the point of view of quantity. . . . Quantity of time is a sign of slackened existence. . . . In [the] perspective of progression in time, the world tends to reduce the quantitative measurability of beings, not in shortening the duration, but in intensifying it." "Le cosmos comme tendance vers la pensée," 178, 179.
81. See above, note 78.

trary, it brings the person into an extreme sense before his world as world"?[82]

The answer appears to be twofold. After remarking the absorption by Technology of the ideological differences between Marxism and Capitalism, and asking what element of "negativity" there can be in a one-dimensional world that can give impulse to revolutionary, qualitative change, Jeremy Shapiro hits precisely on the consciousness of "meaninglessness," "being lost in existence," "absurdity," "nausea," and "schizophrenia."[83] He adds: "This negative experience is the starting point [today] for radical theory and practice."[84] But precisely how can it be? For experience of this sort is still part of the one-dimensional experience. Rather, we must look into the one-dimensional world for a "projection" toward "authenticity"—to use the Heideggerian phraseology.

In *Sincerity and Authenticity*, Lionel Trilling remarks that "a very considerable originative power had once been claimed for sincerity, but nothing to match the marvellous generative force that our modern judgment assigns to *authenticity, which implies the downward movement through all the cultural superstructures to some place where all movement ends, and begins.*"[85] He concludes his essay by observing that "not the organic, but the mechanical is to be the authenticating principle in modern life."[86] Not, of course, that aspect of the mechanical to which precisely one-dimensionality has been attributed. The "marvellous generative force that our modern judgment assigns to authenticity" and which linked to the mechanical as "the authenticating principle in modern life" is revealed, Trilling suggests, by "the violent meanings which are explicit in the Greek ancestry of the word 'authentic.' *Authenteo*: to have full power over; also, to commit a murder. *Authentes*: not only a master and a doer, but also a perpetrator, a murderer, even a self-murderer, a suicide. These ancient and forgotten denotations bear upon the nature and intention of the . . . culture of the period we call Modern."[87] The second, profound aspect of the ultimate irony is before us: the "human" and authenticating principle is the machine in the capacity it gives man for taking apart the universe (and conceivably putting it together again in a new way). It

82. Martin Heidegger, *Sein und Zeit* (9th edition; Tübingen, 1960), 188.
83. Shapiro, "One-Dimensionality," 175.
84. *Ibid.*, 176.
85. Lionel Trilling, *Sincerity and Authenticity* (Cambridge, MA., 1971), 12.
86. *Ibid.*, 129.   87. *Ibid.*, 131.

does indeed, in Heidegger's language, "bring the person into an extreme sense before his world as world." It perfects the analogy used above between the origin of the world in the explosion of an immense atom and the human empathy in the one-dimensional culture with the pure exteriority of the primeval cosmos, wrapped in its own obscurity: for now the analogy is carried further in the authenticating principle of the machine, which is the capacity it gives man for destroying the universe. Now we see what Roszak means both by "the mere *fact* of the bomb" and the "total ethos of the bomb." The bomb is the ultimate machine as the authenticating principle of modern life, the terrible external sign of a defect at the heart of man's being and the sign of that "self-destruction that is taking place at every level of being." We have, to be sure, as Trilling puts it, assigned a generative force to authenticity that "implies the downward movement through all the cultural superstructures to some place where all movement ends, and begins."[88]

These remarks of Trilling put us in mind, again, of Heidegger. While indeed Heidegger hails Marx's doctrine of alienation as the greatest boon to modern philosophy, he enters an acute but sympathetic critique: Because existence for Heidegger is peculiarly human existence (*Dasein*), the notion of "being" must, to be sure, be approached through the things "at hand" (the *Zuhandene*, the instruments of productions, the complexus of tools and the relations of production) rather than through the world of nature (*Vorhandene*). But Marx failed to understand "the crux of the matter of authenticity, which Heidegger tells us, is the masquerading of spirit as intelligence: "The crux of the matter is the reinterpretation of the spirit of *intelligence*: . . . The spirit falsified into intelligence . . . falls to the level of a tool in the service of others."[89] Marx himself fell prey to the fecundity of thought. In Marx's doctrine of the "generic being" of man, the individual realizes the "general mode" of his generic being in the activity of the generic conscience, and this general mode is the "theoretical form of that of which the living form is the real community," the product of "the total living sensuous activity of all the individuals composing the sensuous world."[90] Thus, "Socialism takes its departure from the theoretically and practically sensible conscience of man in nature, consid-

---

88. *Ibid.*, 8.
89. Heidegger, *An Introduction to Metaphysics*, 38.
90. Marx, *Oekonomische-philosophische Manuskript*, Sec. I. Vol. 3, 125–126. Also see Marx and Engels, *The German Ideology*, 37–38.

ered as *being*. . . . The objective reality becomes for man the reality of human forces, . . . the object of himself." In Marx's view, all that is "natural" (*Vorhandene*)—the forms and products of a consciousness that has separated itself from the "real" world and gone off into ' "pure' theory, theology, philosophy, ethics, etc."—must be overthrown by revolutionary action. But their surrogate—work, considered as the first need of life because by work man makes himself specifically human—is, in Heidegger's view, a perpetuation of man's self-estrangement; he is alienated in processes of production. Spirit is to be found neither in "the regulation and domination of the material conditions of production" nor in "the intelligent ordering and explanation of everything that is present and already posited at any time."[91] Spirit is *anterior* to the division of knowledge into theoretical and practical, as well as to the distinction between subject and object. Heidegger wants from the *Zuhandene*—the complexus of tools and the relations of production—the ground of their being, the *principle of exterior activity*. One must get behind both metaphysics and technics; a "homecoming" must be made to the origins, to the "poverty of existence." Heidegger proposes the destruction of the history of ontology, and therefore it is not the winning—whether speculatively or practically—of the world of that-which-is that engages Heidegger. Rather, he wishes to go behind both metaphysics and technics to the "origins," to the "poverty of existence"—to lay being bare by denuding the world of that-which-is. If, with Marx, philosophy passes into practice by transposing to the practical order all that Aristotle had reserved to the speculative intellect, Heidegger brings us to a simple contemplation of the nudity of the world that is subject to the total power of man. The "being" that is laid bare by Heidegger—the "poverty of existence" that is anterior to both metaphysics and technics—is the purely passive principle that is anterior logically to the activity of nature—to, in Trilling's words, "some place where all movement ends, and begins."

A quite opposite path, and one we shall attempt to trace in the hope of perceiving the true element of "negativity" in the one-dimensional world that will allow for qualitative revolutionary change in our cultural world, is brilliantly set forth in an essay to which we have made some allusion. Its very title suggests the possibility of discovering the ultimate intent of the various posi-

---

91. Heidegger, *An Introduction to Metaphysics*, 38–39.

tions we have been examining: "Le cosmos comme tendance vers la pensée" by Charles de Koninck.[92]

The text of de Koninck gives consideration to the idea of the maturation of the cosmos as a tendency toward thought, in which all its parts "will be united and lived." The cosmos tends thus to compenetrate itself, to touch itself in the intelligence of man in which it is able to realize an explicit return to its first principle. It is apparent that this notion is opposite to what Cassirer called the first premise of the modern spirit, namely, that the nature of man meets nature in the cosmos half-way and finds its own essence there.[93] "Let us imagine," de Koninck writes,

the initial state of our universe as one of pure exteriority. The world, was, so to speak, entirely outside of itself, separated from itself, imprisoned in itself and in its own obscurity. It is dead, empty, an abyss of division. But it is necessary that it arrive at intelligence. This exigency is written into it from the very commencement of things. Intelligence being a kind of compenetration, it is necessary that the universe in some fashion fall back upon itself, that it contract itself, that it interiorize itself. It is exactly this interiorization which will permit it to open itself to itself.[94]

De Koninck then proceeds to the consideration of two inverse phenomena, one of the physical world, the other of the biological world. In the expansion of the universe, the energy contained in the original immense atom that physics tells us of is dispersed by the explosion of this immense atom: the result is a fragmenting of space and a diffusion of time—they dominate the primeval cosmos. Now "in the law of the dimunition of energy this same Physics shows us a universe that is growing old: the energy while remaining altogether the same quantitatively is more and more irreversibly diminished. The world tends toward a complete exhaustion or draining away toward a thermo-dynamic equilibrium."

But there is an inverse phenomenon that biology presents to us in the theory of mutations by which life advances by a series of explosions. "[C]ontrary to the impoverishing dispersion of the world of physics, life breaks forth by bursting open. It continually enriches itself. A flower progresses from the bud, the chick which breaks the eggshell in pushing toward the outside furnishes us with a synthetic image of the way in which life arises in the cosmos. The physical world is like an eggshell."[95]

92. De Koninck, "Le Cosmos,' 169–88.
93. Cassirer, The Philosophy of the Enlightenment, ibid., 44–45.
94. De Koninck, "Le Cosmos," 172.
95. Ibid., 173.

Looking at these two inverse phenomena from the vantage point of a philosophy of the sciences, de Koninck suggests that it is the "thrust" of life that "undoes" the universe in its purely physical aspect: it uses this universe in making space expand. "That which from the point of view of physics is a concentration, is from the point of view of biology a separation: life leads to an organization ever more intense, while the disorganization of the physical world is a falling away, a loss of the cosmos that is being absorbed in life." Because of this contraction the biosphere rises above the fragmentation of space and the dispersion of time. "Speaking absolutely, it is life which, in the effort to touch itself in a consciousness, in a center of pure density, disseminates space-time as the prow of a ship disperses the waters." From the point of view of physics the universe expands, but in this process "the universe turns back upon itself in life, constituting in this contraction centers more and more dense, cores or nuclei more and more heterogeneous."[96] It attains at last to man, in whose nature the world comes to unite all the degrees of cosmic being; and in thought it touches and compenetrates itself. Thus the world joins in human nature its extremities—extremities that have been separated by space and time. In this process nature projects that whole hierarchy of species which paleontology, part of biology, studies.

When it is said that the biosphere rises more and more above time, this statement was not meant to be taken merely metaphorically. "Beings are perfect in the measure in which they are not temporal; transcendance over the diffusion of time is a condition of life, of knowledge, of thought. If the vegetable species are hierarchized according to their approach to animal species, and these in turn according as they approach man, it is necessary to say that the vital drive with which the cosmos is animated from the outside since the beginning extracts from the power of matter composites whose form emerges more and more from matter; that is to say, substances that are more and more simple. But since its existence is proportionate to essence, the duration of cosmic beings is more and more one and simple as it is less and less temporal. As we have said, they are specifically hierarchized in their existence as well as in their essence. The animal is less temporal than the plant."[97]

96. *Ibid.*, 173–75.
97. *Ibid.*, 175–76. Earlier, when comparing the homogeneity of the primeval

The idea of evolution suggests to us that the beings below man are to be considered to be a function of man; by reason of this function, these natures are open to one another, and constitute in their ascension toward man an *élan* more and more determinate and powerful. Thus the natural species below man ought to be regarded as ever more daring efforts to detach themselves from the dispersion of time, and to dominate it:

In assimilating the other in sense knowledge, the animal already breaks the barrier of space which separates; it extends to that which is not itself; it can, as it were, live the existence of the other. In the measure that animals are perfect, the field of their knowledge becomes vaster: that is to say, the world more and more compenetrates itself, becomes in this way more and more present to itself, more and more interior. This increasing interiorization is achieved in true simplicity in the human [intelligence which] embraces and transcends space without being mixed in it. Not that the knowledge of this intelligence penetrates and envelopes space as does the knowledge enjoyed by a pure spirit contemplating the world from outside. For accidentally, at least, the human spirit is joined to a corner of space just as a tree is joined to a corner of space—but with this very profound difference, that man's corner can be displaced. The immobility of human thought is for this reason intermediate between that of the pure spirit and that of the tree, conjoined in man thanks to local movement. And it is here that we find the profound sense of the locomotion of living things—a power which frees them from the boundaries of place, and which in the final analysis is at the service of an exploring intelligence. For this intelligence, immobile in itself, and transcending place, must, none the less, transverse the world in order to assimilate it. The locomotion of living things is a tendency toward ubiquity, toward an intentional omnipresence and a sort of immensity. Although from the point of view of physics local movement from a material point involves the complete abandonment of the preceding position, the conscious center, by its displacement, gathers all to itself and enriches itself by living all the preceding positions together in the very place where it finds itself at the moment. Man is a "microcosm" not only because he contains within

---

world with the "one-dimensionality" of our cultural world, the following lines from de Koninck were cited: "It is understood, of course, that the different durations of natural beings are all of them truly temporal, that is to say, successive and continuous. But some are less so than others. And when we consider the hierarchy of durations in the sense of their lower limit where they become experimentally measurable, we notice that they tend to lose their identity and disappear in physical time to the point of the obliteration of the distinctions between *beings*. If the principle of conservation of energy is true, and if the mass of the universe is constant, physical time is, under this aspect, absolutely one; in this perspective, which abstracts from the real breaks or incisions dividing the world in individuals, the different physical times proper to beings—the life of a cat, for example, are only local condensations of an identical time which goes back to the origin of things." See above, note 71.

his purely natural being all the degrees of being in nature, but more profoundly because he uses the resources of art to draw to himself all the richness of the world diffused in space and time. Thus in the so-called *intentional* order he is the power of all things. The progress in the means of transport and communication, of the instruments of research and all the rest of (technological) advance are so many conquests for the intelligence: The ultimate end of these deliverances, the exploration of the world in view of bringing all things back to one point, is what is meant by contemplation.[98]

In light of the comparison I have made between the homogeneity of the primeval cosmos and the "one-dimensionality" of our cultural world, a crucial argument of de Koninck's presentation of the notion of the cosmos as a tendency toward thought requires careful attention; and this is so because it will suggest what appears to be the true and indeed the only means by which men today may hope to rise above the one-dimensional society which by its very nature makes impossible any "break-out" from the "system." De Koninck warns that from the fact that the beings below man are essentially a function of man, constituting in their ascension toward him an *élan* ever more powerful and determinate, "we may not infer that this function reduces itself to a pure canalization of power or potency for spirit. . . . This interpretation is altogether too simplistic":

A work of nature is necessarily a gift of self, and consequently evolution will be a gift of self in the measure exactly that it is a work of nature; otherwise the concept of nature would lead back to that of an exclusively passive principle. It is true that the inorganic considered in its passive nature, cannot, under that precise aspect, actively give itself. But this manner of isolating passive nature is unnatural and false. Nature is not merely matter. Even inorganic nature is form and matter. Even inorganic nature is form and matter. . . . But it is precisely this essential lack that

---

98. Editor's note: The next three notes, like about a dozen others within this article, were left undocumented by McCoy. The editor supplied the previous documentation by context and source research. We may assume from their context that notes 98 and 99 came from the same source as the preceding notes, i.e., McCoy's translation of de Koninck's "Le cosmos comme tendance vers la pensée." Within the current extensive quotation there is the following footnote: "We may note, then, that in the world of nature the power of the object is not the power of the subject 'objectified' (the principle of all the forms of 'objective consciousness'); rather, man is the power of all things in his act of understanding the whole world—in the 'intentional' order. He may then, indeed, proceed to order his own world—the world of culture and civilization—in imitation of the marvelous order of the universe; and this is the work of the 'practical reason'—the reason engaged with 'doing' and 'making.'"

opens the inorganic world as inorganic to life and intelligence, without which the inorganic would be deprived of its natural end and contradictory. The essential need calls upon the spiritual world for the constitution itself of active nature.[99]

Thus in the original eruption of life, taking its departure from the inorganic, the gift of self, which a work of nature is, is accomplished under the influence of a trans-cosmic agent. We will recall the Heideggerian view that "Spirit" is anterior to "the intelligent explanation and ordering of everything that is present and already posited at any time."[100] Heidegger would bring us back to that "poverty of existence" that is anterior to both metaphysics and technics—that purely passive principle that is anterior logically to the activity of nature and which, as we just saw de Koninck remark, "calls upon the spiritual world for the constitution itself of active nature." If the original eruption of life, taking its departure from the inorganic, is accomplished under the influence of a trans-cosmic agent, the vital drive with which the cosmos is animated from the outside since the beginning extracts from the power of matter composites whose form emerges more and more from matter; this ascension culminates in an intra-cosmic intelligence—in the intelligence of man. It is ultimately in the intelligence of man that nature accomplishes her definitive trajectory.[101]

99. *Ibid.*
100. See above, note 91.
101. See above, note 97. In the *Summa Contra Gentiles,* IV, 11, St. Thomas Aquinas describes the degrees of interiority and communication which are found in nature. He says that we must begin by observing that where things differ in nature we find different modes of emanation, and further, that from the higher natures things proceed in a more interior way. Now of all things the inanimate obtain the lowest place, and from them no emanation is possible except by the action of one on another. After inorganic bodies, that is to say, bodies deprived of organs, there come first plants among which emanation proceeds already from within inasmuch as they form within themselves the seed, and the seed, committed to the earth, produces a plant. Accordingly, we find here the first traces of life: since living things are those which move themselves to act, whereas those which can only move extraneous things are wholly lifeless. It is a sign of life in plants that something within them is the cause of a form. Yet the plant's life is imperfect because although in the plant emanation proceeds from within, that which emanates comes forth little by little, and in the end becomes altogether extraneous. Thus for example, the bud in coming forth in the plant bursts into flower and then becoming a fruit is both wholly distinct from the branch while nonetheless wholly attached to it. And once ripened, the fruit separates itself altogether and falls to the earth in order to produce another plant. Indeed, we can see that the first principle of this emanation is something extraneous; the intrinsic vigor of the plant is drawn through the roots from the soil whence the plant derives its nourishment. It might

Now then, the one-dimensional, technocratic society is like the inorganic world in being unable of itself to transcend itself. To recall Marcuse's critique of it: "Ideas, aspirations, and objectives that, by their content, transcend the established universe of discourse and action are either repelled or reduced to terms of this universe. They are redefined by the rationality of the system and its quantitative extension."[102] Like the inorganic world, the cultural world of the Technocracy "calls" upon the spiritual world for the constitution itself of active nature. "Objective consciousness"—in the form of empathy with the pure exteriority of the one-dimensional society—needs to be "animated" from the outside, as it were, by what the Counter Culture calls "consciousness consciousness."[103] This is why I suggested at the beginning of our considerations that the "life style" of the Counter Culture may indeed appear at first glance to go back to the roots of the Establishment but may, perhaps with more reason, be interpreted in the light of the tendency of the cosmos toward life and intelligence; or, indeed, as a response to the Heideggerian "call" which opens up the lifeless world of our Technocratic culture to "the world-creating im-

---

be well to observe here that this form of life cannot assimilate to itself what is outside of it except by disintegrating it; nutrition destroys the assimilated object.

Above the life of plants there is a degree of life that is higher—that of the animal, the proper emanation whereof begins from without but terminates within. And the further the emanation proceeds, the more does it penetrate within: for the sensible object impresses a form on the external senses, whence it proceeds to the imagination and further still, to the storehouse of the memory. Yet in every emanation of this kind the beginning and the end are in different subjects: for no sensitive power reflects on itself. This degree of life is, then, superior to that of plants in proportion to the advanced interiority of the operation proper to this kind of life. Nonetheless, it is not absolutely perfect life because the emanation flows from one power to another.

The animal has knowledge, but it does not know that it knows; it does not make a complete return to itself. It can never say to itself that it knows. It does not compenetrate itself in a consciousness of self. The supreme and perfect degree of life is, therefore, that of the intelligence, for the intelligence can reflect upon itself, can know itself. But although the human intelligence can know itself, it must draw from the outside that which constitutes the first principle of its knowledge; for it is incapable of knowing independently of sense faculties which are powers provided with bodily organs. Although this intelligence can know itself only by grasping an object other than itself and an object most removed from spirit, it is nonetheless truly conscious in the full sense of the word—it is truly present to itself and touches itself.

102. Marcuse, One-Dimensional Man, 12.

103. Roszak, The Making of a Counter Culture, 62. Charles Reich in The Greening of America uses the phrase "Consciousness III."

pulse of the spirit."[104] The only other authenticating principle of modern culture is the power of man through the machine of the bomb to assert his spirit in the destruction of the universe. But as Roszak remarks, it is against this "absolute evil"—the *fact* as well as the *ethos* of the bomb—that the Counter Culture takes its stand.

104. Heidegger, *An Introduction to Metaphysics*, 38.

III. American
Political Thought

13. American Federalism—
Theory and Practice*

[Charles N. R. McCoy wrote three substantial essays on American theory. In part, this first essay on American Federalism reflects the topics of his doctoral dissertation, "The Law Relating to Public Inland Waters," which he completed in 1940 at the University of Chicago. Already here is revealed McCoy's grasp of theoretical questions and how they relate to issues in American politics. He is at pains to compare the political philosophy of the contract theorists, on which federalism and the Constitution were said to be based, with the more classical view of political philosophy, which did not see the state as something artificial. For McCoy Aristotle's notion that every state is part natural and part artificial or conventional means in American terms that neither a federal nor a regional state can be based wholly on compact. The relation of justice, law, and administration is seen to be the theoretical problem that needed to be worked out in the United States after it settled the question of whether it was one state.

McCoy presents John Marshall as an original thinker aware of the influence of political philosophy on practice. This philosophy can provide a more coherent purpose for the state's activities, particularly in the area of navigation and commerce. He demonstrates that the inadequacies of the compact theories to enable the government to function for its general purpose are supported by Marshall's arguments.]

The appearance in the last decade of such devices for social control as the Government Corporation and the Interstate Authority seems to suggest that the American Federal State system is passing through a critical stage in the course of social metamorphosis. It may be that the Federal State system, succeeding the Confederate system of states, approaches now a Regional system

*This essay originally appeared in the *Review of Politics*, 2 (January 1940), 105–17.

in the course of this metamorphosis. It is at any rate interesting that the Constitutional provision for agreements among the states with the consent of Congress—perhaps the most typical symbol of the old Confederation—is, with the breaking down of the Federal State system, coming strongly into vogue. Where the problems are regional in character and where the jurisdictional framework is not coincidental with the problem area (for example, the Colorado River Valley Problem Area) a regional authority created by concessions of jurisdiction on the part of the several states or on the part of the states and the Federal Government becomes necessary. These considerations determine the manner in which such regional or "sub-national" interests are to be set within "the framework of the American Nation"—a framework, the legal lines of which, in the words of the National Resources Committee, "aggravate the growing points of our national life."[1] Where, on the other hand, the problems themselves being regional in character, Federal jurisdiction is made to coincide with the problem area by means of a legal fiction (for example, the Tennessee River Valley Problem Area) a regional authority created by the Federal Government may be established. As for problems directly affecting the socio-economic life of the entire nation, it is clear that were these problems to be regulated likewise by interstate agreements among the forty-eight states the nature of the Federal Union would reveal itself as decomposing into the elements of the old Confederation. That there are problems of national scope which have appeared to lie within what Professor Corwin has aptly called "the twilight zone" of "no-government"[2] has caused liberals to demand a court ready to restore the Constitution to its rightful role as the original determinant of the principles of Justice.

When it is said that the present Federal State system is possibly in its period of decadence, it is not to be imagined that the Regional system that is envisaged as taking its place will completely destroy the Federal system. There is historical evidence for asserting that our present Constitution is itself merely an amendment to the old Articles of Confederation; and from the point of view of political science the present Federal Union retains elements of the Confederation—it is precisely a mean between a confederation and a unitary state such as France and England. So that just as the structural

1. *Report of the National Resources Committee* (Washington, 1934), Sec. 2, p. 2.
2. Edward S. Corwin, *The Commerce Power vs. States' Rights* (Princeton, 1936).

elements of the Confederation remain in the Federal Union, the American Federal State system will provide the structure for a Regional system. The distribution of powers as it now exists between the Federal Government and the states will remain. Regionalism will be effected by concessions of jurisdiction and by the broadened interpretation of Federal power in relation to problems that cannot be successfully managed either by the states individually or collectively through interstate agreements. An example of the latter is the regulation of electric power development—a subject whose peculiarities illustrate the tendency as well as the need for regional control under Federal jurisdiction. Electric power development sites located on non-navigable waters escape the jurisdiction of the Federal Government; yet the actual business of these power companies may be, and usually is, interstate in character. It would be extremely difficult to achieve agreement among the states of a region or of the entire nation in the regulation of such public utilities. Here the trend toward regional control must be predicated upon an extension of Federal power. We select this particular problem for illustrating in the last half of this paper the point which we shall first make as a general proposition on the nature of the Federal system: That the conventional nature of the American Federal system is unique in that by embodying the principles of the social compact philosophy it impresses its legal (and artificial) division of sovereign powers upon the natural configuration of social and economic realities; with the result that if these problems are to be regulated by law, a harmony of problem area with jurisdictional area must be worked out either through the expansion of Federal power (preferably by judicial interpretation) or by contraction of states' rights achieved—be it noted—by making the concessions of jurisdiction necessary for interstate agreements.

That the developments which have been briefly set forth are crucial for the idea of Federalism must be apparent. But the difficulties which they present in terms of the American Constitutional system can be rightly appreciated only by examining the way in which the compact philosophy of the state stands in relation to the basic concepts of politics. For in the United States we have grown accustomed to discussing social and economic problems in terms much too narrow to support the discussion—in terms of the division of sovereign powers between the Federal Government and the states, in terms, that is, of the compact philosophy of the state, the implications of which so far as regards the political nature of the Union were destroyed by the Civil War, but whose implications for the socio-economic structure remain in the Federal system. Social scientists, for the most part neglecting political philosophy and pursuing their researches independently of the tradition of American political philosophy, are indeed aware of the stultifying effect of "legal logic," but often fail to appreciate the fact that usually it is not the logic that is at fault but the compact philosophy, which is at the very heart of our political structure.

The compact theory of the state, presented from different viewpoints by Locke, Hobbes, and Rousseau, proposed the concept of the state as something wholly artificial.[3] The state arises out of a compact and by a deliberate act of the will; there is no natural element in society.[4] Now at the Constitutional Convention in Philadelphia in 1787 the sovereign colonies of the Confederation contracted to establish a more perfect union. As sovereign colonies each was already established as a state by reason of a compact among the people and between the people and their government. Was the new union, therefore, a true state—that is to say, did it succeed immediately and wholly upon a prior natural condition of the people (as the colonies themselves had after the Revolution) or were the sovereign states themselves in their corporate capacity the parties to the compact? That question occupied the attention of publicists and statesmen for over half a century. What is most important to notice is that irrespective of the position adopted on that question, the compact philosophy was enacted into the constitutional structure by the division of sovereign powers between the Federal Government and the governments of the several states. This was not primarily a device for regional autonomy or for decentralized administration; it was primarily and in its historical setting a device for preserving the legal identity of the sovereign states.[5] Since each of the states was already established by com-

3. The Lockean form found in this country over that of Rousseau. See A. C. McLaughlin, *A Constitutional History of the United States* (New York, 1936), 91 ff.

4. Aristotle and St. Thomas taught that society is at once natural and conventional, that the conventions (constitution, laws, decrees, customs) were simply specific determinations of the principles of natural justice. See Aristotle, *Nicomachean Ethics*, V; Thomas Aquinas, *Summa Theologiae*, II, I, 3rd No. [This reference seems unintelligible. It probably refers to the Treatise on Law.]

5. This is clearly verified by an examination of the proceedings of the Constitutional Convention. The great majority of members failed to see the natural sectional diversity as the true source of future trouble and were concerned with the

pact, the new Federal Union had to be established by an artificiality once removed, namely, by the division of the sovereign powers. The framework of the American nation consisted then not primarily in a coordination of jurisdiction and problem area, but in the coordination of two political jurisdictions conditioned essentially by reference to the rights of sovereignty and only secondarily by reference to the demands of the social economy.

The present movement toward Regionalism and the growing extent of Federal power—twin and correlative reactions against the artifice of the compact philosophy—are not new manifestations of the inadequacy of that philosophy of government. Paradoxically it was the compact theory of the union which in the hands of John C. Calhoun was used to break the Union precisely because the regional (sectional) interests of the South were not adequately protected by the compact state. And it is curious as well as significant to observe that the counter-position of Daniel Webster was on its side likewise hampered by the compact theory: Webster was forced to argue in behalf of a true and natural Union in terms of a compact philosophy which refused to admit the natural element in the formation of society. The fact is that the compact philosophy of Locke was incapable of solving the problem of the nature of the American Union, for it failed to observe the truth of Aristotle's proposition that every state is *partly natural and partly conventional*. It required the Civil War to establish the indissolubility of the Union. And even after the War, in facing the problem of "reconstructing" the southern states, Congress was plagued with the old dilemma: If, as the victorious North had already contended, the states could not secede, they were still in the Union and needed no restoration; and if, as the South had contended, the states could secede, they were in the status of conquered provinces and could be treated as such by the Federal Government. As Professors Morison and Commager point out, half-humorously, "Both sides adopted the proper deductions from the other's premise."[6]

Webster was certainly correct in holding against Calhoun that the action of the states in ratifying the work of the Philadelphia

preservation of state sovereignty. It was the latter concern which dictated the principle of the distribution of powers and the compromise on representation. See McLaughlin, *Constitutional History* 171–72.

6. Samuel Eliot Morison and Henry S. Commager, *The Growth of the American Republic* (New York, 1937), II, 31.

Convention could be interpreted as having effected a real union, a new political entity; but Calhoun was correct in his major premise that the state does not arise out of a compact.[7] So that we are confronted with this curious anomaly in the history of the idea of Federalism—the anomaly of Webster arguing the correct point with the wrong premise, and Calhoun arguing the wrong point with the correct premise, and the close of the War witnessing the adoption in the North and in the South of the conclusions from each other's premises. One can sympathize with Lincoln's characterization of the problem as "a pernicious abstraction."

The perniciousness lay, however, then as it does now, in the compact philosophy and not in logic. The nature of the Union established by the Constitution had to be explained (whether by Calhoun or Webster) in terms inadequate to the problem, since the problem of the nature of the state precedes the problem involved in understanding the nature of a conventional body established by compact. The faultiness of both the Webster Union theory and the Calhoun State Sovereignty theory is due to the fact that the basic concepts of political science are avoided, and for them are substituted the terms of the social compact philosophy.

Our existence as a Union was ultimately settled by the Civil War, and settled of course outside the terms of the compact theory. Nonetheless it remains true that the compact theory is woven into the very structure of the American Union. No artificial doctrine such as the compact philosophy could negate what is proper to nature (it is by nature that man is a political animal and not by reason of any compact), but since society is partly conventional and partly natural, the artificiality of the very compact philosophy can itself be imposed upon the political structure. The difficulties of the Lockean theory are still with us; but that that philosophy creates our present difficulties is largely concealed because the modern and contemporary problems of government no longer turn on the question of the political nature of the Union but on the effective regulation by that Union of social and economic life. Between 1789 and 1865 the main issue before the courts and the country was the question of the political nature of the Union; it came up in all the important cases before the Supreme Court, it

7. Calhoun's argument was: (1) States do not originate in a compact; (2) but the United States originated in a compact; (3) therefore the United States is not a true state. See Charles E. Merriam, *History of American Political Theories* (New York, 1903), Chapter VII.

revealed itself in the Virginia and Kentucky Resolutions, in the nullification of the Tariff Act of 1832, and of course culminated in the War. After 1865—it being settled that no state could legally secede from the Union—the Court was left free from distraction and could devote itself wholly to its proper business of marking off the division of powers between the Federal and state governments of this politically unified nation. In short, while the War incorporated the notion of a single political state into the compact theory, the Federal system still yielded the settlement of the basic problems of society to the logic of the compact philosophy. And these problems, whether they are regional or national in scope, are breaking against the artificial lines of the jurisdictional framework and demanding solutions commensurate with the nature of the problems themselves.

Now a strong national tradition and cultural homogeneity may not give a great measure of unity to society, but if political justice is unattainable for important elements of the national life the essential note of political unity will be lacking. A "polis" in the full sense of that word will not be possible. The Federal system of distributed governmental powers (based on the compact between the states and the Federal Government) has in the course of time succeeded to a greater or lesser degree in meeting the demands for regulating an expanding industrial economy. But this division of sovereignty creates the ever-present possibility that certain problems will escape the jurisdiction of both Federal and state governments: namely, problems of regional scope and problems of a national scope which fall within the legal sphere not of the nation but of the states. The effect is that justice (initial or distributive justice in the Aristotelian sense) is subordinated wrongly to a legal system; so that the Constitutional arrangement by its division of powers may limit the consideration that can be given to socioeconomic problems by subordinating justice to law and in effect subordinating law to administration. Economic and social problems, which constitute the matter of justice, are not considered in terms of the principles of justice, but consideration of these problems is constrained by what is essentially an administrative arrangement. The settlement of important issues is thus too often left to a logic bound to the employment of terms inadequate to the basic problems. It follows that while the United States is politically one (the achievement of the Civil War), it remains so essentially affected by the compact philosophy that its unity is vitiated—or

at least continually threatened—by the confusion of the proper
relation that should maintain among justice, law, and administration.

Chief Justice Marshall, perhaps more than any other man influ-
ential in our Constitutional history, appreciated the unique situation of the Federal State system and the need to correct its inherent
tendency toward impotence by construing the terms of the Constitutional grant in the light of the more general concepts of political science. And curiously enough, the basic arguments for
Federal action and the cooperative balance of the Federal system
are set forth by Marshall in a case which involved the extent of
Congress's power over navigation—a power which today has been
construed, if narrowly and with some uncertainty, to justify the
far-reaching activities of the Federal Government in the Tennessee
River Valley. An examination of the arguments of Marshall in this
leading case and the way in which they have fared in subsequent
case law on the navigation power will illustrate the general considerations already set forth in this paper.

"If from the imperfection of human language," wrote Marshall
in *Gibbons* v. *Ogden*,[8] "there should be serious doubts respecting
the extent of any given power, it is a well-settled rule that the
objects for which it was given . . . should have great influence in
the construction." This statement succinctly presents Marshall's
attitude toward the whole problem of constitutional construction.
It illustrates the important role that Marshall assigned to extra-
constitutional arguments in understanding the force of the Constitutional grant—the need, as we have said, to construe the terms
of the Constitution in the light of the more general concepts of
Political Science. For Marshall there was always a presumption
which regarded the Constitutional text as instrumenting the objectives of the Union; and where the text itself might be construed
otherwise, he imposed the conditioning rule which looked to the
workability of the Central Government as the guarantee of the
Union. This is made evident too in his analysis of the word "regulate" in the grant of Congressional power "to regulate commerce
with foreign nations, and among the several states." Indifferent
to the grammatical and logical niceties of the position subsequently
stated by Madison,[9] which insisted upon the negative character of

8. 9 *Wheaton* 1 at 188, 189.
9. Madison maintained that the interstate commerce power was not of the same

the interstate commerce power, Marshall preferred to accept the word "regulate" as a governing concept implying the paramountcy of Federal power and excluding the notion of concurrency of this power between the states and the Federal Government. Here was a priority of priorities, and Marshall seized upon it for the sake of the great objects of the Federal Government.

It has been argued[10] that it is difficult to derive from the words of the Constitutional grant any limitation on the power of the several states to enact legislation not interfering with the operation of authorized Congressional acts. There appears to be no grammatical or logical justification in the compact between the states and the Federal Government preventing a concurrent exercise of the interstate commerce power; for the clause implies a simple grant to the Federal Government and is silent on the matter of other governmental bodies concurrently exercising the same power. This is a perfectly valid observation, and yet, as Professor Sharp has pointed out, "the development of negative limitations on the powers of the states, from these affirmative words alone, (The Congress shall have Power . . . etc.) has been a striking accomplishment of the Supreme Court."[11] Marshall's opinion that the grants of the interstate commerce power to the Federal Government implied a denial of this power to the states has come generally to be accepted by the courts, but not until after the period of Chief Justice Taney.

Of even greater importance than Marshall's views on the question of concurrency was his theory of Federal paramountcy. Should conflict arise, he pointed out, in the regulation of interstate commerce between a state of the Union and the Federal Government, "it [would] be immaterial whether the laws of the state were passed in virtue of a concurrent power 'to regulate commerce . . . among the several states' or in virtue of a power to regulate their domestic trade and police. . . . In one case and the other, the acts of the state must yield to the law of Congress."[12]

The genius of Marshall consisted in his insight into the necessity of minimizing the implications of the compact theory in interpret-

---

nature or extent as the power over foreign commerce. This position is expressed by Madison in a letter to J. C. Cabell, February 13, 1829. *Letters and Other Writings of James Madison* (Philadelphia, 1865), IV, 14–15.

10. See Malcolm P. Sharp, "Movement in Supreme Court Adjudication—a Study of Modified and Over-ruled Decisions," *Harvard Law Review*, XLVI, 593 ff.

11. *Ibid.*, 593.   12. 9 *Wheaton* 1 at 210.

ing the nature of the Union, and of permitting the prior principle of ultimate social purpose to predominate in construing the terms of the Constitutional grant. Thanks to Marshall's decision, which established the range and possibilities of the commerce and navigation powers, the courts—up to the beginning of the present century at any rate—had made use of this excellent precedent for finding the navigation power capable of satisfying new demands of the socio-economic life of the nation. The social and economic conditions of the eighteenth century were not radically altered until the latter part of the next century. The case law of this period is characterized for the most part by an orderly development from precedent. New situations arose for judicial determination, but these required merely new particular applications of well-settled and clearly defined ranges of legal opinion. The far-reaching decision of *The Daniel Ball*,[13] resulted in an extension of the Federal Government's jurisdiction over water courses, was an advance in the law as defined in *Gibbons* v. *Ogden;* and yet in no way was the law distorted. This does not mean to imply that the law during this phase developed without doubt or hesitation as if to some pre-ordained end; but in comparison with the difficulties of our contemporary period its progress was simple. Again, the concept of navigability announced by Taney in *The Genesee Chief*[14] was still a development within the basic formulation of the law: germane to the tradition, yet withal novel.

As long as the problems raised by the navigation power were substantially related to the maintenance and development of waterways, the law expanded without violence either to itself or the facts it presumed to govern. Two historic movements, however,—the rapid industrialization of the past fifty years and the growth of the Far West—brought with them new problems in the control of American waters. These problems—the control of waters in electric power development and in irrigation—have forced an attenuation of the law; so that, having retained its basic formulation, the law has arrived at the stage of fiction. The Court in the T.V.A. Case[15] and in *Arizona* v. *California*[16] preferred to justify governmental control of power development on the basis of a legal

13. 10 *Wall* 557 (1871).
14. *Propeller Genesee Chief v. Fitzhugh*, 12 *How.* 143 (1851).
15. *Ashwander et al. v. The Tennessee Valley Authority et al.*, 8 *Fed. Sup.*,893; 297 *U.S.* 325.
16. 283 *U.S.* 423.

fiction that narrowed the issue of government regulation to the simple question of navigation.[17] There was ample precedent in *Gibbons* v. *Ogden* to justify the Government's control and operation of public utilities as such.[18] The T.V.A. decision was not a liberal decision; on the contrary, it failed to adjust the commerce power to a contemporary problem by failing to employ the basic principle of Marshall: the interpretation of the commerce power in the light of the great objects for which it was established in the Federal Government.

The power business may well be regarded as a public business. If, as Mr. Arthur E. Morgan of the T.V.A. has maintained, the nature of water as *res communis* implies that the generation and distribution of electric power is a "public business"[19]; if it be conceded that in relation at least to such "public business" the Federal Government has the right "to establish public institutions . . . for the promotion of . . . commerce"[20]; if in addition, the substantially instantaneous character of conversion and transmission of water power in interstate commerce be recognized as "an inseparable part of a transaction in interstate commerce"[21]; if these points be conceded, then it would be possible for the Federal Government to enter the power business on an interstate scale. Such an application of the commerce power would have no trouble finding its place within the tradition of Marshall. Remarkably enough, the power interests themselves have suggested that the generation and transmission of electric power comes under the jurisdiction of the Federal Government[22]; this contention nicely brings to light the possible impotencies of the Federal system—the passing of the buck, if we may use the phrase, between the two agents of the social compact. For the power interests protest against state regulation by claiming that electric power is withdrawn from the competence of the states by the Constitution; and Federal jurisdiction

17. The precarious use of the navigation power for upholding Federal control of electric power sites is exemplified by an interesting lower court decision in the New River Case, *Appalachian Electric Power Company v. Members of the Federal Power Commission*.

18. 297 *U.S.* at 340. See the discussion of this case in Charles A. Beard and Mary R. Beard, *America in Mid-Passage* (New York, 1939), 271 ff.

19. "The Tennessee Valley Authority," Information Service, Department of Research and Education, Federal Council of the Church of Christ in America, XIV, June 22, 1935.

20. M. Farrand, *Records of the Federal Convention*, II, 321, 322.

21. *Utah Power and Light Company v. Pfost*, 286 *U.S.* 165.

22. *Ibid.*

is challenged by these same interests on the basis of the Madisonian principle that the interstate commerce power is merely a negative and restraining power.[23]

The power problem is a regional problem. It cannot be satisfactorily managed by forty-eight separate jurisdictions. When a navigable stream is involved, Federal jurisdiction can, it is true, be justified on the basis of the navigation power. But where the Court holds a stream to be non-navigable, the only proper basis for Federal control lies in the adaptation of the commerce power to embrace electric power development on an interstate scale. And it is obvious that the best power sites are not found on our broad navigable waters but along riotous non-navigable streams. In using the navigation power to uphold the right of the Federal Government to regulate private power companies and to own and operate its own plants, the Court has not followed in the liberal tradition of Chief Justice Marshall. With respect to the issue of electric power, an interpretation of the commerce power which would honor the tradition of Marshall would proportion itself to the needs and problems of a power age as Marshall's application of the interstate commerce clause to navigation was proportioned to the needs and problems of the age of the steamboat. Unless the Court returns to the wisdom of Marshall, impregnating its decisions with Marshall's understanding of "the genius and character of [our] whole government," the inadequacy of the compact philosophy will be perpetuated in the public law of a nation that passed through fire and sword to reject forever the political implications of that philosophy.

---

23. The consequences of the Madisonian view are well illustrated by a parallel problem presented by the states using their police power to set up interstate trade barriers in the form of inspection laws and taxation measures. Many authorities are now asking for interstate agreements or Congressional action to remove these obstructions to interstate commerce. These measures cast light on the Confederate substructure which the compact theory preserves in the Federal system.

14. American Political Philosophy After 1865*

[This essay begins with the thesis that there was no major theoretical statement of political philosophy in the United States between 1865 and 1945. During this period there were fundamental social changes which were revealed in practice. These changes served to undermine the eighteenth-century foundations on which the nation was built. McCoy bases his analysis on the notion that a constitution is constituted by the morals and customs of a people. These presuppose some sort of intellectual rectitude or orientation. The American founding fathers understood the place and significance of wealth, but America in the beginning was not an oligarchy in the Aristotelian sense, which it seemed to become after the Civil War. Nor was wealth something seen in Hegelian fashion, to be achieved down the ages. It was something present, similar to the middle-class state of Aristotle. McCoy saw the controversy that took place during this period between the notion of general welfare and the Gospel of Wealth to be a confusion about the theory of natural law. He did not hesitate to find the origins of natural law in Aristotle. The difference between natural law and natural rights theory is developed here in the context of American political philosophy.]

The period between 1865 and the present is one in which no systematic American political philosophy is produced; rather, there is a kind of contrary situation in which, to use Walter Lippmann's phrase, "the acids of modernity" begin to destroy the whole fabric of eighteenth-century life—political, social, economic, intellectual, and religious. The political philosophy of this period is not to be found, then, in any *ex professo* treatment of the subject, but is to be found rather in a great miscellany of things—in cultural changes, and in changes in the applied sciences and mechanical

*This essay originally appeared in *Thought,* 21 (June 1946), 249–71

arts which constitute a civilization; and in the various expressions of these changes, found in writings of scientists and scholars, in the speeches and writings of political leaders, leaders in industry and labor and agriculture, in the judicial opinions of the great Supreme Court justices. All of these express and reflect the changing character of American society after 1865; or better, they reflect the change in what de Tocqueville called the "manners" of the early democracy—its social habits and ideals. Changes of this sort are the most profound for political philosophy, for it is the social habits, institutions, and ideals of a people that determine fundamentally the constitution of a State.

In our political science textbooks we deal necessarily with the physical structure of the American government, and our considerations are there constrained to an appreciation of the positive character of the law. When we speak of changes in the Constitution of the United States we there have in mind either the formal amendment process, judicial interpretation, administrative decisions, or one of the other ordinary means by which the Constitutional document undergoes alteration. And yet, even in the restricted field of constitutional law it has been evident from the beginning that "broad constructionists" and "strict constructionists" derived their theories of interpretation from a political philosophy which they considered as existing prior to the written document and which the written document was intended to express and guarantee. Ultimately, as Aristotle wisely pointed out, the constitution of a country rests upon and gives expression to the moral conditions and capacities of a people; and since rectitude in moral matters presupposes some scientific rectitude by which we know the nature of the thing to be directed and of the end, the constitution of a country is to that extent also affected by the state of intellectual wisdom.

The task, therefore, of examining American political philosophy of the period after 1865 is a much more difficult and complicated one than the task of exposition and analysis of some formal treatise on the nature of the State. It becomes necessary to inquire into the transformations that took place after the middle of the nineteenth century in eighteenth-century culture and civilization. By culture I understand primarily the condition of speculative knowledge and the liberal arts; by civilization, the condition of the applied sciences, the mechanical arts, and the civic or moral virtues. Obviously this is a tremendous task, calling for a great deal of study and reflection. But it is a challenging and rewarding one for the person who is interested in contributing toward an understanding of the nature of contemporary American life.

It is rewarding because a grasp of tradition is always, as Mr. Santayana suggests, "a great advantage, conducive to mutual understanding, to maturity, and to progress."[1] My effort here must necessarily have the character of an essay summarizing, in the preliminary portions, the determining features of the period after 1865, and then suggesting how the canons of traditional western European political philosophy may be used to give a just appreciation of the direction of American life.

The most notable feature of the post-Appomattox years was, perhaps, the changed attitude toward wealth. Property interests, it is true, had had an important share in shaping the work of the Fathers at the Philadelphia Convention, and giving direction to the early legal and political development in the United States. But wealth was not the gospel of the men of these early years, as it was of the leaders in public life after the middle of the century. If we can agree with Beard's *Economic Interpretation of the Constitution,* that agreement involves no more than what the ancient traditional political philosophy of western Europe had always acknowledged. Had not Aristotle explicitly said that the family exists to satisfy the needs of everyday life, that the village serves to provide the "non-daily" needs, and the State comes into existence to make possible a sufficiency of these same needs? But the Fathers of the New England statesmen, who inherited the classical tradition through Locke and Hooker, were just as well aware of the rest of the Aristotelian doctrine, namely, that although the State first came into existence to provide for a sufficiency of material wants, it continues in existence for the sake of the good life. And the difference for Aristotle and for the whole western political tradition between wealth and the good life as principles of a society was precisely a constitutional difference—the constitutional difference between oligarchy and aristocracy. In the *De Regimine Principum* St. Thomas Aquinas remarks that if wealth were the purpose of social life then financiers should be kings. And in the last decade of the nineteenth century financiers were very nearly kings in America; at least they were "robber barons." The United States passes, after 1865, from an aristocratic democracy to an oligarchical democracy.

1. George Santayana, *Character and Opinion in the United States* (New York, 1920), 7–8.

For the men of the early republic the "good life" was not an empty phrase. They had the habits and institutions necessary for guaranteeing it. Wealth was anchored in the soil, and although there were rich and poor the extremes were not predominate, and those who were makers were makers for use according to the very prescription of Aristotle's first book. When the Fathers talked of the pursuit of happiness and the blessings of liberty, they were not, like the liberal Hegelians, waiting for these things to turn up in the historical cards; they were guaranteeing them—or hoping to guarantee them. For the Fathers, the role which Divine Providence had assigned the United States was that of making the good life possible for larger and larger numbers of people.

The reader of Henry Adams's autobiography finds there the most sensitive and profound reaction to the change which came upon the whole of American social life after 1865. Returning from England in the late 1860's, Adams was quickly disillusioned and, as a consequence, lost his ambition to carry on the family's tradition of public service. "What Henry Adams thought he saw," writes Mr. Van Wyck Brooks, "was true. The old idealism had been burnt away, the hopes of the patriot fathers, the youthful and generous dreams of the early republic. The war, with its fearful tension, draining the national vitality, had left the mind of the people morally flabby. The indifference to the public welfare was as marked as Henry Adams thought, and a low type of 'business ethics' prevailed over the old ethics, in a larger and larger measure as time went on."[2] The new civilization which came into being with the factory system, the opening of the west, and foreign immigration

"abounded in practical benefits, railroads and steamships, the gaslight, telegraph wires and friction matches, sewing machines and reaping machines and what-not. Its disastrous effects, however, were apparent at once. With the growth of the stock-exchanges and the corporations, the great centralized industries, the factory owners moved to the cities and lost their connection with the country. They ceased to feel responsible for the welfare of their workers. . . . As absentee directors, they ruled a foreign population. The bond between the masters and the workers, wholly abstract and financial, was full of the seeds of the class war of the future."[3]

Sanctifying and justifying the new civilization was the new Gospel of Wealth. This was the way Andrew Carnegie described his

2. Van Wyck Brooks, New England: Indian Summer (New York, 1950), 97.
3. Ibid., 96–98.

philosophy in an article on Wealth which he wrote for the *North American Review* in 1887. But we must not suppose that the new gospel was preached and embraced only by the promoters and gamblers in stocks, the war-profiteers, like Jay Gould, Jay Cooke, and Jim Fiske. The Gospel of Wealth

was, in fact, not merely the philosophy of a few rich men but a faith which determined the thinking of millions of citizens engaged in small enterprises. . . . This faith and philosophy became the most persuasive siren in American life. It filled the highways with farm boys trekking to the city. It drained the towns and countryside of Europe. It persuaded the educated young men that the greatest rewards of life were to be found in the business world. It taught the ambitious that power lies in wealth.[4]

It is not possible to understand the depth and permanence of this change unless we appreciate how important for the life of the country had been the "universal republic of letters" over which the New England writers had held unquestioned sway before 1865. Mr. Van Wyck Brooks admirably states the nature of their humanizing influence upon the nation:

The New England authors were teachers, educators, bringers of light, with a deep and affectionate feeling of obligation towards the young republic their fathers had brought into being. . . . There was something in their temper that made them seem friends of the human spirit. They stood for good faith and fair play and all that was generous and hopeful in the life of their time. The hold they gained and kept over the nation possessed extra-literary sanction, as if they were voices of the national ethos. If they found themselves 'done up in spices, like so many pharaohs,' as Holmes remarked in later years, it was because they were looked upon as classics,—

In whom is plainest taught, and easiest learnt,
What makes a nation happy, and keeps it so.[5]

The great lesson that the New England authors had communicated to the young republic had been that a truly human life and the things of the spirit are the lasting objectives for man. The statesmen of the earlier age—men like Webster, Sumner, Charles Francis Adams, Motley—themselves schooled in the classical tradition, acknowledged the tutelary role of the New England authors not because the New England authors were men of letters but because

4. Ralph Henry Gabriel, *The Course of American Democratic Thought* (New York, 1940), 153, 155. See Brooks, *New England: Indian Summer*, 98.
5. Van Wyck Brooks, *The Flowering of New England, 1815–1865* (New York, 1936, 529.

as men of letters they best expressed "what makes a nation happy and keeps it so."

Art is judged by principles proper to itself since its excellence resides in the work done. In this respect art differs from virtue, which depends upon the excellence not of what is done but of the doer. And yet art is always under the rule of virtue since the end of men and of societies is the perfection not of things but of men, which perfection is the work of virtue. Therefore if art is divorced from the moral context of a civilization it contributes toward destroying the order of the common good. It is thus, I think, that we must understand that as the ties of New England to the soil and to reform were loosened, the new interest in aesthetics which ceased to be allied to the larger preoccupations, moral, political, religious, contributed toward a weakening of the sense of political common good which was so strong in the leaders of the early republic. But more; as the industrial era progressed, and in time took on the character of finance-capitalism, this change in American civilization was signalized by the new dominance of money and techniques over what had traditionally been the primary element in American civilization, the virtues of citizenship. And money and "numbers," unhindered, rapidly assumed the role of arbiter of public affairs as the economic and political exploitation of the country set earnestly in.

But is there a deeper relationship between the new Gospel of Wealth and the new interest in aesthetics which ceases to be allied to the larger considerations of morals and politics? Did the robber barons of the Gilded Age, whose relations were close with writers, musicians, painters, sculptors, allow their vanity to cause them to see themselves as creative spirits, makers of civilization? They were patrons of the arts; but more, were they not empire-builders? Had they, through contact with the myriads of artists who had visited Italy, learned to think of liberty as that concept had been elaborated under the aegis of Renaissance art, learned to think of it with Pico de Mirandola, as injured when man's mind is subject to the causality of nature or to any other determination which he has not established? Did they, in their own tremendous activity, feel with the man of the Renaissance that the world of culture is the work of genius, in which we meet up with an irrational, a power which cannot be reduced?[6] It is not unlikely that the influ-

6. See Ernst Cassirer, *Individuum und Kosmos in der Philosophie der Renaissance*

ence which Professor Howard Mumford Jones sees as having possibly turned the attention of American wealth to the importance
of patronizing the arts and education, research and philanthropy,
communicated also to the man of wealth the new spirit of independence in the arts and contributed the high justification by
which he, in company with all artists, remained unaccountable
except to his own genius.[7]

If Professor Jones suspects that the relation between wealth and
culture after 1865 is "closer to Cosimo dei Medici than it is to John
Calvin,"[8] the reason undoubtedly is to be found in the evident
disturbance to the order of the common good that marks the careers both of the men of the Renaissance and of late nineteenth-
century America: the disturbance precisely that occurs when the
creative power of man is given complete autonomy, freed from
every determination from without and allowed to decide according
to the inspiration of its genius, the good for man.[9] The result must
be monstrous. And the picture of the Gilded Age, as we all know
it, is, exactly, monstrous. Professor Jones asked rhetorically whether
the career of Cosimo De' Medici does not suggest

the days of economic exploitation, combines, trusts, the Heinz-Daly cop-
per war in Montana, the fight of Jim Hill to dominate a railroad empire
in the Northwest, the buying up of courts and legislatures, Senatorial
elections and appointments to the federal bench, the manipulation of
stock markets, the use of rebate and simulated panic, of artificially lowered
prices and artificially increased taxation to crush competitors—in sum, all
the cruelty and epic struggle of the Gilded Age and its aftermath? But
does it not also call up the founding of libraries and art museums, hos-
pitals and institutions, the patronage of opera and orchestra, the creation
of schools, colleges, and universities, the purchase of newspaper publicity
and magazine propaganda, the patronage, half-scornfully, half-enviously,
extended to writers, musicians, painters, sculptors, decorators, fashion
designers and cooks, the beginning of vast foundations for scholarship,

---

(Leipzig, 1927), for an exposition of this conception of liberty and the dignity of
man.

7. Howard Mumford Jones, *Ideas in America* (Cambridge, 1945), 148.

8. As everyone knows, the Gospel of Wealth of the Gilded Age owed much to
the Puritan doctrine of property. See Gabriel, *The Course of American Democratic
Thought*, 149–50. Calvinism—even original Calvinism—had too much forgotten that
some of the vices opposed to prudence bear striking resemblance to that virtue—
craftiness, guile, fraud—all of which can be of help in making money. See Thomas
Aquinas, *Summa Theologiae*, II–II, 55.

9. The identification of the liberty of a moral agent (which is in the choosing of
the means) with the liberty of art to choose the end involves at root a general denial
of the primacy of the speculative over the practical. See Charles de Koninck, *De la
primauté du bien commun* (Quebec, 1943), 85–90.

research, medicine, public charity—in sum, all the intellectual benefits that have come to the nation through the fortunes of the robber barons?

It is possibly even a bit pedantic to insist upon "influences" where, without influences the behavior is the authentic thing. It is sufficiently clear that the new oligarchical democracy was at the same time creating a civilization in which the applied sciences and the mechanical arts were assuming first place among the values of civilized life. The fact is basic. The critical part played by invention and technology in the rise of modern capitalism, and the peculiarly new vocation of the entrepreneur with its emphasis upon productive energy, skill, and insight, gave a direction to economic life which reversed the traditional order by putting "making" over "doing" and profits over men.

If the Gospel of Wealth summed up the general folk philosophy in the era after Appomattox, how do we account for the deepening revolt, expressed in political action and writings and reflected in constitutional history, against the dominance of the money power? Professor Gabriel writes:

The date, 1887, of Carnegie's essay (on Wealth) is not without significance. It followed the revolt of the Grangers by more than a decade and a half. Twelve years before it appeared had occurred the railway strikes of the frightening summer of 1878. It was written three years after the Haymarket Riot in Chicago, the signal for a nation-wide crusade against anarchism. Its timing suggests that it was an apologia. In spite of the evidence to support this contention, the hypothesis does not seem to fit the facts. Carnegie formulated a folk philosophy which was not only being accepted, but was being acted upon by the farmers who joined the Grange and by the more able and ambitious laboring men. . . . The steelmaster gave words to an economic philosophy which was dominant in the United States of the Gilded Age.[10]

I have suggested that the oligarchical principle as it was put to work in the careers of the robber barons was in fact more than merely the oligarchical principle—more because, it is important to note, oligarchy, insofar as it is a form of rule, is proffered on the basis of a certain interpretation of justice, namely, that land and other forms of wealth, being essential elements entering into the composition of a State, should determine the allocation of political power in the hands of the rich. The point that I am suggesting is that the struggle against the robber barons of the Gilded Age and against the industrial and financial magnates of the subsequent

10. Gabriel, *The Course of American Democratic Thought*, 146–147.

decades, seen in the labor movement, the Grange and populist movements, in Bryanism and New Dealism, was a struggle not against the Gospel of Wealth as such, not, that is, against the oligarchical principle, but against a more deeply amoral attitude, against the belief that culture and civilization belong to great men who, by reason of their genius, are accountable to nobody. The doctrine of the General Welfare State and the policy of governmental intervention, by which the popular movements were defended, were essentially efforts to re-establish the traditional mores of the republic to the extent at least of reaffirming the primacy of the common good. It is quite beside the point *how* this common good was now conceived, that it was or may have been conceived in terms of the Gospel of Wealth, that it had as its ideal an oligarchy of the many rather than the few. The point rather is that it was a conception of common good that the doctrine of the General Welfare State represented and which it opposed to an amoral and tyrannous conception.[11]

Now the controversy between the Gospel of Wealth—or as it later came more properly to be described, "rugged individualism"—and the exponents of the doctrine of the General Welfare State, aired in the courts, in political speeches and programs, in the writings of scholars, had necessarily to be fought out in terms of the nature and purpose of the American Constitution and of the doctrine of natural law from which the Constitutional document received its inspiration. The tremendous confusion in the literature of this controversy is principally due to the eighteenth-century misconception, through Locke, of the classical and medieval doctrine of natural law—a misconception which is held down to the present by writers who do not go beyond Locke.[12] Without intending to call attention to the character of this misconception, Professor Ralph Barton Perry describes it perfectly when he presents the traditional notion as one that is sufficiently understood in terms of a "set of categorical maxims" apprehended as a set of "intuitive principles" by which a regime of "natural harmony" is discovered in social relationships if these are but left undisturbed.[13]

11. It would have been to the interest of the robber barons of the Gilded Age and their heirs to have studied the counsels which Aristotle offered to oligarchs. See *Politics*, V, 6, 1305a38; 8, 1307b30; 1308b20; 1309a20; VI, 5, 1320al–37.

12. Santayana, *Character and Opinion*, 9. See also George H. Sabine, Introduction, Carl Becker, *Freedom and Responsibility in the American Way of Life* (New York, 1945).

13. Ralph Barton Perry, *Puritanism and Democracy* (New York, 1945), 147 ff.

For this formidable strait-jacket Professor Perry offers a solvent in terms of "experimental utilitarianism" which through the "spirit of free inquiry" seeks to establish a condition of "happiness for sentient beings."[14] It is of course notorious that the English Utilitarians set out to destroy the notion of natural law, taking the eighteenth-century conception of it as genuine, and ended up with a conception of their own; what is less well appreciated is that the Utilitarian conception contained the essential errors of the eighteenth-century conception; and what is scarcely at all appreciated is that the eighteenth-century doctrine was a bad presentation of the traditional medieval and classical doctrine.[15] Professor Perry writes that experimental utilitarianism transforms the "pietistic and intuitive" ethics of the eighteenth century and frees the natural law doctrine from its errors without weakening its essential contentions.[16] But it is clear that the ethics of Aristotle is not "pietistic and intuitive"; nor is it an experimental utilitarianism; and yet the doctrine of natural law is originally Aristotle's. Evidently, the doctrine of natural law has been basically misunderstood both by the eighteenth century and by the nineteenth century—and, one must add, by the twentieth.

What concerns us here is the need to realize that the eighteenth-century understanding of the natural-law doctrine (and its nineteenth-century revision by the Utilitarians) jeopardized the western European tradition of political philosophy at its most crucial point by assimilating the diverse ends and methods of speculative and practical science, and more particularly by assimilating the subject matters of physical science and political and moral science.[17] According to the traditional political philosophy, *nature* is found in political and moral problems at two extremes: in the natural powers and passions of individual men, and in the natural associations which preserve life and guarantee the ends of living.[18] Thus the subject matter of ethical and political science is not fixed

14. Ibid., 418.

15. See statement of T. E. Cliffe-Weslie cited in Perry, *Puritanism and Democracy*, 532.

16. *Ibid.*, 418.

17. It is instructive to notice that the twentieth-century revisions of nineteenth-century Utilitarianism seek particularly to restore the practical character of politics which both nineteenth-century Utilitarianism and the eighteenth-century concept of natural law overlooked. Ironically, it is the practical character of politics that is at the root of the classical and medieval doctrine of natural law.

18. See Richard McKeon, "Aristotle's Conception of Political Philosophy," *Ethics*, 51 (April 1941), 253–90.

by natural properties or natural movements as is the subject matter of physics, since the habits and institutions which preserve the end in practical matters (human good) are brought about by voluntary action. Since virtues, actions, and institutions—the subject matter of political and moral science—are not fixed natures, these sciences must be concerned both with the individual conditions—the capacities and potentialities of individual men—and the social conditions—existing social groups and group relationships—affecting the achievement of the ends of individual and communal life. How radically misconceived, therefore, was the eighteenth-century natural-law doctrine implying a discoverable, ready-made "natural harmony" in the social domain!

The natural-rights doctrine which was employed before the courts of the country in defense of property rights and individual liberty was the deeply distorted eighteenth-century version whose basic assumption was natural harmony of interests; and it was a doctrine suited precisely to give scope to a liberty unrestrained save by natural force and selection, a conception of liberty which was, I have suggested, at the core of the social philosophy of the robber barons. At the same time the effect of this policy was exactly to contribute to the destruction of those natural bases of society—the individual man with his intelligence and feelings, the family, and voluntary associations—which the traditional medieval and classical doctrine of natural law sought to preserve through good habits and good institutions. Thus it was that we saw grow up in the United States—and in the name of natural rights and Americanism—the impersonal corporation, the sacrosanct stock exchange, widespread and chronic unemployment and the great slum areas which destroyed individual and family life.

Speaking of the Fourteenth Amendment, the first section of which was heavily relied upon to support the Gospel of Wealth before the courts, Professor Andrew C. McLaughlin remarks that "the difficulty in working out the scope of the amendment arose out of the fact that the protections were thrown about personal liberty at the very time when there was new need of determining what was the nature or the limits of liberty."[19] The appearance of corporation cases in great numbers, Professor McLaughlin says, laid bare "the heart of the modern problem" by showing that the

19. Andrew C. McLaughlin, *A Constitutional History of the United States* (New York, 1936), 724.

"distinction between the old fashioned belief that a person is entitled to his liberty and to the possession of his property and the new belief that large capitalistic interests are likewise to be protected" was, in the late nineteenth century, an actual distinction but not a legal one: Corporations were persons.[20] That was indeed the very heart of the problem. But the complexity of the problem can be appreciated only if we see the manner in which the Court proceeded to adapt the old principles of law to the new facts. It is significant that for nearly twenty years after the adoption of the Fourteenth Amendment there appeared no tendency to give the first section any serious weight, despite not a few opportunities for doing so; there seemed to be, for example, no intention of construing the Amendment so as to protect industries from State regulation by bringing them under the protection of the national government. Justice Miller, giving the opinion of the Court, had declared in 1878: "In fact it would seem from the character of many cases before us, and the arguments made in them, that the clause under consideration [the first section of the Fourteenth Amendment] is looked upon as a means of bringing to the test of the decision of this court the abstract opinions of every unsuccessful litigant in a State court of the justice of the decision against him, and of the merits of the legislation on which such a decision may be founded."[21] And as late as 1885, the conservative Justice Field had stated that "it is hardly necessary to say that the hardship, impolicy, or injustice of State laws is not necessarily an objection to their constitutional validity."[22]

The change came soon after Field's statement was made. "Just why it came at that time," says Professor McLaughlin, "it is difficult to say." But evidently the new tendency to use the Amendment to save private enterprise from governmental interference cannot, in the light of the early history of the Amendment before the Court, be laid to the fixed mentality of a legal apriorism. Before adverting to the reasons which may be offered to explain the change, it would seem proper to consider for a moment the nature of the judicial process. It is fairly evident that the job of interpreting and applying law to particular cases is calculated to give the judge a rather good comprehension of the essential nature and meaning of law. And I suggest that the abstract and wholly imaginative

20. *Ibid.*, 749.
21. *Davidson v. New Orleans*, 96 U.S. 97, 104 (1878).
22. *Missouri Pacific Co. v. Humes*, 115 U.S. 512, 521 (1885).

conception of natural law which is relayed in the books of social historians and scientists and which is attributed by them to the members of the Court is almost wholly absent from the opinions of the justices. Obviously, however, when marking the boundaries of personal liberty and governmental control it is necessary that the courts perform their task in legalistic fashion by adapting old principles and precepts of law to new facts. Now among the new facts which were being impressed upon the Court in the late nineteenth century were the newer forms of property under finance-capitalism, the social unrest of the period, the activity of the Knights of Labor and the whole ferment of social thought and speculation which boded ill for the old order. If these things were not the things which brought the Court after 1885 "to gather the spirit of free institutions and of personal liberty under the protective wings of 'due process'" then, as Professor McLaughlin says, it is difficult to say what were the things. Certainly not an attachment on the part of the justices to "categorical maxims" and "intuitive principles"; for during the first twenty years under the Amendment the Court was oppositely and liberally disposed. No. Granted that it is necessary for the courts to perform their task in legalistic fashion by adapting old principles and precepts of law to new facts, the Court's expressions of the nature and purpose of law—throughout this period—could in many instances not have been better; indeed, the dicta of the Court frequently show considerable appreciation of the changing character of society. But as we have observed, protections were thrown about liberty at a time when the new institutions of industrial society—particularly the new forms of property under finance-capitalism—required a reconsideration of the nature and limits of liberty. The "old order" had come, not unnaturally, to be identified with the dominant institutions of a highly industrialized society—so subtle is Aristotle's observation that a constitution rests ultimately on the social habits and moral conditions of a people—and fearful of what appeared to be an unwarrantable assault upon the old order, the Court was led toward a position calculated to serve not the ends of human life but large and abstract capitalistic interests. Precisely, indeed, what the Court was doing in these decades was applying the general principles of natural law not in any timeless and irrelevant fashion but quite in an experimental and utilitarian fashion, to the institutions and habits of an oligarchical society. The "old order" was the new order. Could anything be more liberal than that? More experimental? More utilitarian? Or are those who attack the reaction of the Court maintaining that there are inalienable natural rights of man independent of times and forms of government?

Is there a joker here in the historical cards? I have said that the work of applying and adapting general principles and precepts of law to new facts conduces to an appreciation of the practical character of law and political science, and I have suggested that it is for this reason that the opinions of the Supreme Court justices are quite free from the wholly abstract and imaginative conception of natural law so generally credited to them.[23] Now the objective of contemporary American political philosophers is to save the essential contentions of the natural-law doctrine by freeing that doctrine from its "abstract assumptions," its "intuitive principles" and "categorical maxims." This twentieth-century revision of the eighteenth-century natural-law doctrine and the nineteenth-century Utilitarian version seeks to free the natural-law doctrine from its "errors"[24] by insisting on the practical character of law and political science. But if the belief of contemporary American political philosophers is that the "essential contentions" of the natural-law doctrine are saved, and the "errors" are expunged simply by restoring to law and politics their practical character, then the eminently practical work of the courts in adapting the general principles of law to new facts should have sufficiently served to protect the essentials of humane living. But as we have seen, the experiment of adapting the general principles of law to a changing so-

23. I have not said that the eighteenth- and nineteenth-century natural-harmony conception of natural law did not influence or even control the thinking of the Court in these decades. What I say is that from the very nature of the case, judicial opinions discussing the applicability of general principles of law to new facts must show an effective appreciation of the practical character of law and of the changing character of social institutions. If natural-law principles are understood as providing a means of comprehending a natural harmony in the social order, then the experimental work of applying these principles entails finding the measure of the law in the ruling institutions of society. And the right, which is the essence of law, by which the dominant elements in society impose themselves will simply derive from the power they possess in the nature of things. This, as I have indicated, was in fact the direction of American constitutional law in the last decades of the nineteenth century.

24. The primary error of the eighteenth and nineteenth-century schools has been to assimilate the diverse ends and methods of speculative and practical science. But it is necessary to notice that the contemporary efforts are not precisely aware of the exact nature of the error since they are not aware of the dimensions of medieval and classical doctrines.

ciety—and to a society precisely insofar as it was changed—so that
the new dominant institutions were protected, had the effect of
serving not the ends of human life, but large capitalistic interests.

The practical character of politics is, indeed, at the root of the
classical and medieval doctrine of natural law; it is at the root of
the doctrine because the general principles of natural law—human
action not taking place in the abstract—need to be specifically determined. But this specific determination will be made in terms of
ends conformable or not conformable with right reason. Thus it is
that the practical—or experimental—aspect of law is as much in
evidence in a society whose determining principle is wealth as it
is in one whose determining principle is virtue. And in this sense
every society, good and bad, rests upon a *moral* foundation, meaning thereby that society is founded upon natures which are not
fixed by natural properties or natural movements with respect to
the achievement of their ends. So that indeed what Professor Perry
includes as the first of the "essential contentions" of the natural-
law doctrine—namely, that political institutions rest upon a moral
foundation—is simply the condition proper to all men and societies of not being *by their natures* at once and perfectly determined
to their ends. Thus the moral foundation of political institutions
precisely means that political institutions can be bad or good; this
"essential contention" of the natural-law doctrine is exactly what
experimental utilitarianism does indeed preserve. An oligarchical
society, the principle of whose constitution is wealth, is as much
a determination of the principles of natural law as is a society
whose end is virtue. How then can it be that, as Professor Perry
suggests, these different practical determinations themselves constitute an experimental finding of the end, namely, civil perfection,
which formerly it had been supposed natural law appointed?[25]

The attempt to correct the eighteenth- and nineteenth-century
schools of natural law by seeking to give back again to political
science its practical character is only a step in the right direction.
It is not enough to see that political science is a practical and not
a speculative science. One must also see that while the classical
and medieval tradition distinguished sciences as speculative and
practical this distinction involved a subordination of the practical
to the speculative: the practical is practical precisely and only as
directing action toward an end known by the speculative intelli-

25. Perry, *Puritanism and Democracy,* 164.

gence; so that in fact if practical regulation were, *per impossibile,* independent of speculative truth, then practical science would no longer be science and simple practical knowledge would no longer be truly practical.[26] In the classical and medieval doctrine of natural law the rectitude of practical regulation presupposes the rectification of the speculative intelligence.

We have noticed the marked character of the disturbance to the order of the common good where an oligarchical system fails to observe the precautions necessary for its continued existence. Although oligarchy frequently gives rise to movements of mass revolt, because of the mass oppression which characterizes them, the natural direction of the oligarchical regime is toward tyranny. The reason is that the pursuit of wealth as such constitutes a "means" unfixed by the ends of the human life to which the natural bases of society—the individual and the natural associations— are ordained. Thus the oligarchical regime inherently tends to take society out of the "ethical" order and into the "productive" order where the end becomes simply what the producer, the maker, wants it to be. This is the meaning of the observation that tyrannical rule is rule by pure political artists. Now the distinction between prudence, which is concerned with right living, and art, which is concerned with right making, is accompanied in the traditional political philosophy by the further observation that property and possessions are instruments of living and not of making. They are instruments subordinated to and employed in behalf of an end already known but yet to be achieved, namely, the virtuous living of men in community.

In the classical and medieval understanding of natural law the family, as one of the natural associations necessary for securing the ends of life, uses property and possessions as instruments for living in a way comparable to the way in which the artist uses instruments in making. The right of private property precedes the State precisely in terms of the early association of the family assuring to itself the daily needs of life. The succeeding associations of village and State come into existence in order to insure, in the first case, the non-daily needs, and in the second a *sufficiency* of these needs. It should be particularly noticed that according to the traditional doctrine, the State *first comes into existence* in order to make possible a sufficiency of material needs: this function is in

26. De Koninck, *De la primauté du bien commun,* 85–86.

no way used to distinguish different kinds of States as good and bad; providing a sufficiency of material needs is a *sine qua non* of all States, both good and bad. The distinction of forms of State is only made upon a further consideration, namely, the end or purpose which is given primary value in the society and which the institutions of the society are designed to achieve.

The root of the relationship between private property and the natural associations necessary to secure the ends of living is, then, the notion of property as an "active," not a "factive," instrument— that is, as instrumental to "doing" and living and not to making. It is for this reason that the citizen, unlike the artist, does not dominate the end for the sake of which the instruments of property and possessions are designed. Thus, according to the traditional doctrine, even before the State comes into existence, the institution of private property under the familial organization undergoes a modification as families gather into villages.[27] Since the purpose of the village is to guarantee non-daily needs (an end necessary for the family but one which the family organization is inadequate to procure) the village organization prescribes new economic activities for the families that compose it in view of the new end of the larger association. Similarly, when the State comes into existence to make possible a sufficiency of all needs the economic structure of the village is subject to modification by the general community in the interest of the common good. It is in this way that the natural law, according to the traditional doctrine, receives increasing determination and the individual with the natural associations necessary for securing the ends of living is strengthened and perfected in view of the common good. These were the economic and political notions which were manifested in the economic institutions of medieval Europe and also of early Capitalism, as Werner Sombart has shown in *Der Moderne Kapitalismus*. Professor Nussbaum, in his *The History of Economic Institutions of Europe* observes that "the object of medieval economic life . . . was not profits but men. In the Middle Ages, this purpose was expressed in an economy the object of which was the nourishment and sustenance of all the individuals in the group" (p. 28).

The Industrial Revolution and the Renaissance did not have their influence in America until after the middle of the nineteenth century. The one, by virtue of the Gospel of Wealth propagandizing

27. See Heinrich Rommen, *The State in Catholic Thought* (St. Louis, 1945), 401.

(and propagandizing in) a market which enabled the entrepreneur to dominate the forces in capitalistic enterprise, and the other, by virtue of the new interest in creative work, contributed to giving primacy to the mechanical arts and the applied sciences over the exigencies of political common good. It was not until these influences made themselves felt in America that the inadequacy of the eighteenth-century natural-law doctrine—made emphatic in the nineteenth century by the Utilitarian revision—could show its disastrous practical consequences. For then it was that as American life came under the rule of money and technics a natural-law doctrine which viewed society as determined to its end by fixed natural properties and natural movements was found to have surrendered the practical to the productive. For, as we have seen, where the subject matter of practical science is assimilated to that of speculative science then human good and society will be simply what we want to make them, and "we" will be whoever has the power over us. The irony of our times is that the cultivation of man and his world, bearing such wonderful fruit in the arts and sciences, has been unaccompanied by the profound sense of governance that characterized less sophisticated times. The roots of that irony are deep, but we have stumbled on some of them.

15. The Doctrine of Judicial Review and the Natural Law*

[In view of the anti-natural-law direction the courts have subsequently taken, this essay on the doctrine of natural law and judicial review is of particular significance. McCoy distinguishes jurisdiction and the other powers of government. This is an essay on rule, but on limited rule. What this means is: that rule concerns means to ends which do not themselves fall under the authority of the ruler. For this McCoy finds John Marshall a guide. He notes the way Marshall used the principles of natural justice in his fundamental cases. He traces the way this position of Marshall was undermined by subsequent "Jacobin" theories, which held that any reliance on the natural law tradition through the common law tradition closed the channels of thought. McCoy rightly points out the totalitarian nature of this latter trend which denied the distinction between jurisdiction and government, only to end up by making whatever the government enacted to be "law." McCoy pays particular attention to how the notions of religion and property were affected when this newer, more radical interpretation of Marshall was in effect. McCoy argued that judicial review is justified only when we can account for the limitation of the state, when natural law is not a mere fiction.]

The title of this article suggests that judicial review bears a unique relation to natural law, that it is related in a way that the legislative power and the executive power are not. This is indeed the case: judicial review immediately evokes the idea of *jurisdiction;* on the other hand, "legislative power," "executive power" signify *government.* The distinction between government and jurisdiction is at the heart of the whole theory of constitutional or limited government.

*This essay originally appeared in *Catholic University of America Law Review,* 6 (December 1956), 97–102.

Before speaking of John Marshall's use of judicial review in establishing the jurisdiction of government, it might be well to spend a moment inquiring into the original source of this notion of *government limited by jurisdiction*. Professor Charles H. McIlwain has spoken of the "riddle" of constitutionalism: this riddle is expressed most strikingly in the dictum of medieval courts that the king is above the law and under the law; it may be expressed in more contemporary fashion by pointing out that limited government is not one which is not in full control of affairs. We know for example that Marshall not only established effective limits to the authority of government, but that he made the authority absolutely effective within its limits—within the limits of its jurisdiction. It might be well to make a preliminary glance at the source of this important political conception.

As in other matters, so in these it is Aristotle who, by attending to the most elemental things, attained the most profound and far-reaching. And so, although it may seem at first irrelevant, a consideration of Aristotle's doctrine is, on the contrary, most useful for a beginning understanding of the meaning of limited government.

In the first book of his *Politics*, Aristotle observes: "There are many kinds both of rulers and subjects . . .; for in all things which form a composite . . . and which are made up of parts . . . a distinction between the ruling and subject element comes to light. Such a duality exists in living creatures; but not in them only; it originates in the constitution of the universe. . . . At all events, we may . . . observe in living creatures a . . . constitutional rule; for . . . the intellect rules the appetites with a constitutional and royal rule."[1] Now the term "royal" here signifies (as could be demonstrated if we went back to Aristotle's psychology and ethics) *the full perfection of the governing principle;* the term "constitutional" signifies *the jurisdiction under which the governing principle operates.* The virtuous man is said to rule himself "royally" because he is in full control of himself—he does the good easily and with pleasure. His self-government is not weak—he is not weak. At the same time he is said to rule himself "constitutionally" *because what he does easily and with pleasure is what he ought to do*—what he is *bound* to do by the constitution of his nature, by the law of his nature, by the natural law. It is the things that he *ought* to do that

---

1. Aristotle, *Politics*, I, 5, 1254a20–54b1.

he does with full control. Now the virtue by which a man chiefly does what he ought to do is the virtue of prudence—a virtue which St. Thomas Aquinas says is the virtue proper to all government. Prudence—the virtue proper to government—operates with respect to means, not to ends: hence when we say that government is in full control of affairs it is with respect to finding the means to ends which are fixed by man's constitution as a rational animal, by the law of his nature, by the natural law. These ends may very conveniently and appropriately for our purposes be summed up by the terms "substantive rights" and "procedural rights." By the first is meant all that is implied in living and living well; and by the second, all the procedures that prudence entails—e.g., deliberation, counsel, judgment.

As I said at the beginning, judicial review is related to natural law in a way that the legislative power and executive power are not. This is not to say that government itself is not also related to natural law: the decrees and statutes of government are said to be derived from natural law by way of *determination* of common principles of the natural law; for example, one's substantive right to life is made determinate by the statute providing for a living wage, social security, etc. As St. Thomas points out, a positive law derives its force from human agreement, from human determination or convention; or does not of itself have the force of natural law. But—and this is the important point—"the human will can, by common agreement, make a thing to be just provided it be not, of itself, contrary to natural right."[2] And within this area lies the function of judicial review.

When John Marshall established the doctrine of judicial review in 1803 in the case of *Marbury v. Madison*,[3] he not only confined the authority of the Federal government to the jurisdictional limits imposed by our written Constitution (this is a somewhat complicating point arising out of our unique Federal system, and a point of comparative unimportance since Marshall might have interpreted the Judiciary Act of 1789 in such a way as to allow the Court jurisdiction in the Marbury Case); but also—and this is the important point—Marshall held the authority of the Federal Government bound by a jurisdiction more fundamental than that of the written constitution. To understand this we must examine briefly

2. Thomas Aquinas, *Summa Theologiae*, II–II, 57, 2, ad 2.
3. 1 *Cranch* 137 (U.S., 1803).

the issues involved in *Marbury v. Madison*. The facts of the case were briefly these: near the end of the term of his office President Adams nominated William Marbury to the office of Justice of the Peace in the District of Columbia. The nomination was confirmed by the Senate, the commission signed by the President and the Great Seal affixed. On the expiration of Adams' term, Marbury applied to the Secretary of State—now James Madison under President Jefferson—for the delivery of his commission. Jefferson refused, holding that the appointment had not been completed since the commission had not been delivered. Marbury moved for a writ of mandamus before the Supreme Court to have Madison deliver the commission.

The legal issue turned out to be a very simple and narrow one: Marbury had moved for a writ of mandamus before the Supreme Court; the question was: does the issuing of a writ of mandamus fall within the original jurisdiction of the Court? Now the importance of the case lies not so much in the answer given by the Court to this question nor in the Court's finding that the Judiciary Act of 1789 Sec. 13 was void because contrary to Art. III, §2 of the U.S. Constitution. The deeper significance of the case lies in Marshall's answers to two questions which he raised before coming to the special legal issue. Paradoxically, after having concluded in his own mind that the Court was without jurisdiction, Marshall proceeded to decide the merits of Marbury's claim. And it is this portion of the decision that is of greatest import.

Marshall approached the decision by asking three questions. The first question asked was: had the applicant a right to the commission? The second question was: if he had a right, and that right had been violated, did the laws of this country afford him a remedy? The third question contained the legal issue: if the laws of his country did afford Marbury a remedy, was this remedy a mandamus issuing from the Supreme Court?

In answering the first question, the Court, having come to the conclusion that the appointment was made when a commission had been signed by the President, and that the commission was complete when the seal of the United States had been affixed to it by the Secretary of State, declared that the right to the office was in the person appointed and therefore to withhold his commission was "an act deemed by the Court not warranted by law, but violative of a vested legal right."[4] The thing to be observed is that

4. *Ibid.*, at 162.

this ruling was based neither upon the special language of any statute nor upon the language of the Constitution. It was based on principles of natural justice.

The answer to the second question was likewise reached not by a study of federal statutes but instead by an application of common law principles. Marshall observed: "The government of the United States has been emphatically termed a government of laws, and not of men. It will certainly cease to deserve this high appellation if the laws furnish no remedy for the violation of a vested legal right."[5] Note then, that Marshall is saying that the laws *must* furnish such a remedy (for the violation of a vested legal right) whether there is specific statutory provision or not. As Professor Carl Brent Swisher puts it: "Having made this assumption, which was based on no constitutional or statutory provision, he examined the case to see if there was anything in it to exempt it from the general rule, and he found nothing."[6] Hence, note the argument of the Court: Marbury has been found to have a legal title to the office, "a refusal to deliver which is a plain violation of that right, for which the laws of his country afford him a remedy"—*the laws of his country,* although, as we have seen, no specific statute so provided.

We may observe then, that there was a federal statute (the Judiciary Act of 1789) which provided Marbury with a procedural right (the writ of mandamus) but the issuance of such a writ *by any court* would depend on proof of neglect of ministerial duty in the Secretary of State, which neglect would itself depend on proof of Marbury's substantive right to the office to which he had been appointed. It was this substantive right that was not provided for in any statute, but which, according to Marshall, the laws of the country must enforce.

Having said all this, Marshall found (somewhat amusingly it must be conceded) that the Court lacked original jurisdiction to issue a writ of mandamus. It was the first time that the Supreme Court had declared void a law of Congress, and it was not to do so again for over half a century. Now the greatness and significance of the Marbury decision are usually said to lie in this invalidation of the federal statute. This was indeed significant, but it was not the matter of deepest significance; it involved, after all, merely finding one written law (the Judiciary Act of 1789) incom-

5. *Ibid.*, at 162.   6. *Ibid.*, at 163.

patible with another written law (the United States Constitution). Furthermore, we may notice that it would not have been at all impossible for Marshall—had he been so disposed—to have found the Judiciary Act of 1789 §13 quite constitutional. The specific legal issue before the Court was this: the Court was acting in this case not as an appellate tribunal but as a court of original jurisdiction. Section 2, Art. III, of the Constitution listed types of cases in which the Supreme Court was to have original jurisdiction. It stated that in all other cases within the judicial power of the United States the Supreme Court should have appellate jurisdiction, with such exceptions and under such regulations as Congress should make. There was doubt as to whether the power of Congress to make exceptions applied both to the original and appellate jurisdiction of the Court, or only to the latter. Marshall concluded that it applied only to the latter. The description of the original jurisdiction of the Supreme Court in the Constitution, he reasoned, was complete. Congress had no power to add to that jurisdiction. Among the items listed in it he did not find authority to issue writs of mandamus. The relevant provision of the Judiciary Act was, therefore, not authorized by the Constitution. This line of reasoning enabled Marshall to expound the principle that an act of Congress repugnant to the Constitution is void. Granted the significance of this principle, it is still subordinate to the other principle that Marshall laid down in answering his two preliminary questions, namely, that the authority of government is regulated by a jurisdiction more fundamental than any written law—even that of the Constitution.

I should like to add a brief *coda* to the considerations we have been making. I think we have seen that the Constitution is not of itself a guarantee of basic natural rights. The Constitution needs always to be interpreted and applied. The principles of constitutionalism are philosophical principles, but they were inherited in this country through the legal structure—especially the common law—of England. The philosophical principles underlying constitutionalism were, in the eighteenth century, undergoing that corruption whose full issue is now evident in what Mr. Walter Lippmann calls our Jacobin education. I may point out that Professor Carl Brent Swisher, a very distinguished authority in the field of Constitutional law, in speaking of those portions of Marshall's decisions which rest on natural-law principles, uses the terms "fictions," "assumptions," and "devices," and observes that we find in Marshall "an intermingling of conceptions of *law as emanating from government* and of laws as emanating from a source superior to any earthly government *which effectively closes the channels of thought and reasoning*."[7] This view expresses what is by no means an uncommon contemporary appreciation of Marshall. Professor Swisher's position leads directly to the abandonment of the distinction between government and jurisdiction: the only law that counts is what the government says. The unfortunate truth is that today, behind the magnificent facade of our legal structure, the substance of what Mr. Lippmann calls the "Public Philosophy" is fast being eaten away by "the acids of modernity." Let me illustrate this point by concluding with two questions relative to two basic rights guaranteed by the Constitution—that of property and that of religion. Is the right of property, as guaranteed by the Fourteenth Amendment, a right that understands property as an instrument of living and fundamentally instrumental in the perfection of family life? Or is it to be understood in the Lockean sense, which is primarily designed to protect large and abstract financial interests? I needn't say that it was the Lockean sense that largely determined the opinion of the Court from 1900 to 1930 and has been responsible for the breakdown of the social structure which the Popes have ceaselessly sought to have remedied. Secondly, is the guarantee of religious freedom by the First Amendment a declaration—as Father John C. Murray, S.J., seems to believe—of the traditional doctrine of the independence and superiority of the spiritual? Or is it, as Karl Marx understood it (and he was an astute student of the eighteenth-century revolutions) a formal relegation of religion to what he called "the refuse heap of arbitrary private whims"? If students and scholars of the caliber of Professor Swisher have come to think of natural-law principles as "devices," "fictions," "assumptions" that effectively close the channels of thought and reasoning, what—one wonders—becomes of supernatural principles? I mention these unpleasant things merely as a caution against supposing that John Marshall's fine spirit must inevitably animate the laws of our land.

7. Carl Brent Swisher, *American Constitutional Development* (New York, 1943), 162.

iv. Catholic Social Questions

16. Social Justice in *Quadragesimo Anno**

[This careful critique of the notion of "social justice" adds a welcome perspective to recent discussions of justice and politics. McCoy is interested in the claim that in the encyclical of Pius XI in 1931, *Quadragesimo Anno*, some new sort of justice, not known to the classics or to Aquinas, was to be proposed. McCoy insists that social justice did not refer to a virtue directly but to a proper disposition of parts within a whole, within society. Understanding Aquinas is crucial. Commenting on the nature of creation, Aquinas noted that inequality does not necessarily imply injustice. Nothing is originally "owed" so that the result is the product of something deeper than justice. Social justice is not, then, an aspect of distributive justice. The justice of the regime includes the order of parts within it, including the family, and these exist in their own right even within the whole. McCoy's clarification of general and particular justice is well taken, for the tendency to identify distributive justice with general justice is often at the root of problems with what is called "social justice." The insistence that distributive justice be not wholly identified with the state is a further pertinent element in this discussion. McCoy seems to have provided a way for the notion of innovation to be seen as itself an element of distributive justice.]

The following observations have been prompted by the review by Father Bernard W. Dempsey of Father William F. Drummond's book, *Social Justice*.[1] I wish to call attention to a number of considerations which bear on the problem of defining social justice and which, for some unaccountable reason, have been scarcely adverted to.

The many students of this question seem not to have been impressed with the possibility that the phrase "social justice" may

*This essay originally appeared in *Social Order*, 7 (June 1957), 258–63.

1. Bernard W. Dempsey, "The Range of Social Justice," *Social Order*, VIII (January 1957), 20. This was a review of *Social Justice* by William F. Drummond (Milwaukee, 1956).

not primarily signify justice as a virtue but rather a certain rectitude or order in the disposition of the parts of that whole which is society; and that the name of the *virtue* derives from its relation to this primary meaning. There has been so much discussion of the *virtue* of social justice that to make the suggestions I do may appear extremely rash.

It will perhaps not appear so if we consider—allowing for all the travail of pushing the "frontiers of research"—the fruitless effort to reach a common understanding of what the "newness" of this virtue precisely is; but more telling in behalf of what I suggest is the fact that the passages from St. Thomas to which Pius XI refers[2] in speaking of the "true guiding principle of social and economic activity" are not the passages in which St. Thomas treats of justice as a virtue (whether legal, distributive, or commutative); they are, rather, passages in which he speaks of another meaning of justice—"the justice of the regime"—a meaning which does not take justice as a virtue. These two senses of justice are explained by the Angelic Doctor as follows:

Since justice, by its very nature, signifies a certain rectitude of order, it may be taken in two ways: First, inasmuch as it signifies a right order in man's act; and thus justice is placed among the virtues—either as particular justice, which directs a man's acts by regulating them in relation to his fellowman, or as legal justice, which directs a man's acts by regulating them in their relation to the common good of society.

Second, justice is so-called inasmuch as it signifies a certain rectitude of order in the interior disposition of a man . . . insofar as . . . the inferior powers of the soul are subject to the superior; . . . and this disposition the Philosopher calls *justice metaphorically speaking*.[3]

We may note parenthetically that the reason why this justice is called "metaphorical" is simply that the due ordering of the parts of this whole is not an ordering of active "agents" or "persons" and hence there is not strictly speaking justice, which is always "toward another"; nevertheless "metaphorically in one and the same man there is said to be justice . . . *in general insofar as . . . to each part of man there is ascribed what is becoming to it.*"[4]

We may observe next that this metaphorical justice is found in the initial constitution of the universe and implies, indeed, a *kind* of distributive justice in the creation of various and unequal na-

2. Pius XI, *Quadragesimo Anno*, #81–91.
3. Thomas Aquinas, *Summa Theologiae*, I–II, 113, 1.
4. *Ibid.*, II–II, 58, 2.

tures. I say a *kind* of distributive justice because here nothing is conferred on "another" according to any preceding merit since nothing was before creation. Against the argument of Origen that justice is violated by an inequality in the parts of the universe, two points, St. Thomas says, are to be observed: In distributive justice something is given to a private individual insofar as what belongs to the whole is due to the part and in a quantity that is proportionate to the importance of the position of that part in respect of the whole. But "in the constitution of things there is no inequality of parts through any preceding inequality . . . [and, therefore, it must needs be that] inequality comes from the perfection of the whole. This appears also in works done by art; for the roof of a house differs from the foundation, not because it is made of other material; but in order that the house may be made perfect of different parts, the artificer seeks different material; indeed he would make such material if he could."[5] The justice spoken of here, then, is also "metaphorical" and not really distributive justice, since there is no real consideration of what is *owed* to the part.

Now, that this kind of justice (metaphorical) applies also to the rectitude of order of the parts—natural and quasi-natural—of that whole which is society is evident from the fact that it is to the doctrine contained in these passages that Pius XI alludes in speaking of the restoration of "the true directive principle of social and economic activity."[6]

The Pope refers also to this passage, in which St. Thomas is speaking of that metaphorical justice which is the rectitude of the order of the parts of the universe: "In every government the best thing is that provision be made for the things governed, according to their mode: *for in this consists the justice of the regime.*"[7] The Pope refers to this passage immediately after making the following observations:

. . . the demand and supply of labor divides men on the labor market into two classes, as into two camps, and the bargaining between these parties transforms this labor market into an arena where the two armies are engaged in combat. To this grave disorder . . . a remedy must evidently be supplied. . . . But there cannot be question of any perfect cure except this opposition be done away with, and *well-ordered members of the*

5. *Ibid.*, I, 47, 2 ad 3; II–II, 61, 2; see I, 65, 2 and ad 3.
6. *Quadragesimo Anno*, #84.
7. Thomas Aquinas, *Summa Contra Gentiles*, III, 71. This was cited in *Quadragesimo Anno*, #84.

social body come into being anew . . . binding men together . . . according to the diverse functions which they exercise in society. . . . These groups, [vocational and professional] in a true sense autonomous, are considered by man to be, if not essential to civil society, at least its natural and spontaneous development.[8]

This is that "justice of the regime" in which "provision [is] made for the things governed, according to their mode" that appears to be the primary signification of "social justice." It is more fully described by Pius XI when he says that

all the institutions of public and social life must be imbued with the spirit of justice and this justice . . . must build up a juridical and social order able to pervade all economic activity. . . . If then the members of the social body be thus reformed, and if the true directive principle of social and economic activity be thus re-established, it will be possible to say, in a sense, of this body what the Apostle said of the Mystical Body of Christ: "The whole body being compacted and fitly joined together, by what every joint supplieth, according to the operation in the measure of every part, maketh increase of the body, unto the edifying of itself in charity.[9]

Thus, applied first to the order of the parts of the universe—which St. Thomas compares (C.G. III, 71) to the justice of social order—"the justice of the regime" is used by the Pontiff in sections 83 through 90 to signify "the true directive principle of social and economic activity" (n. 90); and the exposition culminates in the statement:

If then the members of the social body be thus reformed, and if the true directive principle of social and economic activity be thus re-established, it will be possible to say . . . of this body what the Apostle said of the Mystical Body of Christ.

It appears, then, that the "true directive principle of social and economic activity" is that "justice of the regime" whereby the members of the social body are formed and re-formed according to what in part, at least, is "a natural and spontaneous development."

We may note that in treating of the relation of "social organization" to the *virtue* of social justice, Father Drummond himself observes that "Pope Pius XII was later to call the section of *Quadragesimo Anno* which contains the social policy embodying the idea of an occupational, corporative order of the whole economy the

---

8. *Quadragesimo Anno*, #83.   9. *Ibid.*, #88, 90.

'chief part' of the encyclical."[10] Would it not be strange indeed if in an encyclical on social justice the chief part of it were not devoted to social justice?

Reconstruct Society

If the professional and occupational organizations, "the well-ordered members of the social body," are in a sense institutions of natural law, they are not, however, "brought in" by nature: man has a share, as St. Thomas pointed out, not only in the disposition of Divine Providence but in its execution as well; for this is man's "self-government." It can happen then that "the highly developed social life, which once flourished in a variety of prosperous institutions organically linked with each other, has been damaged and all but ruined, leaving thus virtually only individuals and the State, and social life [has] lost its organic form."[11] The real task, then, is the reconstruction of the social order itself. When Father Drummond takes the social justice of the encyclical to be simply the virtue "whose formal object is the social aspect of property," he has no grounds for denying (although he is right in denying) as primary a role to the State in the exercise of this virtue as to "owners and administrators of property."[12]

In order to do this, it is necessary to invoke the concept of social

10. Drummond, *Social Justice*, 104.

11. *Quadragesimo Anno*, #78.

12. St. Thomas indeed viewed as the purpose of the civil law of property that it "accustom men to give of their own to others readily" (*Summa Theologiae*, I–II, 105, 2, ad 1) and men are made accustomed through the discipline and training of laws. For a man acts "unlawfully" and "sinfully" if in anticipating someone in taking possession of something which at first was common property he excludes others from a share (II–II, 66, 2, ad 2). And so St. Thomas observes, "As the Philosopher says, the regulation of possessions conduces much to the preservation of a state. . . . Consequently, . . . it was forbidden by the law in some of the pagan states that anyone should sell his possessions except to avoid a manifest loss. For [if such were to happen] . . . possession might come into the hands of a few so that it might be necessary for a state to become void of inhabitants." (I–II, 105, 2, ad 3) St. Thomas, in this passage, goes on to point out that the Law of the Old Testament adequately provided for the regulation of possessions, and he gives, among many examples, the limit placed upon possessions. Against the objection that the distribution of common goods to the many is hurtful to the morals of the many, his immediate reply is simply that the State, like a private individual, is praised for moderation in this and blamed for excess; his second reply—which is important for the considerations later made in this chapter—is that distribution may be made "by the authority of a private individual." (II–II, 66, 1, ad 1 and 3).

justice as signifying the organic form, the rectitude of order of society. After fully acknowledging the duty of the State "to specify . . . what is licit and what is illicit for property owners in the use of their possessions," Pius XI gives the reason why the discharge of this duty may not be arbitrary. The reason is this: "that the domestic household is antecedent, as well in idea as in fact, to the gathering of men into a community."[13] Thus it is only on condition of understanding social justice as "the justice of the regime," in which "provision is made for things governed, according to their mode," that we can begin to inquire into the role played by the *virtue* of justice in ensuring the rectitude of the intention of the end.

It was precisely, I suggest, the failure to advert sufficiently to the notion of justice as signifying the proper order of society that created the need to find a—in some sense—new species of the *virtue* of justice. The intention of *Quadragesimo Anno* was to restore to professional associations and occupational groups the task of administering private property for the common benefit of all. Now the use of material goods, privately owned, for the common benefit of all is without question a species of the virtue of justice. Hence it is quite understandable that one would be led to suppose that the novelty of the term "social justice" was to be found in some novelty of the virtue signified. That such is not the case appears, I believe, not only from the considerations thus far made, but from the deficiency of the definitions commonly given of social justice as a virtue.

Issue Misconceived

There are some who think that it is for the following reason that the Holy Father denominated the virtue in question "social justice": Since a family wage (it is argued) is due the worker in strict or commutative justice, but since economic conditions may not in fact allow businesses to pay the worker a family wage, the obligation upon them to do so derives from a new kind of "general" (or legal) or "contributive" justice which, because of its novelty, the encyclical denominates "social" justice. This appears certainly to be a misconception. Throughout *Quadragesimo Anno*, Pius XI speaks repeatedly of the equitable *distribution* of goods:

13. *Quadragesimo Anno*, #49, 50.

Wealth, therefore, which is so constantly being augmented by social and economic progress, must be so distributed among the various individuals and classes of society that the common good of all . . . be thereby promoted. . . . By these principles of social justice one class is forbidden to exclude the other from a share in the profits.[14]

It seems clear that the demand of social justice that economic conditions be so adjusted that business will be able to pay workers a family wage is a demand upon the common purpose of material goods: it is a directing of common goods to particular individuals; and this is St. Thomas's definition of distributive justice.

Moreover, the above argument appears to involve a radical misconception of legal or general justice. Although general justice directs acts of individuals to the common good, *it is not about common goods* and does not have as special matter "the things that are about social life," as St. Thomas clearly says.[15] Considering the objection that since matters pertaining to the community belong to legal justice, it would seem that distributive justice is part of legal justice and not of particular justice, St. Thomas replies: "Movement takes its species from the term *whereunto*. Hence it belongs to general (legal) justice to direct to the common good those matters which concern private individuals; whereas, on the contrary, it belongs to particular justice to direct the common good to particular individuals."[16]

Others, among whom is Father Drummond, think, more plausibly, that the requirement that material goods privately owned serve the common use of all must be called social justice because, while it resembles distributive justice in securing an innate right through the directing of common goods (the use of property privately owned),[17] it differs from distributive justice in being exercised not by the state but by owners and administrators of property. Father Drummond seems also to feel that social justice cannot be distributive justice because "its duties are based not on the determinate claims of any definite individuals."[18] These views, too, appear to be untenable for the following reasons: In treating of distributive justice, St. Thomas points out that the distribution of common goods is not necessarily made by the State; it can be

14. *Ibid.*, #57
15. Thomas Aquinas, *Summa Theologiae*, II–II, 58, 8, *sed contra*.
16. *Ibid.*, II–II, 61, 1, ad 4.
17. *Ibid.*, II–II, 66, 2. See also Drummond, *Social Justice*, 68.
18. Drummond, *Social Justice*, 66.

made "by the authority of private individuals," and this is the case in what St. Thomas considered to be the primary economic association—the domestic household.[19] Secondly, St. Thomas makes it clear that "particular individuals" to whom common goods are distributed signifies the relating of this virtue *immediately* to individuals as parts and *mediately* to the whole of which they are parts: In directing a man toward the common good, *legal justice* directs him only *mediately* toward individuals; "Wherefore there is need for particular justice to direct a man *immediately* to the good of another individual."[20] The requisite "definiteness" of individuals for distributive justice is to be understood, then, in contrast to "the others in general" to which legal justice is directed. Social justice is *immediately* concerned with individuals and mediately with the common good. It would seem, then, that the reasons offered by Father Drummond for denominating social—rather than distributive—the justice by which the economic wealth of society, augmented under the system of private property, be equitably distributed are insufficient reasons. Finally, St. Thomas says that it is distributive justice—not general or legal justice—that is "specially about those things that belong to social life."[21] It appears, then, that distributive justice itself is the species of the virtue of justice that is entitled to the name "social."

Justice and Order

Thus, both the absence of any necessity for the new definitions of social justice and their unsuitability argue that the novelty of the phrase "social justice" must lie elsewhere. We have already noticed the similarity between the metaphorical justice which is "the justice of the regime" and the virtue of distributive justice. Both are concerned with the relation of the whole to the parts— metaphorical justice, in the original constitution of diverse *ordines*, distributive justice in the distribution of common goods to the parts insofar as what belongs to the whole is due to the parts. Since, however, as we have observed, the establishment of the "order"—through according to the inclination of nature—may fail of achievement, its institution becomes something "due." Hence Pius XI writes:

19. Thomas Aquinas, *Summa Theologiae*, II–II, 61, 1, ad 3.
20. *Ibid.*, II–II, 58, 7, ad 1.   21. *Ibid.*, II–II, 58, 8, *sed contra*.

But just as in the living organism it is impossible to provide for the good of the whole unless each single part and each individual member is given what it needs for the exercise of its proper functions, so it is impossible to care for the social organism and the good of a society as a unit unless each single part and each individual member . . . is supplied with all that is necessary for the exercise of his social functions. If social justice be satisfied, the result will be an intense activity, in economic life as a whole, pursued in tranquillity and order.[22]

I suggest, then, that the novelty of the phrase "social justice" lies in the relating of the virtue of distributive justice to the governing principle of order, the "justice of the regime."

Thus, the *virtue* of social justice derives its name from the order under which it operates and which at the same time it helps to procure—the "provision that things be governed, according to their mode," the "true directive principle of social and economic activity."

22. Pius XI, *Divini Redemptoris*, #51.

17. *Humanae Vitae:*
Perspectives and Precisions*

[On the surface, this essay deals with the famous controversy that centered around the encyclical of Paul VI, *Humanae Vitae,* on the nature of marriage. However, it is something more. It has direct overtones in political philosophy. The reasons Leo Strauss gave for his doubt about the relation of reason and revelation in Aquinas were the indissolubility of marriage and birth control. McCoy was not directly concerned with the Straussian problem, because he understood that the argument from natural law needed to be posed properly by Catholics themselves, and it was being subject to considerable confusion. The scope of argument was quite narrow. It dealt with the "pill" ostensibly as a means to control or regulate a woman's irregular cycle. This consideration enabled McCoy to clarify the meaning of the natural-law position. In the Straussian view, the Catholic position was available only to those of the "faith," whereas for McCoy, it is precisely the natural-law argument that is to the fore. McCoy sees the confusions among Catholic theologians and thinkers reinforcing the assumptions of the political philosophers. Consequently, it is most important to restore the argument to its proper dimensions before the subject of the relation of revelation and reason can appear in its proper form.]

Canon F. H. Drinkwater has called attention to the great difference in perspective between the encyclical of 1930 on birth control and *Humanae Vitae. Casti Connubii* was written from the perspective of objective categories, of instant certainties and unyielding orthodoxies; the perspective of *Humanae Vitae* is, on the contrary, "personalistic": objective categories are of course employed, but their weight is balanced by the consideration given to the dignity and responsibility of persons; conjugal love in its great and liberal na-

*This essay originally appeared in *The New Scholasticism,* 44 (Spring 1970), 265–72.

ture is acclaimed; there is no mention of mortal sin, but rather an awareness that the immutable structures of the human person are fewer and more general than previous ages had believed; the *loi déréglée*—the law of the morbific condition, the refractory character of human nature (measured differently, absolutely by the "natural law") is taken into account. "The 1930 Encyclical was followed . . . by a determined campaign to enforce its decrees and to drive 'erroneous consciences' from the sacraments. Nothing like that will happen this time. . . . The watchword is 'compassion' and the official picture is of back-sliders from an ideal summit, admittedly rather unscalable by the average novice-climber. . . . All this amounts to a considerable change of attitude, if not of doctrine, during one generation."[1]

It is not then curious that the large and liberal perspectives of this changed attitude should have issued in the severe doctrinal ruling of the encyclical? The apparent incongruity of the "personalist" philosophy of the encyclical's pastoral section and the severe doctrinal ruling caused both shock and dismay. I should like to argue that although the doctrinal ruling excludes the use of the pill as an action that exposes the mission of generating human life to the arbitrary will of men, there remains nonetheless a use of the pill that is not intrinsically evil and that is, therefore, in accord with the *central idea* of *Humanae Vitae*—that the use of matrimony must always by itself be oriented toward the procreation of human life.[2] Nor does this view imply that the encyclical is inconsistent with itself; it simply means that it has not (for reasons which I hope to make clear) brought forth certain precisions that are latent in it.

Father George Tavard has suggested that the Holy Father had "bad tools to work with." On the one hand he was given by his commission a majority report that, "leaving aside scholastic considerations and categories," took its departure from a philosophy of the human person and from this philosophy evolved a new theology of the marriage relationship. On the other hand, the minority report had too easy a time of it in rejecting the new "problematic" by a "massive reliance on the old theology."[3] The stage was set by the framework of the new problematic in such a way

1. Canon F. H. Drinkwater, Letter to the Editor, *The Tablet*, 222 (August 10, 1968), 798.

2. Paul VI, *Humanae Vitae*, 17, 11.

3. George Tavard, *National Catholic Register* (October 2, 1968), 9.

that the question at issue became that of the licitness of man acting as principal cause of a state of infertility, chosen by himself as a goal to be pursued without regard for the purpose of nature. This is evident from the fact that the new problematic reopened the whole question of birth control, and not merely the new problems presented by the pill; even the explicitly disallowed means of contraception were again to be examined. The means of birth regulation posed no special problem; the "principle of totality" justified making the marriage act infecund in order to promote the overall good of human life. From the point of view of the new theology of marriage, it became a matter of indifference whether man acted as principal or merely instrumental cause in bringing about infecundity; the mutual love of the partners, expressed in the marriage act, was considered on an equal level with the orientation of the marriage act toward the procreation of human life.

It is important to recognize that many theologians have been brought so much under the persuasion of the new theology of the marriage relationship that even when they think they are criticizing the encyclical from the point of view of its objective categories they give a quite new interpretation to these. Father Tavard says that he has "adopted the objective categories of the encyclical" in his criticism of it. Nonetheless he seems to be equally the victim of the bad tools that the Holy Father had to work with. He says that "according to all Catholic theology in our times, the subjective purpose of sexual intercourse may simply be the expression of love, apart from any positive intention to procreate." But he expressly takes this quite unimpeachable statement to imply that the use of sexuality need not always be open to the transmission of human life—a notion of conjugal love that is peculiar to the new theology of the marriage relationship. It is this inference that makes Father Tavard find the encyclical inconsistent with itself in teaching that the use of matrimony must always be oriented toward procreation and at the same time allowing the use of natural rhythm. Father Tavard supposes that the licitness of the "safe period" implies that the use of the marriage act may be considered apart from its orientation toward the procreation of human life. He thus employs, indeed, an "objective category" of the encyclical—the end of the marriage act—but he reads it in the light of the overhauled theology of marriage. This is not, of course, the perspective of the encyclical. The use of natural rhythm may not be separated from procreation for the following reason: The infertility of the "safe period" is itself for the sake of spacing births, and hence it is oriented toward procreation—taken as including not only the mere existence of the child but its nurture and education.[4] This is the moral category concerning the use of natural rhythm; it may be abused—the licitness of means, taken in general, in no way guarantees that their employment will invariably be an act of virtue. But it *is* the principle that is involved and it is the perspective from which all questions of the validity of direct intervention for the procurement of infertility must be looked at. Those theologians who hold that the encyclical must perforce sanction the use of the pill *on the ground that* infertility as a natural fact (and the use of natural rhythm is permitted) separates the *use* of the marriage act from procreation have changed an objective category under the influence of the new theology of the marriage relationship.

The same point is again evident in the criticism that the encyclical is inconsistent with itself when it would sanction the regularizing of the cycle (as being not against nature) but would prohibit irregularizing the cycle. *Humanae Vitae* appeals to medical science to seek out means of birth control that are according to nature—that is, based on the observance of natural rhythms.[5] The reason why the intervention of medical science can be necessary is that nature, with no means but her own, is unequal to the task of achieving her objective. Here art and reason serve as instrumental causes in bringing about what nature works for as principal cause; and art imitates nature, acting as instrumental cause in employing the same means. "For as nature heals one who is suffering from cold by warming him, so also does the doctor."[6] Since nature aims at infertility for the sake of spacing births with a view to the proper nurture and education of offspring, its intention can be effective only if the cycle is regularized. Thus the regularizing of the cycle is nature's own aim, and medical science acts as instrumental cause in bringing about infertility only if it is designed to help nature's intention of regularizing the cycle.

Now if from the fact that, as Father Tavard puts it, "women whose cycle is irregular find themselves so *by nature*," we were to infer that irregularity of the cycle is as much nature's intention as is regularity, we would be radically changing the "objective cate-

4. *Ibid.*   5. *Humanae Vitae*, 24.
6. Thomas Aquinas, *De Veritate*, XI, 1.

gory" employed in deciding the moral question of licit means of bringing about a state of infertility. Father Tavard writes:

[The encyclical] does not show why regularity should be considered more natural than irregularity. . . . If man is free to regularize the cycle with progesterone pills (and thus to make contraception through rhythm possible) he is just as free to irregularize it or to regularize with longer periods with similar medication (and thus to make contraception possible without rhythm). Both regularity and irregularity of ovulation are natural. By the same token, each, for adequate reasons, may be medically induced, and the period may be medically shortened or lengthened.[7]

Again, this change of the objective category is done under the aegis of the new theology of the marriage relationship, and the effect of the change is indeed, unfortunately, to verify the argument of the encyclical that permission to use the pill would expose "the mission of generating life . . . to the arbitrary will of men. . . ."[8] This becomes, in fact, the precise ground on which any use whatever of the pill is forbidden by the encyclical. It is, to be sure, an example of what Father Tavard rightly enough calls a "massive" reliance on the old theology; it conceals certain precisions (they are indeed there, but latent) which would distinguish the use of the pill by man acting as instrumental cause and acting as principal cause of infertility, chosen, in the latter case, by himself as a goal without regard for the purpose of nature which ought to be his guide. The new theology of the marriage relationship doesn't make that distinction, and so the encyclical in disallowing all use of the pill did not feel the need to make it either—it worked with the bad tools handed it. A massive reliance on the old theology was all that was necessary to combat an undiscerning permissiveness; it was combatted with an equally—and, in a sense, deliberately— undiscerning prohibition.

Now let us try to draw the precisions that lie latent in the blanket condemnation of the pill. Any use of the pill whatever is prohibited by n. 14 which excludes "every action that . . . in anticipation of the conjugal act . . . proposes, whether as an end or as a means, to render procreation impossible." Natural rhythm is allowed because its use is not an action that "proposes" to render procreation impossible. Nature's own measure and rule dominates the conjugal act in the use of natural rhythm so that the act itself (the structure of sexuality) remains of itself oriented toward procreation. This is the case, we may note, even where there is abuse of

7. Tavard, *National Catholic Register*.   8. *Humanae Vitae*, 17.

natural rhythm, for the abuse itself has to take account of nature as principal cause of infertility. Now if the pill were used by man acting as merely instrumental cause of infertility, i.e., regularizing the cycle in the way in which nature herself tries to do, it would (a) still be forbidden by n. 14 as an "action that . . . in anticipation of the conjugal act proposes . . . to render procreation impossible." But (b) although forbidden for that reason, it would not (as would the use of the pill for irregularizing the cycle) be "of itself contrary to conception" anymore than would natural rhythm *for such use would equally relate to the structure of sexuality.*[9] In short, the use of the pill by man acting as instrumental cause, in behalf of nature acting as principle cause in bringing about infertility, is indeed in accord with the *central idea* of the encyclical: that the use of the marriage act must always be oriented by itself toward the pro-creation of human life. Such use of the pill does not fall under the condemned "principle of totality" any more than does natural rhythm itself. The "principle of totality" is a principle of the over-hauled theology of marriage which alters the objective categories I have spoken of.

What then precisely is the reason for its prohibition if the pill is not, in the use of it as instrumental cause, intrinsically evil? I have said that the reason is simply that its use *"exposes"* the mission of generating human life to the arbitrary will of man.[10] But now again, it is necessary to note that the blanket prohibition of the pill con-ceals two quite different uses in the encyclical of the word "arbi-trary." If the pill were used by man taking nature as a guide it would not be an arbitrary use—it would not be itself contrary to conception anymore than nature herself is during the "safe pe-riod." But if it were used by man acting as principal cause of infertility—chosen as a goal without regard for the purpose of nature, its use would be arbitrary. But there is a second use of the word "arbitrary," according to which *each* of the above uses of the marriage act is arbitrary. This second use derives from the fact that although the pill acts biologically to affect the feminine cycle (un-like a chemical or physical artefact) its use is not tied to the struc-ture of sexuality in such a way that it is compelled (as both the use and abuse of natural rhythm are compelled) to take account of nature as principal cause of infertility: the determination whether it will be used arbitrarily in the first sense of the word or not so

9. *Ibid.,* 15.   10. *Ibid.,* 17.

used is itself a decision left to the arbitrary will of man. It is this second use of the word, and not the first, that is employed in n. 17 ("the mission of generating human life may not be *exposed to . . .*"), that the use of the pill as instrumental to nature remains (hidden there in the encyclical) as a means neither by itself contrary to conception nor intrinsically evil.

These considerations account, I think, for what would otherwise be quite inexplicable: the counselling by some national hierarchies that persons are free to form their consciences on the issue of birth regulation. This could be the case only if there remains within the context of the encyclical a use of the pill that is compatible with the central idea of the encyclical—a use that would be neither of itself contrary to conception nor intrinsically evil. The Canadian, English, and Austrian hierarchies took advantage of the precisions that lie dormant there in the encyclical. The eclipse of these precisions by the blanket prohibition of n. 14 is to be attributed to that massive reliance on the old theology in opposing the overhauled theology of the marriage relationship—which the Holy Father took as announcing a right to exercise an arbitrary will with regard to the mission of generating life. Certain freedoms are permitted persons who have a sense of moderation and responsibility that are forbidden to others. The new theology of marriage removes, of itself, that sense of moderation and responsibility. The consciences that national hierarchies have said are free to make their own decisions in this matter are free precisely to form themselves not arbitrarily but by using nature (and indeed the central idea of *Humanae Vitae*) as their guide.

If the perspective of the person and personal responsibility in the pastoral section appears to have been abandoned in the doctrinal section of the encyclical, this appearance hides the basic intention of preserving the very structure of the person. "In allowing full range to man's historical existence and creativity," Father Richard McCormick has written, "we must retain the courage to be concrete. Otherwise we can be left with a natural law so refined that it contemplates with equanimity the notion that one man goes in for golf while another likes chopping up Negroes and Vietnamese, and that is all there is to say about the matter."[11] If in the final analysis the problem of human existence is one whose solution does not indeed lie in any science as such—in a mere mechanical

11. Richard McCormick, "The New Morality," *America*, 118 (June 15, 1968).

interconnection of things—moral science is, nonetheless, not a matter of indifference. We cannot place ourselves outside of all science and, in the full existentialist sense, retreat to the inner structure of the free resolve in its freedom; to do so would be to engage the person in that process of self-destruction that Gabriel Marcel has said is going on today at every level of being. If the moral world is one that has to be constructed by free personal responses, it is not from nothing that it is made. The "true values of life" of which the encyclical speaks, are there, in the nature of man, to be brought forth and realized. If today we have come to understand that the abiding structures of the human person are fewer and less specific, less powerful and effective than earlier ages had supposed, the old understanding nevertheless remains: that man makes the moral world as God made the physical universe, and that both take time. ". . . [A]nimals which live but a short time are perfected in a short time. But if happiness consists in a perfect operation according to perfect virtue, whether intellectual or moral, it cannot possibly come to man except after a long time."[12] The direction of personalistic ethics against "systems," "methods," "orthodoxies" that would find value arising from a mere mechanical interconnection of things and oppose all that is ineffable, incommunicable and obscure, is certainly laudable in intention; but in its extreme form it leads to that conscience by which, as Heidegger puts it, man stands outside himself and communicates total "irrelationality" of the cosmos to himself. In exercising arbitrarily the mission of generating life, man does indeed communicate total "irrelationality" of the cosmos to himself.

And yet, the personalist philosophy has contributed to a renaissance, suggested by the encyclical itself, of the traditional concept of the divine law as a law that reaches the individual in that which is most determinate and proper, most profound and obscure in him—the interior movements of the soul. Unlike the civil law which, finding the common denominator, extends indifferently to all, and unlike the natural law which measures human nature absolutely, the divine positive law extends to individuals in their very diversity, in their not being all alike.[13] In this doctrine, of venerable tradition, the divine law, by providing the ultimate safeguard against mere conformity and conventionality, makes possible the ultimate verification of human freedom.

12. Thomas Aquinas, *Summa Contra Gentiles*, III, 48.
13. Thomas Aquinas, *Summa Theologiae*, I–II, 91, 4.

18. Liberation Theology and Political Philosophy

[This posthumous essay is edited by John J. Schrems from its hand-written original. McCoy comments about Christian theologians who had begun to use Marx without full attention to the profundity of Marx, the profundity of Classical-Christian tradition, or the deliberate but pro-found change that Marx made in the tradition. The suggestion put forth by liberation theologians of a Christian ideal of citizenship only recently available is the result of the "dismaying ignorance" of both tradition and Marx from whom their inspiration springs. On its own the argu-ment here is almost cryptic. When read in the light of McCoy's corpus it is an aspect of the faith and reason issue. It might best be read in conjunction with McCoy's "The Dilemma of Liberalism" (Chapter 6).]

I do not intend in this essay to judge except indirectly liberation theology, with which indeed, I have some sympathy. I want, rather, to give consideration to two matters that, I suggest, sig-nificantly account for the strong attraction that liberation theology has for so many "intellectuals." The first of these contributing factors is the truly appalling neglect of the great tradition of Clas-sical-Christian political thought. A careful study of that tradition would have revealed it as containing what one writer suspects as having emerged only in the nineteenth and twentieth centuries and what he calls, with Marxist overtones, a *"Praxis-weltan-schauung."* This notion of a contemplation of the world that passes into practice was, as I shall try to show, not only contained in the Classical-Christian tradition but is to be found there with a far greater acuity and depth than in its aberrant modern expressions.

The second factor that contributes, in a positive way, to the appeal of liberation theology is the central fact that Karl Marx, unlike the political philosophers in the modern Western democratic tradition, retained as a constitutive part of his social doctrine the theological elements of Greek-medieval political thought. It is the dismaying ignorance of these elements, and consequently the ignorance of their use and profound transformation by Marx, that accounts for the vacuity of so much present-day writing in the area of Christian political philosophy.

We may begin by examining the extraordinary "thesis" put forward by Father John A. Coleman, S.J. His thesis is that "Christianity lacks an adequate moral ideal of citizenship."[1] This is incredible and simply absurd. To refute so false an assertion we need only cite two passages from the treatise on justice and prudence of Thomas Aquinas. Asking whether justice stands foremost among all the moral virtues St. Thomas answers that it does so because of the preeminence of civic virtue:

If we speak of legal justice, it is evident that it stands foremost among all the moral virtues, *for as much as the common good transcends the individual good of one person.* . . . But even if we speak of particular justice it excels the other world virtues . . . because the other virtues are commendable in respect to the sole good of the virtuous person himself, *whereas justice is praiseworthy in respect of the virtuous person being well-disposed towards another,* so that justice is somewhat the good of another person.[2]

And here he cites Aristotle to the effect that " 'The greatest virtues must needs be those which are most profitable to other persons, because virtue is a faculty of doing good to others.' "[3] Next, treating of prudence, he maintains that the prudence that extends to the good of the political community is a higher virtue than the prudence that is concerned only with the good of the individual:

Some have held that prudence does not extend to the common good . . . and this because they thought that man is not bound to seek other than his own good.

But this opinion is opposed to charity, which seeketh not her own. . . . Moreover it is contrary to right reason, which judges the common good to be better than the good of the individual.[4]

In answer to an objection to the contrary, he writes:

He that seeks the good of the many seeks *in consequence* his own good, for two reasons. First, because *the individual good is impossible without the common good of the state.* . . . Second, because, since man is a part of the

1. John S. Coleman, S.J., "The Christian as Citizen," *Commonweal* (September 9, 1983), 458.
2. Thomas Aquinas, *Summa Theologiae*, II–II, 158, 12. Italics added.
3. *Ibid.*   4. *Ibid.*, II–II, 47, 10.

. . . state, he must needs consider what is good for him by being prudent about the good of the many.[5]

If these statements do not constitute "an adequate moral ideal of citizenship" I do not know what does. But the author of its denial calls as witnesses to his "thesis" such improbable characters as Machiavelli and Rousseau who complain that Christianity is not conducive to good citizenship.

On the contrary it is rather, as exhibited by Father Coleman, precisely the inattention to the Christian moral ideal of citizenship that ought indeed be complained about. Fundamental reasons of a metaphysical nature are offered by Professor Thomas O'Dea to account for the alleged absence of a Christian moral ideal of citizenship. In *Alienation, Atheism, and the Religious Crisis* Professor O'Dea tells us that Christianity left man bereft of a self-definition that would relate him to the larger rhythms of nature and the community.[6] It is not, then, so much the collapse of religious values that has left man bereft of an adequate self-definition as it is that those values were not satisfactorily secured to begin with. They have left man separated from himself and from the larger rhythms of nature and the community. This, of course, is the Marxist humanist concept of human alienation and it dominates contemporary revolutionary efforts. These efforts are intent upon exploring new ways of understanding the human enterprise and putting forth a fresh definition of what it means to be man—a definition that will relate him to the larger rhythms of nature and the community.

That past religious values were in themselves inadequate to furnish significant interpretation of man's worth in the world, that those values were unsatisfactorily secured to begin with is surely a profoundly mistaken view, and I should like to adduce evidence to show that the traditional values were indeed rich in insights and in significant interpretations of the human enterprise.

It is necessary here to give brief preliminary consideration to the profound connection established by classical social thought (that of Aristotle in particular) between concrete worldly activity and theological realities. The neglect of this point is no doubt to be attributed to the fact that, as the Greeks understood it (and prop-

5. *Ibid.*, ad 2. Italics added.
6. Thomas F. O'Dea, *Alienation, Atheism, and the Religious Crisis* (New York, 1969).

erly), no *analytical* connection exists between "first theology" (metaphysics) and concrete conduct—that is, no connection such that in order to act well in this world one must subscribe to some theological doctrine. Theological doctrine does not come under any civil law, nor is adherence to it required for citizenship. But in the order of things themselves there was considered to be a profound connection. The implication of these principles may be seen from the fact that when Aristotle inquires into the worthwhileness of political life he offers two different lines of consideration: The first is proper to political science and consists in analyzing the nature of the political community as one of free men having the freedom of "moral action," that is, action which depends not on a natural power determined to its act, but on a power that is indifferently disposed to many different things contained under the notion of the good, whether true good or having the appearance of good.

The second approach to the ground of the goodness of the political life is theological; it is to be found in considerations that lie beyond the directly pertinent ones of political science. In the opening chapters of the *Ethics* Aristotle maintains that the ultimate end of all things we do is the first principle or first reason for doing all the lesser things: whether building a ship or curing the body or engaging in politics, and in the Tenth Book the ultimate thing of all that we do turns out to be the contemplation of the order of the universe and of that principle upon which the order depends.[7] For man is "a little world," Aristotle points out, not only in the sense that he contains all the degrees of natural being within himself, but more profoundly in that he uses the resources of art to draw to himself all the richness of the world, diffused in space and time. The goodness of the political life is here said to consist ultimately in the goodness of the political order being an imitation of the order of the universe, in which—together with God upon whom the order depends—consists the highest good. And this indeed is why Aristotle says in the *Ethics* that if the good is the same for a single man and for a whole community, that of the whole community of man is *"more divine"*; he calls it more divine because it is a more perfect likeness of the good of the universe and of the ultimate essential goodness which draws all things to itself.

There is, then, in the thought of Aristotle a theological dynamic

---

7. Aristotle, *Ethics* X, 8, 1178b25; see *Metaphysics* XII, 1, 1075a12.

that explains, sustains, and perfects political life, but it is not part of political science strictly speaking: none of it is required for citizenship, nor does it come under any law. In the felicitous words of Charles Krauthammer, this supra-political dynamic "is meant to infuse communal life with a religious dimension." With altogether justifiable misgiving, Mr. Krauthammer ascribes the origin of the notion of a religious dimension to political life to Rousseau. It is found in Aristotle with superb clarity of understanding, while Rousseau's civic religion is nothing but a hodge-podge of sentimental and dangerous political "pieties."[8]

In exposition of this doctrine of Aristotle, St. Thomas points out that in the contemplative life (which Aristotle places first)[9] man shares in the life of God by "union and informing," whereas in the political life man participates in the life of God by way of "proportion"—that is to say, by standing in relation to what he produces in the political community as God stands in relation to His work in holding together the universe.[10] Indeed, the activity of both the speculative and practical reason is nothing but a participation of man's intellect in the life of the Prime Intellect, upon whose perfect freedom "depend the heavens and the world of nature." This is the original, elementary, and essential meaning of the "primacy of the spiritual" and it was indeed part of Greek wisdom. But in our secular intellectual milieu these ideas are considered even by theologians to be "brittle answers" and "thin abstractions."

As I have been attesting, this profound spiritual root of the concept of political common good has been lost in the West in modern times. We have come to the impression that the Classical-Christian tradition has man bereft of a definition that relates him to the larger rhythms of nature and community. The contrary is true. Indeed, the theological principles that we have been examining present us with a kind of contemplation that passes into practice.

Alone among the modern political philosophers Marx retained—if, indeed, in profoundly perverted form—this theological element of the Classical-Christian tradition: the primacy of the "spiritual." Marx saw that the Enlightenment had indeed repudiated "the essentiality of God," but that it had not affirmed "the essentiality of

8. Charles Krauthammer, "America's Holy War," *The New Republic* (April 9, 1984), 16–17.
9. Aristotle, *Ethics* VI, 7, 1141a20.
10. Thomas Aquinas, *Summa Theologiae*, I–II, 3, 5.

man." It left man indeed with a freedom of conscience, but a freedom of conscience that must make itself the decisive religious attitude and thus threw religion on the refuse heap of arbitrary private whims. The primacy of the spiritual is retained by Marx's acclaiming the "essentiality of man." Man's religious freedom is, with Marx, achieved by affirming his own "self-origin" and himself as being. Man comes to see that he is all that he knows and that he is the act whereby all things are made—all things humanly significant, which becomes the totality of significance.

v. Conclusion

19. A McCoy Analysis: What Is Political Philosophy?*

[No doubt, the best concise description of the work of Charles N. R. McCoy is that written by McCoy himself in the two essays on political philosophy that he did for the *New Catholic Encyclopedia* (1967). The first of these essays on "political philosophy" is included here as a final review and statement by McCoy himself for the way he understood the discipline and the central issues of its "structure."

The second essay in the *New Catholic Encyclopedia* (a reference work usually available in all good libraries) is devoted to the "History of Political Philosophy." This essay is an excellent brief survey of the general material covered in *The Structure of Political Thought*. This latter essay likewise can enable the reader to see how McCoy saw the parts and the whole of the discipline in its various relationships and would be well worth consulting by any interested student of McCoy's works.]

The Nature of Political Philosophy

[Political philosophy is] the part of philosophy that treats of political society, its nature and end—the proper human common good. It is distinguished from political science in the modern sense of that discipline by its concern with the first general principles of all practical activity, to which any circumstantial and detailed study must ultimately be referred. It is in this way a philosophical science rather than an experimental science. Like the propositions in any philosophical discipline, those in political philosophy are such that a necessity can be shown to exist in the relation of their terms. One can say, for example, that if there is to be a "man," he must of necessity be "rational animal"; one cannot say that he must of

*This essay originally appeared under the title, "Political Philosophy," in the *New Catholic Encyclopedia*, 1967, V. 11, 510–16.

necessity be two-footed and smooth-skinned. Similarly, one can say that whenever many persons are constituted in such a way that a community results, a ruler-subject relationship will manifest itself; one cannot, on the other hand, say with regard to this community precisely what this ruler-subject relationship will be.

Political Science as Practical

Political science is a practical rather than a speculative science. A speculative science has as its object simply the truth of what is, whereas a practical science, though concerned with the truth of what is, is further ordained to action for the sake of some end. But practical reason can be engaged in action (1) either by making things, in which case the action passes into external matter and is governed by art, or (2) by doing, in which case the action is immanent in the agent and is governed by prudence. In art it is the excellence of the thing made that is the criterion of truth. The truth of an artistic judgment depends simply on the conformity of the intellect with the work that the artist intends to produce. In this, art very much resembles the habits of the speculative intellect, because both are concerned simply with the disposition of the things considered by them and not with the disposition of the will toward these objects. The situation is quite different in the case of action intrinsic to the agent—in doing, or in human behavior. For here the good in question is within the man himself: he has to be joyful and sad about the right things, about things that ought to please or displease him. Truth depends here primarily on the rectitude of the man's will, on conformity of his desire with what is known to be truly good.

This distinction between art and prudence entails other important consequences for political philosophy. The freedom of prudence does not, like the freedom of art, extend to the end itself of action. If one wishes to use the term art in a broad sense to include moral action, then it must be understood that the art of politics does not aim at any good other than that of man's nature. One cannot, morally, brainwash men, even though there is an art of doing it. Art, taken in the strict sense, bears on contraries. The art of medicine is just as effective in killing as in curing an individual, or a whole community, as is known from the threat of biological warfare. That art be put to right use thus requires moral virtue. If practical truth bore on contraries, as does art, then the judgment of the morally corrupt man would be just as valid as that of the morally good man. Man is indeed free to become good or bad, but this liberty of contrariety is not a mark of the perfection of human nature. The art of living, for the individual as for the community, does not extend to the first principles of man's nature. As Aristotle observes—and it is an observation that stands as a barrier to every form of tyranny—"the state does not make men, but taking them from nature, perfects them."

The reason why man's self-government and liberty are limited in the way just described is that man himself is produced by nature and can perfect only the nature he has. The "self" of which man is the cause in "self-government" is that of his "second nature," which is constituted by the political virtues. This essential and elemental meaning of the limited character of man's government over himself is brought out most strikingly by Aristotle's comparing the first principles of practical science with mathematical axioms. It is precisely because the ends of human life are unchangeable starting points for the infinitely variable judgments of political prudence that they can be compared in their fixity with mathematical hypotheses. Aristotle, in effect, here safeguards the fundamental requirements of man's nature by withdrawing such matters from the province of political art.

Proper Human Common Good

The chief good and end of man is discovered by examining his nature with respect to the function proper to that nature. Human life, as distinguished from other animal life and from vegetable life, is characterized by the activity of a rational element. Man's proper good consists in the activity of his soul according to reason. But this activity is twofold. On the one hand, the human reason considers an order of things for the sake of knowledge of the truth; here the reason, perfected through the speculative virtues, produces the speculative sciences. On the other hand, the appetitive part of the soul participates in rationality in the sense of being obedient to reason; thus the rational principle in the virtuous man is the object of praise for urging him aright and toward the best objects. In the latter sense man has a capacity for self-government that is manifested through the "political virtues"—justice, temperance, courage, and prudence. Now then if, as Aristotle puts it, the good is the same for a single man as for a State, that of the State seems to be something more complete. This doctrine of the primacy of the common good is based on the consideration that since man is part of a family and of the State, he must of necessity consider what is good for him by being prudent about the good of the many.

NOTION OF THE COMMON GOOD. Three aspects of this doctrine of the common good require special attention. One must first take note that the doctrine does not mean that the individual exists for the sake of the state. The common good, which Aristotle calls more "godlike" than the private good, is not taken in opposition to the good of a single man. The unity of this common good is not the unity of the logical whole, which absorbs the real parts in an indeterminate genus, as John and Paul are indeterminately contained under man. On the contrary, the common good extends to many not by reason of any indetermination of individuals, but extends to them in their very diversity and by reason of this diversity. As Aristotle observes in speaking of the order of the universe, "[A]ll things are ordered together somehow, but not all alike." But this very diversity comes from the order of the parts in any whole; and thus the common good is the good of individuals as parts and members of society, and is sought by them precisely as members of society and as being not all alike. The common good is common, then, as a universal cause whose power extends to many different kinds of effects.

As a consequence of this, a second point about the common good becomes clear. If it indeed extends to what is most determinate and actual in individuals, it is not for that reason to be identified with the singular, private good of these individuals; rather, it is common by reason of its communicability to these many different individuals, and not because it includes the singular good of all of them. The good of the family is better than the singular good of its members not because all the members of the family find their singular good therein; the good of the family is better because, for each of its members, this good is also the good of the others.

Finally, it should be understood that the attainment of the common good of an association of human beings differs from the common good of an organic whole and of a collectivity of animals. The unity of an organic whole and of a collectivity is a simple unity, whereas the unity of human society is a unity of order. In an organic whole, in a collectivity, there is no action of the parts that is not either simply or principally the same as the action of the whole. In a composite, the movement of the part is principally of the whole (one does not say that the eye of man sees, but that man sees with his eye); and in a collectivity, such as a society of bees or ants, the action of the parts is principally of the whole because the parts have no principle of self-government within them and act by the necessity of nature for the common good. A society of human beings, on the other hand, has a unity of order, for its unity is brought about by the collaboration of parts that are self-governing. Therefore the direction to the human common good is not accomplished except by self-government; the action of the ruling element in the political community is in no sense divorced from the participation of citizenry.

FAMILY VS. POLITICAL COMMUNITY. The first order of common good to which the individual directs his action is the good of that association without which man cannot exist at all—the family, or household. The procreation and education of children is impossible without the collaboration of several persons, and nature has instituted a society for attaining this end in marriage and the family. The family is thus said to be natural to man in a much more primordial way than political society. The family and its management (the "art of acquisition") are designed primarily to safeguard the very living of men; and property is an instrument of mere life, which pertains to economic associations.

If the task of the household is that of procuring the indispensable daily needs of life, the diversity of trades and activities that comes from a union of families marks the beginning of the political community. For the political community first comes into existence to make possible a full sufficiency of material goods, and it continues in existence for the sake of the perfection of life in the virtues and the arts. For the state is a community—a communication—of men, not for mere activity of life, but for activity of life according to the highest virtues. The political community is organized for the procurement of this common good of its members: the good of the virtues, both speculative and moral, and of the arts. For this reason the art of politics is declared by Aristotle to be "the most authoritative art."

Politics as Architectonic

Politics is called architectonic because its authoritative character is that of a master art with respect to autonomous subordinate arts. As there are many actions, arts, and sciences, their ends also are many—the end of the medical art is health; of shipbuilding, a vessel; of strategy, victory; of economics, wealth. The art that directs all of these autonomous activities to the human common good is the most authoritative.

One may discern two properties of an authoritative art: (1) such an art prescribes what the sciences under it ought to do (as the art of medicine directs the pharmacist), and (2) it uses the subordinate sciences for its own end. Now because political science is itself a practical science, it is authoritative with respect to all other sciences only insofar as these deal with things that are operable by man; it follows, then, that politics is authoritative with a difference in regard to speculative and practical sciences. In regard to the speculative sciences, the first of the above-mentioned properties belong to politics only to the extent that the state prescribes that they be pursued; the state may issue orders for the sake of truth, but not to it. It ordains, for example, that some should teach geometry and lays down qualifications for teachers, but it does not prescribe for geometry what should be the conclusion concerning the triangle; for this is a matter that does not come under the will of man (the sphere of practical science) but depends on the very nature of things (the sphere of speculative science). In regard to practical sciences, politics may prescribe for them not only with respect to putting them to use, but also with respect to the determination of their work—what kind of roads to build and where to build houses or where not to build them.

The second attribute of an authoritative science (viz., that it uses the subordinate sciences for its own end) pertains to politics only with respect to the practical sciences; thus military science, economics, and the science of agriculture fall under the direction of the state. The speculative sciences, on the other hand, may not be used by the state for its own end. This is because the end of the speculative sciences is a good that lies outside the sphere of the human will; it is an end that the human intellect only considers but does not make, viz., the truth of things. The contemplative life, most perfectly ordained to this intelligible good, is the life to which the political virtues and the arts themselves are ordered.

Political and Contemplative Life

The participation of the appetitive part of the soul in the rational part produces the virtues of the political life. Now the part of rationality that is not so by participating but by possessing and exercising thought is more principally rational. And because activity according to reason is the principal good of man, his happiness consists in what is essentially rational rather than in what is rational by participation. This happiness is that of the contemplative life, the life of the speculative virtues, and most particularly of the virtue of wisdom.

Beyond the directly pertinent considerations, already examined, that establish the goodness of the political life, the ultimate reason for this goodness derives from the absolute superiority of the contemplative life. If man—as Aristotle observes—were the best thing in the universe, then political science and prudence would be the most perfect knowledge; but the most perfect knowledge is, rather, of the highest object. The contemplative life surpasses all others because its object is that very life—the life of God—upon which the whole order of the universe depends.

Again, this order of the universe is "more divine" than a particular good of the same order because it is a better imitation of the ultimate final cause that draws all things to itself. Similarly, the common good of men is "more divine" than a particular good of the same order because it is a more perfect imitation of the ultimate essential goodness that draws all things to itself. Thus above the political common good is the life devoted to knowledge about God, who is the extrinsic common good of the whole universe. And the activity of this life is most leisurely and contains happiness within itself, whereas political actions aim at a happiness different from the actions themselves and sought as being different—whether honors, or power, or even virtue itself. As Aristotle puts it, among virtuous actions political and military actions are distinguished by nobility and greatness, but these are unleisurely and aim at an end and are not desirable for their own sake; however, the activity of reason, which is contemplative, seems both to be superior in serious worth and to aim at no end beyond itself, and to have its pleasure proper to itself, as evidenced by the self-sufficiency, leisureliness, unweariedness, and all other attributes ascribed to the supremely happy man; therefore, it follows that this will be the complete happiness for man. The activity, indeed, of both the speculative and the practical intellect is nothing but a participation of man in the life of God, upon whom depends the whole order of nature.

Constitution of the Political Community

In nature there is evident both a universal and a particular form of government. The universal is that by which all things find their place under the direction of God, who, by His providence, governs the universe. The particular form of government in nature is present in man himself; he is a microcosm of the government of the universe, for, in a sense, reason is to man what God is to the universe. The political community is, then, one of self-governing men. Since law as a measure and rule of human acts must be homogenous with what it measures, the homogeneity of human law with the community whose acts it rules is found initially in the derivation of the specific form of constitution from the community of free men. For free men, who are equal in having the disposal of themselves, are of such nature as to make it impossible that any one of them in particular should have a natural right to rule over others; therefore the specific form of government is a matter of free choice. And because the individual good is impossible without the common good of all, this good is an end that belongs to all, and therefore it is within the competence of the whole multitude to make the very first law—that of the constitution by which the government (whatever its form) is set up. And if any one person or group of persons should presume to found a state, this action is justifiable only on the ground of their representing the whole people.

POLITICAL AUTHORITY. Although the question of the natural and primary subject of political authority is very old, it did not receive full and explicit treatment until the sixteenth century. At that time there were two categories of opinion: (1) that power comes to the ruler directly from God and (2) that power is naturally and in the first instance in the people. The first view has come to be known as the designation theory, the second as the transmission theory. The transmission theory has the oldest roots and was represented in the sixteenth century by St. Robert Bellarmine and F. Suárez. Bellarmine held that political power is in its "universal essence" originally in the whole multitude. But because "the *respublica* cannot exercise political power considered in its universal essence, it is bound to transfer it to one person or to a few. Thus the power of the princes, considered in its genus, is . . . of natural and divine right, and the human race could not, even if all men were gathered, make a decree to the contrary."[1] The whole people is said to be "bound" to transfer political power because the transference is done "by the same law of nature" by which it is originally, in its universal essence, in the whole people. Political power as residing immediately in the whole people does not constitute a form of government.

It should be noted here that a thing is said to be derived from the natural law in either of two ways. In one way, it is derived by determination of common principles; e.g., the law of nature has it that the evil-doer should be punished, but that he be punished in this or that way is a determination of the common principle. Things that are derived from the law of nature in this way have no force other than that of human law. These are the things that, Aristotle observes, are originally a matter of indifference, but when once laid down are not matters of indifference. It is not in this way that political power is transferred from the whole people: the transference is not a matter of indifference; the people are "bound." Secondly, a thing is derived from the natural law in such a manner that it is contained in human law not as emanating therefrom exclusively, but as having some force from the natural law also. Thus, that one must not kill is derived from the principle that one should do harm to no man, and this has the force of the natural law itself.

The transference of political power from the whole people is of the natural law in the second sense. The same law of nature by which political power is, in its universal essence, in the multitude also establishes the forms of government considered in their genus. If the natural law thus binds the multitude to transfer political power to some distinct governing personnel, the meaning of "transfer" becomes clear from consideration of the fact that the genus must be specified; the specification of the genus—the determination of the particular kind of government—by the whole people justifies the term transfer. Elements of the transmission theory here combine with elements from the designation theory. Taken with respect to its particular cause, authority may fittingly be said to be transmitted by the community; but with respect to its universal cause, authority is in the person designated as having it. Because the act of instituting a particular government bears with

1. Robert Bellarmine, *Controversiarum de Membris Ecclesiae* 3.6, *Opera* (Paris, 1870), 3:10–12.

it something of the force of natural law itself, it is an act that belongs not simply to positive law (a position taken by the seventeenth- and eighteenth-century social contract theories of T. Hobbes, J. Locke, and J. J. Rousseau) but to the *ius gentium*, which is partly natural law and partly positive law. As Bellarmine says, "[N]otice . . . that distinct kinds of government, taken in their peculiarity, concern the law of nations, not the law of nature."[2]

ELEMENTS OF CONSTITUTIONAL GOVERNMENT. Two elements of constitutional government thus emerge: the first is the element of consent, based on man's moral freedom; the second, the principle of rule to which consent is given. Whenever things are constituted of many parts—whether the parts are continuous, as are the conjoined members of a body, or discrete, as one army is constituted from many soldiers—there is always found a ruling and a subject element. In a natural composite the ruling and subject parts are designated by nature itself, and the commensuration of one with respect to the other is natural by an absolute commensuration. Thus the intellect is by its very nature, considered absolutely, commensurate with the sense appetites to regulate them; the male, with the female to beget offspring by her; and the parent with the child, to nourish it. But in a community where ordering to the common good is among persons in whom there is no absolute commensuration of one as ruler with another as subject, this relation is introduced by the natural reason in imitation of what nature elsewhere effects. It is in this way that the political community is said to be natural to man and that man is said to be by nature a political animal.

There is, finally, a third element of constitutionalism: The element of possibility, which corresponds to man's physical freedom. Comparing the art of gymnastics with that of politics, Aristotle observed that a man may not desire the best habit of body even though this be physically possible to him; and a man for whom there is a physical impediment to acquiring the best habit of body may desire what the circumstances permit or may desire something even less than the circumstances permit. The same principle holds equally in medicine, shipbuilding, and the arts generally. On the basis of that comparison, Aristotle argued that political science has to consider what government is best and of what sort it must be, to be most in accord with man's aspirations, and this

2. *Ibid.*

if there is no external impediment; it must also consider what kind of government is adapted to particular states. Thus political science deals even with states that are neither the best under the circumstances nor the best absolutely, but of an inferior type, much as medicine is concerned to know to what degree a person can in fact attain health. And since the moral sciences bear on the contraries of good and evil only in the sense that they pursue the one and avoid the other, a constitutional government cannot be one that is simply bad, though it may be neither the best absolutely nor the best in the sense of being best suited to the majority of states, nor even the best in the circumstances. But it cannot be simply bad; for no free man, if he can escape from it—as Aristotle says—will endure tyranny. The element of possibility allows for the choice of a government that may indeed be quite inferior, but it does not extend to permitting what of itself is contrary to natural law, viz., the tyranny that no free man, if he can escape from it, will endure. The incompetence of a primitive people is analogous to the incompetence of a corrupt people; and as St. Thomas Aquinas points out, if a people are thoroughly corrupt and entrust the government to scoundrels and criminals, the right of appointing their public officials is rightly forfeit and the choice devolves upon a few good men. Such a people do not, then, have a constitutional government that is properly political, for they are not competent to share in government. Politically immature or corrupt, they may be likened to brute natures that need to be directed to their proper end by an intelligence extrinsic to them. But the seeds of political life are there. They have the kind of government that their nature and condition require for growth in political maturity. For again, as St. Thomas says, different things are expedient to different men because of the difference of their condition. If indeed political science deals first and formally with human acts, i.e., with actions that proceed from human volition according to the ordinance of reason, it must also take into consideration nonrational aspects of human nature in making the prudential judgment of the politically possible.

Best Form of Government

The problem of the best constitution is that of combining the elements of consent and possibility with the perfection of the governing principle—the unity, effectiveness, and stability of the form of government. Aristotle found each of the simple forms of good government defective in relation to the common welfare on the score either of inadequate allowance for the elements of consent and possibility or of inadequate provision for effectiveness in the governmental structure—the two aspects of constitutional government. The simple form of monarchy—which Aristotle considered, absolutely speaking, the best form because it best imitates the perfection of the governing principle of the rational soul over the appetites—has the curious disadvantage that there are no citizens in such a state; neither the ruler nor the subjects are true citizens, for the virtue of a citizen includes both ruling and obeying. Despite its acknowledged primacy from the point of view of the perfection of the governing principle, this form, if it is transferred to a community where the ideal prerequisites for it are lacking, loses its advantage of unity of rule by a lack of interest in the common welfare on the part of the members of the community, who do not share in the government. On the other hand, democracy, the simple political form, in which citizens rule and are ruled in turn, has for Aristotle the more serious disadvantage that by dividing political authority among equals it tends to ostracize the better element and to seek equality in everything.

ARISTOTLE'S PROPOSAL. To retain the democratic principle of ruling and being ruled in turn—without, however, retaining the democratic principle of absolute equality and the social instability that it entails—Aristotle suggested a substitute for absolute kingship modeled on the substitute that the continent man employs for true virtue. The kind of consent to true rule and the possibility of it that are found in the average (continent) man were made to serve as the model for the average political community. The unity of rule that is exemplified in the virtuous man's government of himself is imitated in the continent man by a somewhat precarious combination of the two extremes that lie outside the intermediate of true virtue. The man who is self-indulgent by nature moves toward the opposite extreme of total abstinence and thus, by a combination of the two extremes, imitates the intermediate condition of true temperance. In similar fashion the extremes of freedom and equality on the one hand and wealth on the other are brought together in a large middle class by a wide distribution of property. This large middle class is capable of the unity of absolute kingship; for, just as the continent man does not live by virtue precisely but by something less, so the middle-class polity lives by the steadying effects of property values. Both overcome the division of soul within them.

AQUINAS'S THEORY. St. Thomas agrees with Aristotle's prescription for the best constitution under most actual conditions, viz., that it should combine features of all the good forms with the forms that are not altogether corrupt and that it should be based on a wide distribution of property. But St. Thomas supplies for a serious deficiency in Aristotle's solution. That solution achieves a substitute "unity of rule" by means of the middle-class government; yet this unity is such as to preserve stability but not to secure effective legislative direction. St. Thomas's task was to devise, on the basis of Aristotle's principles, a form of government that would combine stability of middle-class government with the need for effective policy-making authority. To the device of middle-class government (which combines the elements of consent and possibility, the political elements of constitutional government, with stability, one of the two elements of royal rule) St. Thomas adds the second element of royal rule, namely, effective governing authority. And he does this by restoring the exercise of government to the one best-qualified man, conceived now, by the tying of the instruments of his power, as representative of the people. It is this latter conception that introduces the political element into the concept of royal rule itself in St. Thomas's thought on constitutionalism.

The key to this theory of the best form of government is to be found in the concept of the people sharing in rule without dividing the government, of introducing the political element through the concept of representation. If one were to suppose that a genuinely mixed regime cannot be had without the existence of two independent and competing organs of government, then he would be justified in declaring St. Thomas's mixed regime no different from pure monarchy. But if one considers the possibility of pure monarchy's being tempered by tying the instruments through which it acts, then this monarchy, while retaining the purity of the form (for the authority is not divided) is "mixed" with the political element; it is in this way distinguished from pure monarchy, which signifies simply the form as such of monarchical government untempered. This latter was called simply royal, whereas the former was called royal and political. Distinguishing between common political prudence (which is in all subjects and enables them to govern themselves in their own individual acts in accordance with the governance of the ruler) and legislative prudence (which is the virtue proper to the ruler), St. Thomas teaches that more than common political prudence is required of the subject who is a free man; for as a free man having the disposal of himself, he shares in the legislative prudence of the ruler by being taken into counsel in the formulating of the law: he is represented by the ruler as a slave is not represented by his master. St. Thomas would have the ruler of the one best-qualified man tempered in part by the elective process and in part by the ratifying process; in effect, this would be "law sanctioned by the Lords and Commons."

Intrinsic Limitations on Positive Law

It must finally be noted that the canon of consent, based on man's moral freedom, and the canon of possibility, based on his physical freedom, place intrinsic limitations on positive law. Aristotle defined positive law as the legal part of political justice, of which the other part is natural, viz., "having the same force everywhere and not such by people thinking this or that."[3] Positive law does indeed, as part of its function, declare natural right, but it does not establish it. Its main function is to declare the legally just, that "which is originally indifferent, but when it has been laid down is not indifferent." For positive law derives from the natural law not in the way of conclusions from its first principles, but by way of determination of these common notions. It derives from the natural law in such fashion simply that what it prescribes may not of itself be contrary to natural right.

In its function of establishing the legally just, human law is a product of the practical reason, and its dependence on natural law is only one of the properties of which its structure must take account. Human law falls short of the natural law's participation in the objective order of essences that is the natural law, for it is applied to very refractory material, to the common condition of men. As has been seen, law as a measure and rule must be homogenous with what it measures, and human law as a work of the practical reason ought to be imposed on men according to their condition. Now, that condition is such as to make the attainment of perfect virtue extremely difficult, and therefore human law does not forbid all vices, from which the virtuous abstain, but only the more grievous ones, from which it is possible for the majority to

3. Aristotle, *Nicomachean Ethics*, 1134b18.

abstain, and chiefly those that are injurious to others, without the prohibition of which human society could not be maintained. There is, then, a distinction between the juridical order and the moral order. The purpose of law is indeed to make men virtuous, but the good that the law can achieve is the human good of a multitude of persons the majority of whom are not perfect in virtue. It is enough, then, for the common good of the state that the citizens be virtuous enough to obey the commands of the government. More than this does not come under the precept of human positive law. Nonetheless, the virtuous performance of virtuous acts "is the end at which every lawgiver aims."[4] The end that the law seeks is, then, a common good predicated not on force and fear of the law but on a free advance to the perfection of the virtues directed to the common good of each and all. What law accomplishes is an extrinsic and remote disposing of the citizen for inward growth in the virtues; force and fear only supply motives for regulating the passions and developing true virtue. The ultimate aim of the law is accomplished only through one's interior freedom. That a whole people have a sense of moderation and responsibility depends essentially on a free commitment to the ends appointed by the natural law.

Natural Society of States

The idea of a natural society of states seems to be wholly lacking in ancient Greek philosophy. But the idea of a natural human society is found as early as the period known as the anthropological, which extends from 450 B.C. to the third century A.D. Socrates is said to have called the whole world "the common fatherland of men." Aristotle admits the existence of a universal society with an unwritten law applying to all peoples.[5] Cicero greatly developed this idea of a universal human society; and Tacitus, Philo, Seneca, and Marcus Aurelius are in the same tradition. St. Thomas appears to have been the first to have a clear idea of a universal society of which the members are states: ". . . and between a single bishop and the Pope there are other grades of dignities corresponding to the grades of unions insofar as one congregation or community includes another one, as the community of a province includes the community of the city, and the community of the kingdom in-

4. Thomas Aquinas, *Summa Theologiae*, I–II, 96, 3, ad 2.
5. Aristotle, *Nichomachean Ethics*, 1155a20.

cludes the community of the province, and the community of the whole world includes the community of a kingdom."[6] F. de Vitoria, the founder of modern international law along with H. Grotius, develops this idea of the community of the world constituted of states.

Although the state remains a "perfect society" in the sense that it makes possible the communication of men in the highest goods, this possibility itself depends on the general peace among states and on the diversity of riches—spiritual and material—that the whole inhabited world makes available to all men. There is, then, a collective end that consists in a system of material and spiritual goods corresponding adequately to the basic tendency of human nature toward an ever fuller and higher perfection, which can result only from the peaceful cooperation of states. There is, too, an international common good, distinct from the common good proper to each state; there is, again, a natural society of states that is directed to its end by certain precepts of natural law. But if nature supplies the general lines for the organization of states, this work is to be accomplished by the labors of men. The first efforts have aimed simply at disciplining international activity without concern for the constitution of society itself. Organizations such as the League of Nations and the United Nations seem to point the way toward a more complete and positive organization of international society.

6. Thomas Aquinas, *In 4 Sent.*, 24. 3. 2. 3.

Appendix: Table of Contents of
The Structure of Political Thought
by Charles N. R. McCoy

[As an aid in understanding the order of the thought of Charles N. R. McCoy in these collected essays, it was thought useful to reprint here the Table of Contents of *The Structure of Political Thought*. This is the best brief overall view of the nature and scope of McCoy's work and serves as a guide to the themes, and their development in political philosophy, that McCoy treats in his various essays appearing in this book.]

A Bibliography of Charles N. R. McCoy
by John J. Schrems

1933

"Communication on 'Tickets for Utopia,'" *The Commonweal*, Vol. 18, (August 4), pp. 347–348. [A brief comment concerns social science and the goals of education versus genuine social science as understood by Aristotle.]

1935

"Dialectics of Freedom," *The Commonweal*, Vol. 22, (October 25), pp. 626–627. [A word on dialectics as employed by Fascism and Marxism as opposed to Aristotle and Aquinas.]

1939

Review of Homer C. Hockett, *The Constitutional History of the United States 1776–1826*. Review of Charles A. Beard, *American Government and Politics* in *Catholic Historical Review*, Vol. 25, No. 3 (October), pp. 398–399. [Hockett's work is weak on moral foundations of constitutionalism because of Lockean principles. Beard's text has a vital and stimulating quality.]

1940

The Law Relating to Public Inland Waters, Chicago, (Chicago University Press, 1940). (Dissertation abstract.) 29 pp. [A tightly reasoned, well-written study in the area of constitutional law and history. The study was done in this area because, in the compiler's understanding, the author chose not to write under Charles E. Merriam who taught the political theory area at Chicago at the time.]

"American Federalism—Theory and Practice," *The Review of Politics*, Vol. 2, (January 1940), pp. 105–17. [This article is a theoretical application of the above-cited dissertation. Ramifications of compact theory and practical dimensions of the theory of federalism are discussed.]

Review of Homer C. Hockett, *The Constitutional History of the United States 1826–1876* in *Catholic Historical Review*, Vol. 26, No. 3 (October), pp.

403–404. [This is a follow-up from the earlier reviewed volume. Little theoretical discussion is found here, but it does show McCoy's breadth outside the theory area.]

1941

Review of Arthur N. Holcombe, *The Middle Classes in American Politics* in *The Commonweal*, Vol. 33, (January 10), p. 305. [Shows America in classical terms which Holcombe does not understand, e.g., Aristotle on the middle class, and the weakness of Holcombe's faith in Kant.]

Review of Charles H. McIlwain, *Constitutionalism, Ancient and Modern* in *Catholic Historical Review*, Vol. 27, No. 2 (July), p. 263. [A supportive review of McIlwain's grasp of classical thought.]

1942

Review of F. A. Hermens, *Democracy or Anarchy?* in *Catholic Historical Review*, Vol. 28, No. 2 (July), pp. 293–294. [Review approves Hermens's criticism of the proportional representation system but enters a caveat about Hermens's failure to treat the weaknesses of the majority representation system.]

1943

"The Place of Machiavelli in the History of Political Thought," *American Political Science Review*, Vol. 37, pp. 626–641. [Developed slightly differently, but is essentially the same as the discussion in *Structure*.]

Review of S. Shepherd Jones and Denys P. Myers (editors), *Documents of American Foreign Relations: Volume III, July 1940–June 1941* in *Catholic Historical Review*, Vol. 28, No. 4 (January), p. 557. [A description of a collection by the World Peace Foundation documenting the world at war intended, unfortunately in McCoy's view, to be more persuasive for peace than man's natural intelligence.]

1945

Review of Manley O. Hudson, *International Tribunals, Past and Future* in *Catholic Historical Review*, Vol. 31, No. 3 (October), p. 368. [Descriptive of Judge Hudson's tracing, from experience and the law, efforts for international jurisdiction. Hudson is said to avoid the moral argument, although McCoy "suspects" that he would like to "insist upon" it.]

1946

"American Political Philosophy after 1865," *Thought*, Vol. 21, pp. 249–271. [A treatment of the theoretical foundations and implications of the Gilded Age.]

Review of Carl L. Becker, *Freedom and Responsibility in the American Way of Life* in *Catholic Historical Review*, Vol. 32, No. 1 (April), pp. 98–100. [Points out Becker's confusions and misconceptions about Christian and natural bases for liberty, and democratic government versus pure chance.]

1947

"Democracy and the Rule of Law," *Modern Schoolman*, Vol. 25, No. 1 (November), pp. 1–10. [Aristotle's treatment of democracy.]

"St. Thomas and Political Science," in *Thomistic Principles in a Catholic School.* Edited by Theodore Bauer. (St. Louis: Herder), pp. 264–288. [Organic treatment of Aquinas' politics: man's nature, individual good and common good, essence of law, constitution, good forms of government, end of the state, church and state.]

1948
Review of Ernst Cassirer, *The Myth of the State* in *Modern Schoolman,* Vol. 25, (May), pp. 271–278. [Extended examination of an important work.]
Review of Charles E. Merriam, *Systematic Politics* in *Catholic Historical Review,* Vol. 33, No. 4 (January), pp. 480–481. [Points out that there is no explanation of in what way Merriam's wide-ranging treatment is systematic or how it combines with his "faith" in scientific advances.]

1949
Review of Carl Joachim Friedrich, *Inevitable Peace* in *Modern Schoolman,* Vol. 26, (May), pp. 364–366. [Points out that Friedrich assumes an antithesis of nature and reason in mediaeval thought and goes on to build his peace on Kantian assumptions where reason remakes nature and peace.]

1950
"The Turning Point in Political Philosophy," *American Political Science Review,* Vol. 44, No. 3 (September), pp. 678–688. [First part is dealt with in *Structure,* but link to Hume, Kant, Hegel, and Heine is better presented here.]
Review of Juan de Mariana, *The King and the Education of the King:* (An English Translation and Criticism by George Albert Moore). *Modern Schoolman,* Vol. 27, (May), pp. 329–331. [Moore in his criticism does not understand the fullness of Mariana's attempt to destroy divine-right theory and thus Moore wrongly suggests a "nontheological view of civil society" while acknowledging the "intrusion of God into politics."]

1951
"Ludwig Feuerbach and the Formation of the Marxian Revolutionary Idea," *Laval Théologique et Philosophique,* Vol. 7, pp. 218–248. [Essentially the same as in *Structure.*]
Review of A. C. Ewing, *The Individual, The State, and World Government* in *Modern Schoolman,* Vol. 28, (January), pp. 164–165. [Ewing attempts to create a nontotalitarian ethics of "universalistic utilitarianism" without knowledge of Aquinas.]
Review of Martin J. Hillenbrand, *Power and Morals* in *Modern Schoolman,* Vol. 28, p. 235. [Regards book as worthwhile but full of graduate school jargon and hurried.]
Review of Cornelia Geer Le Boutillier, *American Democracy and Natural Law* in *Catholic Historical Review,* Vol. 37, No. 2 (July), p. 202. [Three brilliantly funny paragraphs about the utter confusion of Le Boutillier.]
"A Serious Indictment," *Social Justice Review,* Vol. 44, (November), p. 236. [About 275 words on tradition, family, property, the purpose of the state, and the robber-baron view which destroys them.]

1953
"Note on the Problem of the Origin of Political Authority," *Thomist*, Vol. 16, pp. 71–81. [Greek-medieval, Thomas, and Bellarmine on Designation and Transmission theory permutations.]
Review of Francis J. Powers (editor), *Papal Pronouncements on the Political Order* in *Catholic Historical Review*, Vol. 39, No. 1 (April), pp. 104–105. [Praises Powers's collection as a useful guide for fundamentals of papal pronouncements on the state.]

1954
"The Logical and the Real in Political Theory: Plato, Aristotle, and Marx," *American Political Science Review*, Vol. 48, pp. 1058–1066. [In *Structure* but developed quite differently.]
Review of Alan Gewirth, *Marsilius of Padua, the Defender of the Peace* in *Modern Schoolman*, Vol. 31, pp. 146–147. [Praises Gewirth's clear and full statement of Marsilius's position and the alternative even though Gewirth does not himself comment.]
Review of Reinhold Niebuhr, *Christian Realism and Political Problems* in *Catholic Historical Review*, Vol. 40, No. 3 (October), pp. 318–320. [Niebuhr, failing to understand the pessimism of liberalism, ought to re-study classical and medieval philosophers.]

1955
"Hegel, Feuerbach, Marx, and the Doctrine of St. Thomas Aquinas," *Sapientis Aquinatis*, Vol. 1, pp. 328–338. [Slightly different development than in earlier article on Feuerbach.]
Review of A. R. M. Murray, *An Introduction to Political Philosophy* in *Catholic Historical Review*, Vol. 41, pp. 359–360. [Criticism of Murray's celebration of no first principles in political theory and his treatment of practical thinking as essentially irrational.]

1956
"The Meaning of Jean-Jacques Rousseau and the Structure of Political Theory," *Proceedings of the American Catholic Philosophical Association*, Vol. 30, pp. 50–62. [In *Structure* Rousseau is dealt with as part of the development of political thought. Here Rousseau is treated or analyzed in light of many others, e.g., Cassirer, Gay, Marx, Thomas, and more Marx.]
"The Doctrine of Judicial Review and the Natural Law," *Catholic University of America Law Review*, Vol. 6, pp. 97–102. [Important treatment of American theory and constitutional law.]
Review of Ewart Lewis (editor), *Mediaeval Political Ideas* in *Catholic Historical Review*, Vol. 42, No. 3 (October), p. 363. [Praised as an excellent delving into the ideas of mediaeval thought.]

1957
"Social Justice in Quadragesimo Anno," *Social Order*, Vol. 7 (June), pp. 258–263. [Is "social justice" new?]
"Comment on 'Sociology of Religion,'" *The Commonweal*, Vol. 67, (November 8), pp. 153–154. [About Fr. Fichter's social science as a theoretic science which then allows "social engineering."]

1960
"The Dilemma of Liberalism," *Laval Théologique et Philosophique*, Vol. 16, pp. 9–19. [Hume, Cassirer, Eddington, Learned Hand, David Riesman, Erich Fromm, Lionel Trilling, and the implications of modern thought.]
Review of Arnold Brecht, *Political Theory: The Foundations of Twentieth Century Political Thought* in *Catholic Historical Review*, Vol. 46, pp. 214–216. ["Intersubjective transmissible knowledge" as the inadequate basis for scientifically constructed truth.]

1963
The Structure of Political Thought: A Study in the History of Political Ideas. New York: McGraw-Hill Book Company, Inc.
"St. Augustine," in *History of Political Philosophy.* Edited by Leo Strauss and Joseph Cropsey. (Chicago: Rand McNally and Co.), pp. 151–159. [Compact study of Augustine as in *Structure.*]
"St. Thomas Aquinas," in *History of Political Philosophy.* Edited by Leo Strauss and Joseph Cropsey. (Chicago: Rand McNally and Co.), pp. 201–226. [Concise treatment of the essential Aquinas.]
Review of Walter Ullmann, *Principles of Government and Politics in the Middle Ages* in *Catholic Historical Review*, Vol. 49, No. 3, (October), pp. 429–431. [Appraisal of an unfortunate excursion into the field of political philosophy.]

1967
"Bodin, Jean," *New Catholic Encyclopedia.* (New York: McGraw-Hill Book Co.), Vol. 2, p. 630. [Different treatment of Bodin than found in *Structure.*]
"Political Philosophy," *New Catholic Encyclopedia.* Vol. 11, pp. 510–516. [Analytical, nonhistorical, treatment of political philosophy.]
"Political Thought, History of," *New Catholic Encyclopedia.* Vol. 11, pp. 525–531. [An adumbration of *Structure.*]
Review of Ralph Lerner and Mushin Mahdi (editors), *Mediaeval Political Philosophy: A Sourcebook* in *Catholic Historical Review*, Vol. 52, No. 4 (January), pp. 593–595. [Praised as a "valuable service" to students of political philosophy, it shows primacy of jurisprudence over theology and philosophy in Muslim and Jewish thought.]

1968
"The Historical Position of Man Himself," found in *Mélanges à la Mémoire de Charles de Koninck.* (Quebec: Les Presses de l'Université Laval), pp. 219–231. [A study of Heidegger, an essential extension of *Structure.*]

1970
"The Value-Free Aristotle and the Behavioral Sciences," *Western Political Quarterly*, Vol. 23, No. 1 (March), pp. 57–73. [A formal treatment of the social sciences previously dealt with briefly in comments or reviews.]
"*Humanae Vitae*: Perspectives and Precisions," *The New Scholasticism*, Vol. 44, No. 2 (Spring), pp. 265–272. [Puts the papal letter on birth control in the context of natural law thought.]

1971
Review of Christopher Morris, *Western Political Thought: Volume I, Plato to Augustine* in *Catholic Historical Review*, Vol. 56, pp. 695–696. [Views the work as an immensely erudite treatment marked by humor and ambivalence, but essentially using political philosophy "for milking."]

1973
"On the Revival of Classical Political Philosophy," *The Review of Politics*, Vol. 35, No. 2 (April), pp. 161–179. [A scholarly critique of Leo Strauss's understanding of Plato and Aristotle.]
Review of Joseph Petulla, *Christian Political Theology: A Marxian Guide* in *The Thomist*, Vol. 27, (July), pp. 624–625. [Critique of the simplistic transferral of alienation, liberation, and praxis to Christian political theology.]

Unpublished manuscripts by Professor McCoy in the possession of the compiler:

"Aristotle and the Medieval Tradition." [The division of the science according to Aristotle and Aquinas.]
"Liberation Theology and Political Philosophy: A Brief Note." [Sympathetic yet critical treatment.]
"The Counter Culture: Its Sense of Life."
"The Counter Culture: Its Place in the History of Political Thought."

Reviews of *The Structure of Political Thought*:

Klubertanz, George, in *Modern Schoolman* 42 (March 1963), 343–44.
McInerny, Ralph M., in *The New Scholasticism* 39 (July 1965), 405–407.
Schwandt, J. A., in *Thought* 41 (Spring 1966), 159–60.
Wilson, Francis Graham, in *Catholic Historical Review* 50 (July 1964), 239–40.

Index

Aberrations, 78, 84

Absolute commensuration, 284

Abstraction, 16

Adams, Henry, 224

Aggiornamento, 99

Alienation, 95

American, Constitution, 229; culture, 2; law, 234; political philosophy, 8, 221; theory, 209

Aquinas, 3, 5, 6, 7, 8, 10, 16, 21, 24, 25, 33, 50, 51, 54, 58, 68, 70, 73, 86, 88, 100, 117, 121, 122, 124, 127, 129, 131, 158, 203, 212, 241, 249, 250, 253, 258, 267, 270, 285, 287, 289; Commentary on the *Physics*, 67; Commentary on the *Politics*, 19, 56, 101; theologian, 37; on natural right, 142; treatise on law, 38; on wealth, 223

Architectonic politics, 25, 279

Arendt, Hannah, 2, 4

Aristocracy, 31, 223

Aristotle, 3, 6, 7, 8, 16, 17, 24, 25, 33, 39, 42, 54, 58, 70, 71, 73, 81, 85, 86, 98, 100, 101, 102, 116, 122, 126, 127, 129, 131, 132, 137, 144, 148, 160, 161, 162–64, 169, 171, 179, 198, 212, 221, 222–24, 233, 240, 267, 269, 277, 281, 283, 284; definition on law, 54; *Metaphysics*, 102; of length, 111; *Ethics*, 35, 102, 269; every state partly natural, 213; on nature, 139; natural law, 230; oligarchs, 229; on physics, 81; *Physics*, 17, 19, 67, 76, 77, 139, 144, 158; political science, 103; *Politics*, 20, 41, 56; value-free attitude, 113, 165; on virtue, 102, 109

Aristotelian, 115, 150, 163, 215, 221

Arithmetic, 188

Arntz, Joseph, 159

Art, 18, 19, 20, 22, 23, 43, 71, 90, 92, 100, 108, 123, 190, 226, 227, 228, 251, 261, 269, 276, 279, 280, 284; of gymnastics, 284; of politics, 23

Articles of Confederation, 210

Artist, 71, 236, 237

Atom bomb, 87, 155, 194, 197, 205

Augustine, 8, 10, 57

Autarky, human reason, 172

Authenticity, 89, 96, 153, 156, 167, 196, 197

Autonomy of nature, 75

Averroist, 125

Barrett, William, 92, 114, 158, 192

Bay, Christian, 106

Beard's *Economic Interpretation of the Constitution*, 223

Becker, Carl L., 47

Behavioral sciences, 2, 3, 8, 100, 101, 106, 163, 165, 188, 193

Bellarmine, Robert, 50, 51, 53, 55, 282

Bentley, Arthur, 111, 188, 193

Berelson, Bernard, 113, 188

Best form of government, 285

Best regime, 31, 101, 133, 135, 140, 144

Biblical tradition, 134

Bibliography, 5

Bill of Rights, 82

Biology, 110, 199

Birth control, 258

Bloom, Allan, 167

Bloy, Myron, 156, 157, 158, 164

Boethius, 21

Brauer, Theodore, 24

Brecht, Arnold, 83

Brecht, Bertolt, 180